Microsoft®
EXCEL® 2010
INTRODUCTORY

Gary B. Shelly

Jeffrey J. Quasney

COURSE TECHNOLOGY
CENGAGE Learning™

SHELLY
CASHMAN
SERIES®

Australia • Brazil • Japan • Korea • Mexico • Singapore • Spain • United Kingdom • United States

COURSE TECHNOLOGY
CENGAGE Learning

Microsoft Excel 2010: Introductory
Gary B. Shelly, Jeffrey J. Quasney

Vice President, Publisher: Nicole Pinard

Executive Editor: Kathleen McMahon

Senior Product Manager: Mali Jones

Associate Product Manager: Aimee Poirier

Editorial Assistant: Lauren Brody

Director of Marketing: Cheryl Costantini

Marketing Manager: Tristen Kendall

Marketing Coordinator: Stacey Leasca

Print Buyer: Julio Esperas

Director of Production: Patty Stephan

Content Project Manager: Matthew Hutchinson

Development Editor: Jill Batistick

Copyeditor: Foxxe Editorial

Proofreader: Chris Clark

Indexer: Rich Carlson

QA Manuscript Reviewers: Chris Scriver,
    John Freitas, Serge Palladino, Susan Pedicini,
    Danielle Shaw

Art Director: Marissa Falco

Cover Designer: Lisa Kuhn, Curio Press, LLC

Cover Photo: Tom Kates Photography

Text Design: Joel Sadagursky

Compositor: PreMediaGlobal

For product information and technology assistance, contact us at
Cengage Learning Customer & Sales Support, 1-800-354-9706

For permission to use material from this text or product,
submit all requests online at **cengage.com/permissions**
Further permissions questions can be emailed to
permissionrequest@cengage.com

Library of Congress Control Number: 2010929240

ISBN-13: 978-1-4390-7846-4

ISBN-10: 1-4390-7846-7

Course Technology
20 Channel Center Street
Boston, MA 02210
USA

Cengage Learning is a leading provider of customized learning solutions with office locations around the globe, including Singapore, the United Kingdom, Australia, Mexico, Brazil, and Japan. Locate your local office at:
international.cengage.com/region

Cengage Learning products are represented in Canada by Nelson Education, Ltd.

Visit our website **www.cengage.com/ct/shellycashman** to share and gain ideas on our textbooks!

To learn more about Course Technology,
visit **www.cengage.com/coursetechnology**

Purchase any of our products at your local college store or at our preferred online store **www.cengagebrain.com**

We dedicate this book to the memory of James S. Quasney (1940 – 2009), who for 18 years co-authored numerous books with Tom Cashman and Gary Shelly and provided extraordinary leadership to the Shelly Cashman Series editorial team. As series editor, Jim skillfully coordinated, organized, and managed the many aspects of our editorial development processes and provided unending direction, guidance, inspiration, support, and advice to the Shelly Cashman Series authors and support team members. He was a trusted, dependable, loyal, and well-respected leader, mentor, and friend. We are forever grateful to Jim for his faithful devotion to our team and eternal contributions to our series.

The Shelly Cashman Series Team

Printed in the United States of America
2 3 4 5 6 7 12 11

Microsoft® EXCEL® 2010
INTRODUCTORY

Contents

Microsoft **Excel 2010**

CHAPTER ONE
Creating a Worksheet and an Embedded Chart

CHAPTER TWO
Formulas, Functions, and Formatting

Appendices

Preface

The Shelly Cashman Series® offers the finest textbooks in computer education. We are proud that since Mircosoft Office 4.3, our series of Microsoft Office textbooks have been the most widely used books in education. With each new edition of our Office books, we make significant improvements based on the software and comments made by instructors and students. For this Microsoft Excel 2010 text, the Shelly Cashman Series development team carefully reviewed our pedagogy and analyzed its effectiveness in teaching today's Office student. Students today read less, but need to retain more. They need not only to be able to perform skills, but to retain those skills and know how to apply them to different settings. Today's students need to be continually engaged and challenged to retain what they're learning.

With this Microsoft Excel 2010 text, we continue our commitment to focusing on the user and how they learn best.

Objectives of This Textbook

Microsoft Excel 2010: Introductory is intended for a first course on Excel 2010. No experience with a computer is assumed, and no mathematics beyond the high school freshman level is required. The objectives of this book are:

- To offer an introduction to Microsoft Excel 2010

- To expose students to practical examples of the computer as a useful tool

- To acquaint students with the proper procedures to create worksheets suitable for coursework, professional purposes, and personal use

- To help students discover the underlying functionality of Excel 2010 so they can become more productive

- To develop an exercise-oriented approach that allows learning by doing

New to This Edition

Microsoft Excel 2010: Introductory offers a number of new features and approaches, which improve student understanding, retention, transference, and skill in using Excel 2010. The following enhancements will enrich the learning experience:

- Office 2010 and Windows 7: Essential Concepts and Skills chapter presents basic Office 2010 and Windows 7 skills.

- Streamlined first chapter allow the ability to cover more advanced skills earlier.

- Chapter topic redistribution offers concise chapters that ensure complete skill coverage.

- New pedagogical elements enrich material creating an accessible and user-friendly approach.

  - Break Points, a new boxed element, identify logical stopping points and give students instructions regarding what they should do before taking a break.

  - Within step instructions, Tab | Group Identifiers, such as (Home tab | Bold button), help students more easily locate elements in the groups and on the tabs on the Ribbon.

  - Modified step-by-step instructions tell the student what to do and provide the generic reason why they are completing a specific task, which helps students easily transfer given skills to different settings.

The Shelly Cashman Approach

A Proven Pedagogy with an Emphasis on Project Planning

Each chapter presents a practical problem to be solved, within a project planning framework. The project orientation is strengthened by the use of Plan Ahead boxes, which encourage critical thinking about how to proceed at various points in the project. Step-by-step instructions with supporting screens guide students through the steps. Instructional steps are supported by the Q&A, Experimental Step, and BTW features.

A Visually Engaging Book that Maintains Student Interest

The step-by-step tasks, with supporting figures, provide a rich visual experience for the student. Call-outs on the screens that present both explanatory and navigational information provide students with information they need when they need to know it.

Supporting Reference Materials (Appendices, Quick Reference)

The appendices provide additional information about the Application at hand and include such topics and project planning guidelines and certification. With the Quick Reference, students can quickly look up information about a single task, such as keyboard shortcuts, and find page references of where in the book the task is illustrated.

Integration of the World Wide Web

The World Wide Web is integrated into the Excel 2010 learning experience by (1) BTW annotations; (2) BTW, Q&A, and Quick Reference Summary Web pages; and (3) the Learn It Online section for each chapter.

End-of-Chapter Student Activities

Extensive end-of-chapter activities provide a variety of reinforcement opportunities for students where they can apply and expand their skills.

Instructor Resources

The Instructor Resources include both teaching and testing aids and can be accessed via CD-ROM or at www.cengage.com/login.

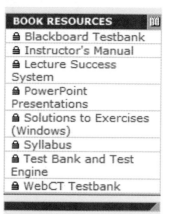

Instructor's Manual Includes lecture notes summarizing the chapter sections, figures and boxed elements found in every chapter, teacher tips, classroom activities, lab activities, and quick quizzes in Microsoft Word files.

Syllabus Easily customizable sample syllabi that cover policies, assignments, exams, and other course information.

Figure Files Illustrations for every figure in the textbook in electronic form.

PowerPoint Presentations A multimedia lecture presentation system that provides slides for each chapter. Presentations are based on chapter objectives.

Solutions To Exercises Includes solutions for all end-of-chapter and chapter reinforcement exercises.

Test Bank & Test Engine Test Banks include 112 questions for every chapter, featuring objective-based and critical thinking question types, and including page number references and figure references, when appropriate. Also included is the test engine, ExamView, the ultimate tool for your objective-based testing needs.

Data Files for Students Includes all the files that are required by students to complete the exercises.

Additional Activities for Students Consists of Chapter Reinforcement Exercises, which are true/false, multiple-choice, and short answer questions that help students gain confidence in the material learned.

SAM: Skills Assessment Manager

SAM 2010 is designed to help bring students from the classroom to the real world. It allows students to train on and test important computer skills in an active, hands-on environment.

SAM's easy-to-use system includes powerful interactive exams, training, and projects on the most commonly used Microsoft Office applications. SAM simulates the Microsoft Office 2010 application environment, allowing students to demonstrate their knowledge and think through the skills by performing real-world tasks such as bolding word text or setting up slide transitions. Add in live-in-the-application projects, and students are on their way to truly learning and applying skills to business-centric documents.

Designed to be used with the Shelly Cashman Series, SAM includes handy page references so that students can print helpful study guides that match the Shelly Cashman textbooks used in class. For instructors, SAM also includes robust scheduling and reporting features.

Content for Online Learning

Course Technology has partnered with the leading distance learning solution providers and class-management platforms today. To access this material, instructors will visit our password-protected instructor resources available at www.cengage.com/coursetechnology. Instructor resources include the following: additional case projects, sample syllabi, PowerPoint presentations per chapter, and more. For additional information or for an instructor user name and password, please contact your sales representative. For students to access this material, they must have purchased a WebTutor PIN-code specific to this title and your campus platform. The resources for students may include (based on instructor preferences), but are not limited to: topic review, review questions, and practice tests.

Course Notes

Course Technology's CourseNotes are six-panel quick reference cards that reinforce the most important and widely used features of a software application in a visual and user-friendly format. CourseNotes serve as a great reference tool during and after the student completes the course. CourseNotes are available for software applications such as Microsoft Office 2010, Word 2010, Excel 2010, Access 2010, PowerPoint 10`0, and Windows 7. Topic-based CourseNotes are available for Best Practices in Social Networking, Hot Topics in Technology, and Web 2.0. Visit www.cengage.com/ct/coursenotes to learn more!

course|notes™
quick reference guide

A Guided Tour

Add excitement and interactivity to your classroom with "*A Guided Tour*" product line. Play one of the brief mini-movies to spice up your lecture and spark classroom discussion. Or, assign a movie for homework and ask students to complete the correlated assignment that accompanies each topic. "*A Guided Tour*" product line takes the prep work out of providing your students with information about new technologies and applications and helps keep students engaged with content relevant to their lives; all in under an hour!

About Our Covers

The Shelly Cashman Series is continually updating our approach and content to reflect the way today's students learn and experience new technology. This focus on student success is reflected on our covers, which feature real students from University of Rhode Island using the Shelly Cashman Series in their courses, and reflect the varied ages and backgrounds of the students learning with our books. When you use the Shelly Cashman Series, you can be assured that you are learning computer skills using the most effective courseware available.

Textbook Walk-Through

The Shelly Cashman Series Pedagogy: Project-Based — Step-by-Step — Variety of Assessments

Plan Ahead boxes prepare students to create successful projects by encouraging them to think strategically about what they are trying to accomplish before they begin working.

Step-by-step instructions now provide a context beyond the point-and-click. Each step provides information on why students are performing each task, or what will occur as a result.

General Project Decisions

While creating an Excel worksheet, you need to make several decisions that will determine the appearance and characteristics of the finished worksheet. As you create the worksheet necessary to meet the requirements shown in Figure 2–2, you should follow these general guidelines:

1. **Plan the layout of the worksheet.** Rows typically contain items analogous to items in a list. A name could serve as an item in a list, and, therefore, each name could be placed in a row. As a list grows, such as a list of employees, the number of rows in the worksheet will increase. Information about each item in the list and associated calculations should appear in columns.

2. **Determine the necessary formulas and functions needed.** Calculations result from known values. Formulas for such calculations should be known in advance of creating a worksheet. Values such as the average, highest, and lowest values can be calculated using Excel functions as opposed to relying on complex formulas.

3. **Identify how to format various elements of the worksheet.** The appearance of the worksheet affects its ability to express information clearly. Numeric data should be formatted in generally accepted formats, such as using commas as thousands separators and parentheses for negative values.

4. **Establish rules for conditional formatting.** Conditional formatting allows you to format a cell based on the contents of the cell. Decide under which circumstances you would like a cell to stand out from related cells and determine in what way the cell will stand out.

5. **Specify how the hard copy of a worksheet should appear.** When it is possible that a person will want to create a hard copy of a worksheet, care should be taken in the development of the worksheet to ensure that the contents can be presented in a readable manner. Excel prints worksheets in landscape or portrait orientation, and margins can be adjusted to fit more or less data on each page. Headers and footers add an additional level of customization to the printed page.

When necessary, more specific details concerning the above guidelines are presented at appropriate points in the chapter. The chapter also will identify the actions performed and decisions made regarding these guidelines during the creation of the worksheet shown in Figure 2–1 on page EX 67.

Plan Ahead

In addition, using a sketch of the worksheet can help you visualize its design. The sketch for The Mobile Masses Store Biweekly Payroll Report worksheet includes a title, a subtitle, column and row headings, and the location of data values (Figure 2–3 on the following page). It also uses specific characters to define the desired formatting for the worksheet, as follows:

1. The row of Xs below the leftmost column defines the cell entries as text, such as employee names.

2. The rows of Zs and 9s with slashes, dollar signs, decimal points, commas, and percent signs in the remaining columns define the cell entries as numbers. The Zs indicate that the selected format should instruct Excel to suppress leading 0s. The 9s indicate that the selected format should instruct Excel to display any digits, including 0s.

3. The decimal point means that a decimal point should appear in the cell entry and indicates the number of decimal places to use.

4. The slashes in the second column identify the cell entry as a date.

5. The dollar signs that are not adjacent to the Zs in the first row below the column headings and in the total row signify a fixed dollar sign. The dollar signs that are adjacent to the Zs below the total row signify a floating dollar sign, or one that appears next to the first significant digit.

EX 86   Excel Chapter 2   Formulas, Functions, and Formatting

To Determine the Highest Number in a Range of Numbers

The next step is to select cell C15 and determine the highest (maximum) includes a function called the **MAX function** that displays the highest value the MAX function using the keyboard and Point mode as described in the p to entering the function is to use the Insert Function box in the formula bar Function box in the formula bar to enter the MAX function.

1

• Select the cell to contain the maximum number, cell C15 in this case.

• Click the Insert Function box in the formula bar to display the Insert Function dialog box.

• Click MAX in the 'Select a function' list (Insert Function dialog box) to select it (Figure 2–19). If the MAX function is not displayed in the 'Select a function' list, scroll the list until the function is displayed.

Figure 2–19

2

• Click the OK button (Insert Function dialog box) to display the Function Arguments dialog box.

• Type c4:c12 in the Number1 box (Function Arguments dialog box) to enter the first argument of the function (Figure 2–20).

Q&A Why did numbers appear in the Function Arguments dialog box?

As shown in Figure 2–20, Excel displays the value the MAX function will return to cell C15 in the Function Arguments dialog box. It also lists the first few numbers in the selected range, next to the Number1 box.

Figure 2–20

Explanatory callouts summarize what is happening on screen.

Navigational callouts in red show students where to click.

To Save a Workbook Using the Same File Name

Earlier in this project, an intermediate version of the workbook was saved using the file name, The Mobile Masses Biweekly Payroll Report. The following step saves the workbook a second time, using the same file name.

1 Click the Save button on the Quick Access Toolbar to overwrite the previously saved file.

Break Point: If you wish to take a break, this is a good place to do so. You can quit Excel now. To resume at a later time, start Excel, open the file called Mobile Masses Biweekly Payroll Report, and continue following the steps from this location forward.

Verifying Formulas Using Range Finder

One of the more common mistakes made with Excel is to include a wrong cell reference in a formula. An easy way to verify that a formula references the cells you want it to reference is to use the Excel Range Finder. Use **Range Finder** to check which cells are referenced in the formula assigned to the active cell. Range Finder allows you to make immediate changes to the cells referenced in a formula.

To use Range Finder to verify that a formula contains the intended cell references, double-click the cell with the formula you want to check. Excel responds by highlighting the cells referenced in the formula so that you can check that the cell references are correct.

To Verify a Formula Using Range Finder

The following steps use Range Finder to check the formula in cell J4.

1
- Double-click cell J4 to activate Range Finder

Q&A What is the effect of clicking the Decrease Font Size button?

When you click the Decrease Font Size button, Excel assigns the next lowest font size in the Font Size gallery to the selected range. The Increase Font Size button works in a similar manner but causes Excel to assign the next highest font size in the Font Size gallery to the selected range.

Figure 2–33

To Change the Background Color and Apply a Box Border to the Worksheet Title and Subtitle

The final formats assigned to the worksheet title and subtitle are the orange background color and thick box border (Figure 2–30b on page EX 92). The following steps complete the formatting of the worksheet titles.

1
- Select the range A1:A2 and then click the Fill Color button arrow (Home tab | Font group) to display the Fill Color gallery (Figure 2–34).

Experiment
- Point to a number of colors in the Fill Color gallery to display a live preview of the color in the range A1:A2.

2
- Click Orange, Accent 1, Lighter 60% (column 5, row 3) in the Fill Color gallery to change the background color of the range of cells (Figure 2–35).

Figure 2–34

Figure 2–35

Textbook Walk-Through

④ Click the OK button (Page Setup dialog box) to set the print scaling to normal.

⑤ Display the Home tab.

Q&A What is the purpose of the Adjust to box in the Page Setup dialog box?
The Adjust to box allows you to specify the percentage of reduction or enlargement in the printout of a worksheet. The default percentage is 100%. When you click the Fit to option, this percentage automatically changes to the percentage required to fit the printout on one page.

BTW Quick Reference
For a table that lists how to complete the tasks covered in this book using the mouse, Ribbon, shortcut menu, and keyboard, see the Quick Reference Summary at the back of this book, or visit the Excel 2010 Quick Reference Web page (scsite.com/ex2010/qr).

To Save the Workbook and Quit Excel

With the workbook complete, the following steps save the workbook and quit Excel.

① Click the Save button on the Quick Access Toolbar.

② Click the Close button on the upper-right corner of the title bar.

Chapter Summary

In this chapter you have learned how to enter formulas, calculate an average, find the highest and lowest numbers in a range, verify formulas using Range Finder, added borders, align text, format numbers, change column widths and row heights, and add conditional formatting to a range of numbers. In addition, you learned to spell check a worksheet, print a section of a worksheet, and display and print the formulas version of the worksheet using the Fit to option. The items listed below include all the new Excel skills you have learned in this chapter.

1. Enter a Formula Using the Keyboard (EX 75)
2. Enter Formulas Using Point Mode (EX 77)
3. Copy Formulas Using the Fill Handle (EX 80)
4. Determine the Average of a Range of Numbers
   ... ange of ... x (EX 86)
   ... nge of ...
   ... to an ... (EX 89)
   ... (EX 91)
   ... a Box ...tle (EX 96)
   ... (EX 98)

12. Apply an Accounting Number Format and Comma Style Format Using the Ribbon (EX 100)
13. Apply a Currency Style Format with a Floating Dollar Sign Using the Format Cells Dialog Box (EX 102)
14. Apply a Percent Style Format and Use the Increase Decimal Button (EX 103)
15. Apply Conditional Formatting (EX 104)
16. Change the Widths of Columns (EX 107)
17. Change the Heights of Rows (EX 110)
18. Check Spelling on the Worksheet (EX 112)
19. Change the Worksheet's Margins, Header, and Orientation in Page Layout View (EX 114)
20. Print a Section of the Worksheet (EX 118)
21. Display the Formulas in the Worksheet and Fit the Printout on One Page (EX 119)

... profile, your instructor may have assigned an autogradable ... so, log into the SAM 2010 Web site at www.cengage.com/sam2010 ... and start files.

Learn It Online

Test your knowledge of chapter content and key terms.

Instructions: To complete the Learn It Online exercises, start your browser, click the Address bar, and then enter **scsite.com/ex2010/learn** as the Web address. When the Excel 2010 Learn It Online page is displayed, click the link for the exercise you want to complete and then read the instructions.

Chapter Reinforcement TF, MC, and SA
A series of true/false, multiple choice, and short answer questions that test your knowledge of the chapter content.

Flash Cards
An interactive learning environment where you identify chapter key terms associated with displayed definitions.

Practice Test
A series of multiple choice questions that test your knowledge of chapter content and key terms.

Who Wants To Be a Computer Genius?
An interactive game that challenges your knowledge of chapter content in the style of a television quiz show.

Wheel of Terms
An interactive game that challenges your knowledge of chapter key terms in the style of the television show *Wheel of Fortune*.

Crossword Puzzle Challenge
A crossword puzzle that challenges your knowledge of key terms presented in the chapter.

Apply Your Knowledge

Reinforce the skills and apply the concepts you learned in this chapter.

Profit Analysis Worksheet
Instructions: The purpose of this exercise is to open a partially completed workbook, enter formulas and functions, copy the formulas and functions, and then format the worksheet titles and numbers. As shown in Figure 2–73, the completed worksheet analyzes the costs associated with a police department's fleet of vehicles.

Vehicle ID	Miles Driven	Cost per Mile	Maintenance Cost	Mileage Cost	Total Cost	Total Cost per Mile
	Village of Scott Police Department					
	Monthly Vehicle Cost-per-Mile Summary					
670543	2,007	$ 0.49	$ 243.80	$ 983.43	$ 1,226.23	$ 0.61
979253	3,192	0.48	446.37	1,532.16	1,978.53	0.62
948173	3,802	0.65	472.47	2,471.30	2,943.77	0.77
837625	3,060	0.62	432.25	1,289.60	1,721.85	0.83
624664	2,475	0.56	369.88	1,386.00	1,755.88	0.71
655385	3,294	0.50	352.05	1,647.00	1,999.05	0.61
836417	3,640	0.70	417.80	2,548.00	2,965.80	0.81
993617	3,395	0.70	390.39	2,376.50	2,766.89	0.81
779468	4,075	0.55	443.17	2,241.25	2,683.42	0.66
Totals	**27,960**		**$ 3,566.18**	**$ 16,475.24**	**$ 20,041.42**	**$ 0.72**
Highest	4,075	$0.70	$472.47	$2,548.00	$2,965.80	$0.83
Lowest	2,007	$0.48	$342.80	$983.43	$1,226.23	$0.61
Average	3,107	$0.58	$396.24	$1,830.58	$2,226.82	$0.72

Figure 2–73

Extend Your Knowledge

Extend the skills you learned in this chapter and experiment with new skills. You may need to use Help to complete the assignment.

Formatting a Worksheet and Adding Additional Charts

Instructions: Start Excel. Open the workbook Extend 1–1 Pack Right Moving Supplies. See the inside back cover of this book for instructions for downloading the Data Files for Students, or see your instructor for information on accessing the files required in this book. Perform the following tasks to format cells in the worksheet and to add two charts to the worksheet.

1. Use the commands in the Font group on the Home tab on the Ribbon to change the font of the title in cell A1 to 22-point Arial Black, green, bold, and the subtitle of the worksheet to 14-point Arial, red, bold.

2. Select the range A3:G8, click the Insert tab on the Ribbon, and then click the Dialog Box Launcher in the Charts group on the Ribbon to open the Insert Chart dialog box. If necessary, drag the lower-right corner of the Insert Chart dialog box to expand it (Figure 1–77).

Figure 1–77

3. Insert a Stacked Area in 3-D chart by clicking the Stack clicking the OK button. You may need to use the scroll dialog box to view the Area charts in the gallery. Move data in the worksheet. Click the Design tab and apply

4. Deselect the chart and reselect the range A3:G8, and th Horizontal Cone chart in the worksheet. Move the cha that each chart does not overlap the Stacked Area in 3- the horizontal axis readable by expanding the size of th this chart than the one you selected for the Stacked Ar

Extend Your Knowledge projects at the end of each chapter allow students to extend and expand on the skills learned within the chapter. Students use critical thinking to experiment with new skills to complete each project.

Make It Right projects call on students to analyze a file, discover errors in it, and fix them using the skills they learned in the chapter.

Make It Right

Analyze a workbook and correct all errors and/or improve the design.

Inserting Rows, Moving a Range, and Correcting Formulas in a Worksheet

Instructions: Start Excel. Open the workbook Make It Right 3-1 SpeedyOfficeSupply.com Annual Projected Net Income. See the inside back cover of this book for instructions for downloading the Data Files for Students, or see your instructor for information on accessing the files required for this book. Correct the following design and formula problems (Figure 3–86a) in the worksheet.

Figure 3–86 (a) Before

Figure 3–86 (b) After

1. The Shipping Cost in cell C8 is computed using the formula =B2*B8 (Shipping % × Sales). Similar formulas are used in cells C9, C10, and C11. The formula in cell C8 was entered and copied to cells C9, C10, and C11. Although the result in cell C8 is correct, the results in cells C9, C10, and C11 are incorrect. Edit the formula in cell C8 by changing cell B2 to an absolute cell reference. Copy the corrected formula in cell C8 to cells C9, C10, and C11. After completing the copy, click the Auto Fill Options button arrow that is displayed below and to the right of cell C11 and choose Fill Without Formatting.

2. The Discount amounts in cells D8, D9, D10, and D11 are computed using the IF function. The Discount amount should equal the amount in cell B3*B8 (Discount % × Sales) if the corresponding Sales in column B is greater than or equal to $2,500,000. If the corresponding Sales in column B is less than $2,500,000, then the Discount amount is 5%*B8 (5% × Sales). The IF function in cell D8

Textbook Walk-Through

In the Lab

Lab 2: Analysis of Indirect Expense Allocations

Problem: Your classmate works part time as an advisor for the ReachOut Neighbors not-for-profit group. She has asked you to assist her in creating an indirect expense allocation worksheet (Figure 3–89) that will help the not-for-profit administration better evaluate the branch offices described in Table 3–11.

Figure 3–89

In the Lab Three all new in-depth assignments per chapter require students to utilize the chapter concepts and techniques to solve problems on a computer.

Table 3–11 ReachOut Neighbor Worksheet Data

	Chicago Branch Office	Dallas Branch Office	Houston Branch Office	Jacksonville Branch Office
Total Donations	735356	98190	178435	212300
Distributed Goods and Services	529750	60891	135589	150895
Direct Expenses	57550	22530	14750	25300
Square Footage	15500	775	7550	8250

Instructions Part 1: Do the following to create the worksh...
1. Apply the Solstice theme to the worksheet. Bold the en... worksheet and using the Bold (Home tab | Font group...
2. Change the following column widths: A = 30.00; B thr...
3. Enter the worksheet titles in cells A1 and A2 and the sy... 14-Mar-01 style.

Cases & Places exercises call on students to create open-ended projects that reflect academic, personal, and business settings.

Cases and Places

Apply your creative thinking and problem solving skills to design and implement a solution.

1: Bachelor Degree Expense and Resource Projection

Academic

Attending college with limited resources can be a trying experience. One way to alleviate some of the financial stress is to plan ahead. Develop a worksheet following the general layout in Table 3–16 that shows the projected expenses and resources for four years of college. Use the formulas listed in Table 3–17 and the concepts and techniques presented in this chapter to create the worksheet.

Table 3–16 Bachelor Degree Expense and Resource Projection

Expenses	Freshman	Sophomore	Junior	Senior	Total
Room & Board	$12,550.00	Formula A			—
Tuition & Books	16,450.00	Formula A			—
Clothes	785.00	Formula A			—
Entertainment	1,520.00	Formula A			—
Miscellaneous	936.00	Formula A			—
Total Expenses	—	—	—	—	—

Resources	Freshman	Sophomore	Junior	Senior	Total
Savings	Formula B				—
Parents	Formula B				—
Job	Formula B				—
Loans	Formula B				—
Scholarships	Formula B				—

Assumptions	
Savings	10.00%
Parents	12.00%
Job	11.00%
Loans	35.00%
Scholarships	32.00%
Annual Rate Increase	8.25%

Table 3–17 Bachelor Degree Expense and Resource Projection Formulas

Formula A = Prior Year's Expense * (1 + Annual Rate Increase)

Formula B = Total Expenses for Year * Corresponding Assumption

After creating the worksheet: (a) perform what-if analysis by changing the percents of the resource assumptions; (b) perform a what-if analysis to determine the effect on the resources by increasing the Annual Rate Increase to 9.95% (answer = $149,520.41); and (c) with the original assumptions, goal seek to determine what the Annual Rate Increase would be for the total expenses to be $175,000 (answer = 20.77%). Submit the workbook and results of the what-if analysis as specified by your instructor.

Continued >

Office 2010 and Windows 7: Essential Concepts and Skills

Objectives

You will have mastered the material in this chapter when you can:

- Perform basic mouse operations
- Start Windows and log on to the computer
- Identify the objects on the Windows 7 desktop
- Identify the programs in and versions of Microsoft Office
- Start a program
- Identify the components of the Microsoft Office Ribbon

- Create folders
- Save files
- Change screen resolution
- Perform basic tasks in Microsoft Office programs
- Manage files
- Use Microsoft Office Help and Windows Help

Office 2010 and Windows 7: Essential Concepts and Skills

Office 2010 and Windows 7

This introductory chapter uses Excel 2010 to cover features and functions common to Office 2010 programs, as well as the basics of Windows 7.

Overview

As you read this chapter, you will learn how to perform basic tasks in Windows and Excel by performing these general activities:

- Start programs using Windows.
- Use features in Excel that are common across Office programs.
- Organize files and folders.
- Change screen resolution.
- Quit programs.

Introduction to the Windows 7 Operating System

Windows 7 is the newest version of Microsoft Windows, which is the most popular and widely used operating system. An **operating system** is a computer program (set of computer instructions) that coordinates all the activities of computer hardware such as memory, storage devices, and printers, and provides the capability for you to communicate with the computer.

The Windows 7 operating system simplifies the process of working with documents and programs by organizing the manner in which you interact with the computer. Windows 7 is used to run **application software**, which consists of programs designed to make users more productive and/or assist them with personal tasks, such as word processing.

Windows 7 has two interface variations, Windows 7 Basic and Windows 7 Aero. Computers with up to 1 GB of RAM display the Windows 7 Basic interface (Figure 1a). Computers with more than 1 GB of RAM also can display the Windows Aero interface (Figure 1b), which provides an enhanced visual appearance. The Windows 7 Professional, Windows 7 Enterprise, Windows 7 Home Premium, and Windows 7 Ultimate editions have the capability to use Windows Aero.

Using a Mouse

Windows users work with a mouse that has at least two buttons. For a right-handed user, the left button usually is the primary mouse button, and the right mouse button is the secondary mouse button. Left-handed people, however, can reverse the function of these buttons.

Figure 1 (a) Windows 7 Basic interface

Figure 1 (b) Windows 7 Aero interface

Table 1 explains how to perform a variety of mouse operations. Some programs also use keys in combination with the mouse to perform certain actions. For example, when you hold down the CTRL key while rolling the mouse wheel, text on the screen becomes larger or smaller based on the direction you roll the wheel. The function of the mouse buttons and the wheel varies depending on the program.

Table 1 Mouse Operations		
Operation	**Mouse Action**	**Example***
Point	Move the mouse until the pointer on the desktop is positioned on the item of choice.	Position the pointer on the screen.
Click	Press and release the primary mouse button, which usually is the left mouse button.	Select or deselect items on the screen or start a program or program feature.
Right-click	Press and release the secondary mouse button, which usually is the right mouse button.	Display a shortcut menu.
Double-click	Quickly press and release the left mouse button twice without moving the mouse.	Start a program or program feature.
Triple-click	Quickly press and release the left mouse button three times without moving the mouse.	Select a paragraph.
Drag	Point to an item, hold down the left mouse button, move the item to the desired location on the screen, and then release the left mouse button.	Move an object from one location to another or draw pictures.
Right-drag	Point to an item, hold down the right mouse button, move the item to the desired location on the screen, and then release the right mouse button.	Display a shortcut menu after moving an object from one location to another.
Rotate wheel	Roll the wheel forward or backward.	Scroll vertically (up and down).
Free-spin wheel	Whirl the wheel forward or backward so that it spins freely on its own.	Scroll through many pages in seconds.
Press wheel	Press the wheel button while moving the mouse.	Scroll continuously.
Tilt wheel	Press the wheel toward the right or left.	Scroll horizontally (left and right).
Press thumb button	Press the button on the side of the mouse with your thumb.	Move forward or backward through Web pages and/or control media, games, etc.

*Note: the examples presented in this column are discussed as they are demonstrated in this chapter.

Scrolling

A **scroll bar** is a horizontal or vertical bar that appears when the contents of an area may not be visible completely on the screen (Figure 2). A scroll bar contains **scroll arrows** and a **scroll box** that enable you to view areas that currently cannot be seen. Clicking the up and down scroll arrows moves the screen content up or down one line. You also can click above or below the scroll box to move up or down a section, or drag the scroll box up or down to move up or down to move to a specific location.

Shortcut Keys

In many cases, you can use the keyboard instead of the mouse to accomplish a task. To perform tasks using the keyboard, you press one or more keyboard keys, sometimes identified as

Figure 2

a **shortcut key** or **keyboard shortcut**. Some shortcut keys consist of a single key, such as the F1 key. For example, to obtain help about Windows 7, you can press the F1 key. Other shortcut keys consist of multiple keys, in which case a plus sign separates the key names, such as CTRL+ESC. This notation means to press and hold down the first key listed, press one or more additional keys, and then release all keys. For example, to display the Start menu, press CTRL+ESC, that is, hold down the CTRL key, press the ESC key, and then release both keys.

Starting Windows 7

It is not unusual for multiple people to use the same computer in a work, educational, recreational, or home setting. Windows 7 enables each user to establish a **user account**, which identifies to Windows 7 the resources, such as programs and storage locations, a user can access when working with a computer.

Each user account has a user name and may have a password and an icon, as well. A **user name** is a unique combination of letters or numbers that identifies a specific user to Windows 7. A **password** is a private combination of letters, numbers, and special characters associated with the user name that allows access to a user's account resources. A **user icon** is a picture associated with a user name.

When you turn on a computer, an introductory screen consisting of the Windows logo and copyright messages is displayed. The Windows logo is animated and glows as the Windows 7 operating system is loaded. After the Windows logo appears, depending on your computer's settings, you may or may not be required to log on to the computer. **Logging on** to a computer opens your user account and makes the computer available for use. If you are required to log on to the computer, the **Welcome screen** is displayed, which shows the user names of users on the computer (Figure 3). Clicking the user name or picture begins the process of logging on to the computer.

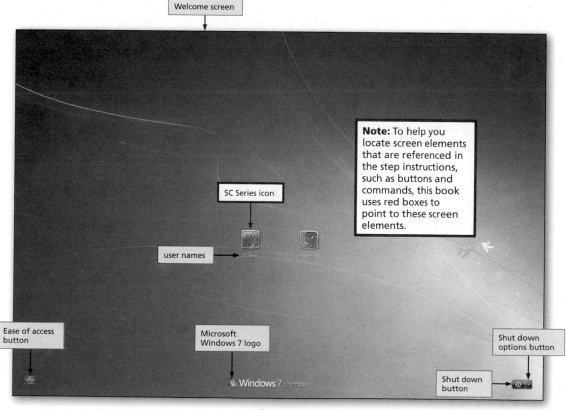

Figure 3

At the bottom of the Welcome screen is the 'Ease of access' button, Windows 7 logo, a Shut down button, and a 'Shut down options' button. The following list identifies the functions of the buttons and commands that typically appear on the Welcome screen:

- Clicking the 'Ease of access' button displays the Ease of Access Center, which provides tools to optimize your computer to accommodate the needs of the mobility, hearing, and vision impaired users.
- Clicking the Shut down button shuts down Windows 7 and the computer.
- Clicking the 'Shut down options' button, located to the right of the Shut down button, displays a menu containing commands that perform actions such as restarting the computer, placing the computer in a low-powered state, and shutting down the computer. The commands available on your computer may differ.
  - The **Restart command** closes open programs, shuts down Windows 7, and then restarts Windows 7 and displays the Welcome screen.
  - The **Sleep command** waits for Windows 7 to save your work and then turns off the computer fans and hard disk. To wake the computer from the Sleep state, press the power button or lift a notebook computer's cover, and log on to the computer.
  - The **Shut down command** shuts down and turns off the computer.

To Log On to the Computer

After starting Windows 7, you might need to log on to the computer. The following steps log on to the computer based on a typical installation. You may need to ask your instructor how to log on to your computer. This set of steps uses SC Series as the user name. The list of user names on your computer will be different.

1

- Click the user icon (SC Series, in this case) on the Welcome screen (shown in Figure 3 on the previous page); depending on settings, this either will display a password text box (Figure 4) or will log on to the computer and display the Windows 7 desktop.

Q&A Why do I not see a user icon?

Your computer may require you to type a user name instead of clicking an icon.

Q&A What is a text box?

A text box is a rectangular box in which you type text.

Q&A Why does my screen not show a password text box?

Your account does not require a password.

Figure 4

2

- If Windows 7 displays a password text box, type your password in the text box and then click the arrow button to log on to the computer and display the Windows 7 desktop (Figure 5).

Q&A

Why does my desktop look different from the one in Figure 5?

The Windows 7 desktop is customizable, and your school or employer may have modified the desktop to meet its needs. Also, your screen resolution, which affects the size of the elements on the screen, may differ from the screen resolution used in this book. Later in this chapter, you learn how to change screen resolution.

Figure 5

The Windows 7 Desktop

The Windows 7 desktop (Figure 5) and the objects on the desktop emulate a work area in an office. Think of the Windows desktop as an electronic version of the top of your desk. You can perform tasks such as placing objects on the desktop, moving the objects around the desktop, and removing items from the desktop.

When you start a program in Windows 7, it appears on the desktop. Some icons also may be displayed on the desktop. For instance, the icon for the **Recycle Bin**, the location of files that have been deleted, appears on the desktop by default. A **file** is a named unit of storage. Files can contain text, images, charts, and symbols. You can customize your desktop so that icons representing programs and files you use often appear on your desktop.

Introduction to Microsoft Office 2010

Microsoft Office 2010 is the newest version of Microsoft Office, offering features that provide users with better functionality and easier ways to work with the various files they create. These features include enhanced design tools, such as improved picture formatting tools and new themes, shared notebooks for working in groups, mobile versions of Office programs, broadcast presentation for the Web, and a digital notebook for managing and sharing multimedia information.

Microsoft Office 2010 Programs

Microsoft Office 2010 includes a wide variety of programs such as Word, PowerPoint, Excel, Access, Outlook, Publisher, OneNote, InfoPath, SharePoint Workspace, Communicator, and Web Apps:

- **Microsoft Word 2010**, or Word, is a full-featured word processing program that allows you to create professional-looking documents and revise them easily.
- **Microsoft PowerPoint 2010**, or PowerPoint, is a complete presentation program that allows you to produce professional-looking presentations.
- **Microsoft Excel 2010**, or Excel, is a powerful spreadsheet program that allows you to organize data, complete calculations, make decisions, graph data, develop professional-looking reports, publish organized data to the Web, and access real-time data from Web sites.
- **Microsoft Access 2010**, or Access, is a database management system that allows you to create a database; add, change, and delete data in the database; ask questions concerning the data in the database; and create forms and reports using the data in the database.
- **Microsoft Outlook 2010**, or Outlook, is a communications and scheduling program that allows you to manage e-mail accounts, calendars, contacts, and access to other Internet content.
- **Microsoft Publisher 2010**, or Publisher, is a desktop publishing program that helps you create professional-quality publications and marketing materials that can be shared easily.
- **Microsoft OneNote 2010**, or OneNote, is a note taking program that allows you to store and share information in notebooks with other people.
- **Microsoft InfoPath 2010**, or InfoPath, is a form development program that helps you create forms for use on the Web and gather data from these forms.
- **Microsoft SharePoint Workspace 2010**, or SharePoint, is collaboration software that allows you access and revise files stored on your computer from other locations.
- **Microsoft Communicator** is communications software that allows you to use different modes of communications such as instant messaging, video conferencing, and sharing files and programs.
- **Microsoft Web Apps** is a Web application that allows you to edit and share files on the Web using the familiar Office interface.

Microsoft Office 2010 Suites

A **suite** is a collection of individual programs available together as a unit. Microsoft offers a variety of Office suites. Table 2 lists the Office 2010 suites and their components.

Programs in a suite, such as Microsoft Office, typically use a similar interface and share features. In addition, Microsoft Office programs use **common dialog boxes** for performing actions such as opening and saving files. Once you are comfortable working with these elements and this interface and performing tasks in one program, the similarity can help you apply the knowledge and skills you have learned to another Office program(s). For example, the process for saving a file in Excel is the same in Word, PowerPoint, and the other Office programs. While briefly showing how to use Excel, this chapter illustrates some of the common functions across the Office programs and also identifies the characteristics unique to Excel.

Table 2 Microsoft Office 2010 Suites	Microsoft Office Professional Plus 2010	Microsoft Office Professional 2010	Microsoft Office Home and Business 2010	Microsoft Office Standard 2010	Microsoft Office Home and Student 2010
Microsoft Word 2010	✔	✔	✔	✔	✔
Microsoft PowerPoint 2010	✔	✔	✔	✔	✔
Microsoft Excel 2010	✔	✔	✔	✔	✔
Microsoft Access 2010	✔	✔	✗	✗	✗
Microsoft Outlook 2010	✔	✔	✔	✔	✗
Microsoft Publisher 2010	✔	✔	✗	✔	✗
Microsoft OneNote 2010	✔	✔	✔	✔	✔
Microsoft InfoPath 2010	✔	✗	✗	✗	✗
Microsoft SharePoint Workspace 2010	✔	✗	✗	✗	✗
Microsoft Communicator	✔	✗	✗	✗	✗

Starting and Using a Program

To use a program, such as Excel, you must instruct the operating system to start the program. Windows 7 provides many different ways to start a program, one of which is presented in this section (other ways to start a program are presented throughout this chapter). After starting a program, you can use it to perform a variety of tasks. The following pages use Excel to discuss some elements of the Office interface and to perform tasks that are common to other Office programs.

Excel

Excel is a powerful spreadsheet program that allows users to organize data, complete calculations, make decisions, graph data, develop professional-looking reports, publish organized data to the Web, and access real-time data from Web sites. The four major parts of Excel are:

- **Workbooks and Worksheets** — **A workbook** is like a notebook. Inside the workbook are sheets, each of which is called a **worksheet**. In other words, a workbook is a collection of worksheets. Worksheets allow users to enter, calculate, manipulate, and analyze data such as numbers and text. The terms worksheet and spreadsheet are interchangeable.

- **Charts** — Excel can draw a variety of charts.

- **Tables** — Tables organize and store data within worksheets. For example, once a user enters data into a worksheet, an Excel table can sort the data, search for specific data, and select data that satisfies defined criteria.

- **Web Support** — Web support allows users to save Excel worksheets or parts of a worksheet in HTML format, so that a user can view and manipulate the worksheet using a browser. Excel Web support also provides access to real-time data, such as stock quotes, using Web queries.

To Start a Program Using the Start Menu

Across the bottom of the Windows 7 desktop is the taskbar. The taskbar contains the **Start button**, which you use to access programs, files, folders, and settings on a computer. A **folder** is a named location on a storage medium that usually contains related files. The taskbar also displays a button for each program currently running on a computer.

Clicking the Start button displays the Start menu. The **Start menu** allows you to access programs, folders, and files on the computer and contains commands that allow you to start programs, store and search for files, customize the computer, and obtain help about thousands of topics. A **menu** is a list of related items, including folders, programs, and commands. Each **command** on a menu performs a specific action, such as saving a file or obtaining help.

The following steps, which assume Windows 7 is running, use the Start menu to start the Microsoft Excel 2010 program based on a typical installation. You may need to ask your instructor how to start Excel for your computer. Although the steps illustrate starting the Excel program, the steps to start any program are similar.

1

- Click the Start button on the Windows 7 taskbar to display the Start menu (Figure 6).

Q&A

Why does my Start menu look different?

It may look different depending on your computer's configuration. The Start menu may be customized for several reasons, such as usage requirements or security restrictions.

Figure 6

2

- Click All Programs at the bottom of the left pane on the Start menu to display the All Programs list (Figure 7).

Q&A

What is a pane?

A **pane** is an area of a window that displays related content. For example, the left pane on the Start menu contains a list of frequently used programs, as well as the All Programs command.

Q&A

Why might my All Programs list look different?

Most likely, the programs installed on your computer will differ from those shown in Figure 7. Your All Programs list will show the programs that are installed on your computer.

Figure 7

❸

- If the program you want to start is located in a folder, click or scroll to and then click the folder (Microsoft Office, in this case) in the All Programs list to display a list of the folder's contents (Figure 8).

Q&A

Why is the Microsoft Office folder on my computer?

During installation of Microsoft Office 2010, the Microsoft Office folder was added to the All Programs list.

Figure 8

❹

- Click, or scroll to and then click, the program name (Microsoft Excel 2010, in this case) in the list to start the selected program (Figure 9).

Q&A

What happens when you start a program?

Many programs initially display a blank file in a program window, as shown in the Excel window in Figure 9; others provide a means for you to create a blank file. A **window** is a rectangular area that displays data and information. The top of a window has a **title bar**, which is a horizontal space that contains the window's name.

Figure 9

Q&A

Why is my program window a different size?

The Excel window shown in Figure 9 is not maximized. Your Excel window already may be maximized. The steps on the next page maximize a window.

Other Ways

1. Double-click program icon on desktop, if one is present

2. Click program name in left pane of Start menu, if present

3. Display Start menu, type program name in search box, click program name

4. Double-click file created using program you want to start

To Maximize a Window

Sometimes content is not visible completely in a window. One method of displaying the entire contents of a window is to **maximize** it, or enlarge the window so that it fills the entire screen. The following step maximizes the Excel window; however, any Office program's window can be maximized using this step.

1

- If the program window is not maximized already, click the Maximize button (shown in Figure 9 on the previous page) next to the Close button on the window's title bar (the Excel window title bar, in this case) to maximize the window (Figure 10).

Q&A What happened to the Maximize button?

It changed to a Restore Down button, which you can use to return a window to its size and location before you maximized it.

Q&A How do I know whether a window is maximized?

A window is maximized if it fills the entire display area and the Restore Down button is displayed on the title bar.

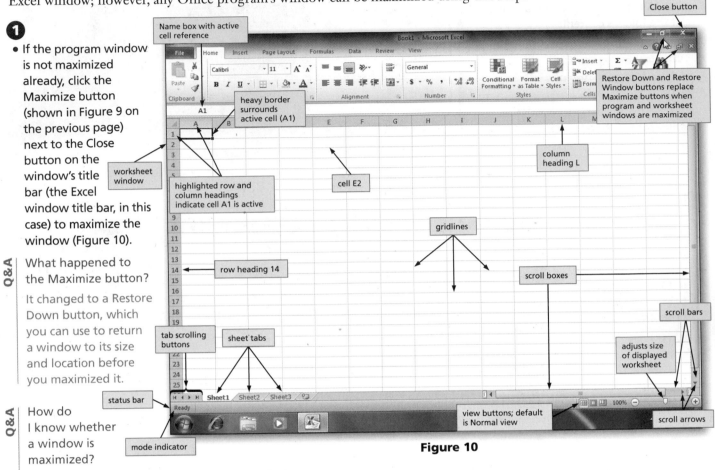

Figure 10

Other Ways

1. Double-click title bar
2. Drag title bar to top of screen

The Excel Worksheet Window, Ribbon, and Elements Common to Office Programs

The Excel window consists of a variety of components to make your work more efficient and worksheets more professional. These include the worksheet window, Ribbon, Mini toolbar, shortcut menus, and Quick Access Toolbar. Most of these components are common to other Microsoft Office 2010 programs; others are unique to Excel.

You view a portion of a worksheet on the screen through a **worksheet window** (Figure 11). The default (preset) view is **Normal Layout view**, which shows the worksheet in a continuous arrangement of rows and columns.

Scroll Bars You use a scroll bar to display different portions of a worksheet in the worksheet window. At the right edge of the worksheet window is a vertical scroll bar. A horizontal scroll bar also appears at the bottom of the worksheet window. On a scroll bar, the position of the scroll box reflects the location of the portion of the worksheet that is displayed in the worksheet window.

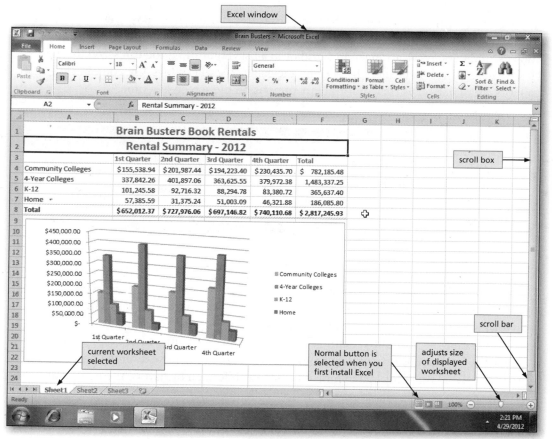

Figure 11

Status Bar   The **status bar**, located at the bottom of the worksheet window above the Windows 7 taskbar, presents information about the worksheet, the progress of current tasks, and the status of certain commands and keys; it also provides controls for viewing the worksheet. As you type text or perform certain tasks, various indicators and buttons may appear on the status bar.

The left side of the status bar in Figure 11 shows the current progress of current tasks. The right side of the status bar includes buttons and controls you can use to change the view of a worksheet and adjust the size of the displayed worksheet.

Ribbon   The Ribbon, located near the top of the window below the title bar, is the control center in Excel and other Office programs (Figure 12). The Ribbon provides easy, central access to the tasks you perform while creating a workbook. The Ribbon consists of tabs, groups, and commands. Each **tab** contains a collection of groups, and each **group** contains related functions. When you start an Office program, such as Excel, it initially displays several main tabs, also called default tabs. All Office programs have a **Home tab**, which contains the more frequently used commands.

In addition to the main tabs, Office programs display **tool tabs**, also called contextual tabs (Figure 13), when you perform certain tasks or work with objects such as pictures or charts. If you insert a picture in an Excel worksheet, for example, the Picture Tools tab and its related subordinate Format tab appear, collectively referred to as the Picture Tools Format tab. When you are finished working with the picture, the Picture Tools Format tab disappears from the Ribbon. Excel and other Office programs determine when tool tabs should appear and disappear based on tasks you perform. Some tool tabs, such as the Chart Tools tab, have more than one related subordinate tab.

Items on the Ribbon include buttons, boxes (text boxes, check boxes, etc.), and tabs (Figure 12). Clicking a button on the Ribbon might display a gallery. A **gallery** is a set of choices, often graphical, arranged in a grid or in a list (Figure 13). You can scroll through choices in an in-Ribbon gallery by clicking the gallery's scroll arrows. Or, you can click a gallery's More button to view more gallery options on the screen at a time.

Figure 12

Some buttons and boxes have arrows that, when clicked, also display a gallery; others always cause a gallery to be displayed when clicked. Most galleries support **live preview**, which is a feature that allows you to point to a gallery choice and see its effect in the worksheet — without actually selecting the choice (Figure 13).

Some commands on the Ribbon display an image to help you remember their function. When you point to a command on the Ribbon, all or part of the command glows in shades of yellow and orange, and an Enhanced ScreenTip appears on the screen. An **Enhanced ScreenTip** is an on-screen note that provides the name of the command, available keyboard shortcut(s), a description of the command, and sometimes instructions for how to obtain help about the command (Figure 14). Enhanced ScreenTips are more detailed than a typical ScreenTip, which usually displays only the name of the command.

Some groups on the Ribbon have a small arrow in the lower-right corner, called a **Dialog Box Launcher**, that when clicked, displays a dialog box or a task pane with additional options for the group (Figure 15). When presented with a dialog box, you make selections and must close the dialog box before returning to the workbook. A **task pane**, in contrast to a dialog box, is a window that can remain open and visible while you work in the workbook.

Figure 13

Figure 14

Figure 15

Mini Toolbar The **Mini toolbar**, which appears automatically based on tasks you perform, contains commands related to changing the appearance of text in a worksheet. All commands on the Mini toolbar also exist on the Ribbon. The purpose of the Mini toolbar is to minimize mouse movement.

When the Mini toolbar appears, it initially is transparent (Figure 16a). If you do not use the transparent Mini toolbar, it disappears from the screen. To use the Mini toolbar, move the mouse pointer into the toolbar, which causes the Mini toolbar to change from a transparent to bright appearance (Figure 16b). If you right-click an item in the worksheet window, Excel displays both the Mini toolbar and a shortcut menu, which is discussed in a later section in this chapter.

(a) transparent Mini toolbar   **(b) bright Mini toolbar**

Figure 16

Quick Access Toolbar The **Quick Access Toolbar**, located initially (by default) above the Ribbon at the left edge of the title bar, provides convenient, one-click access to frequently used commands (Figure 14). The commands on the Quick Access Toolbar always are available, regardless of the task you are performing. The Quick Access Toolbar is discussed in more depth later in the chapter.

KeyTips If you prefer using the keyboard instead of the mouse, you can press the ALT key on the keyboard to display **KeyTips**, or keyboard code icons, for certain commands

Figure 17

(Figure 17). To select a command using the keyboard, press the letter or number displayed in the KeyTip, which may cause additional KeyTips related to the selected command to appear. To remove KeyTips from the screen, press the ALT key or the ESC key until all KeyTips disappear, or click the mouse anywhere in the program window.

To Display a Different Tab on the Ribbon

When you start Excel, the Ribbon displays eight main tabs: File, Home, Insert, Page Layout, Formulas, Data, Review, and View. The tab currently displayed is called the **active tab**.

The following step displays the Insert tab, that is, makes it the active tab.

1

- Click Insert on the Ribbon to display the Insert tab (Figure 18).

🔍 **Experiment**

- Click the other tabs on the Ribbon to view their contents. When you are finished, click the Insert tab to redisplay the Insert tab.

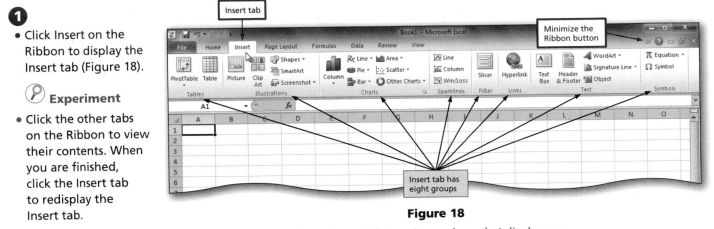

Figure 18

Q&A If I am working in a different Office program, such as PowerPoint or Access, how do I display a different tab on the Ribbon?

Follow this same procedure; that is, click the desired tab on the Ribbon.

To Minimize, Display, and Restore the Ribbon

To display more of a worksheet or other item in the window of an Office program, some users prefer to minimize the Ribbon, which hides the groups on the Ribbon and displays only the main tabs. Each time you start an Office program, such as Excel, the Ribbon appears the same way it did the last time you used that Office program. The chapters in this book, however, begin with the Ribbon appearing as it did at the initial installation of Excel.

The following steps minimize, display, and restore the Ribbon in Excel.

1

- Click the Minimize the Ribbon button on the Ribbon (shown in Figure 18) to minimize the Ribbon (Figure 19).

Figure 19

Q&A What happened to the groups on the Ribbon?

When you minimize the Ribbon, the groups disappear so that the Ribbon does not take up as much space on the screen.

Q&A What happened to the Minimize the Ribbon button?

The Expand the Ribbon button replaces the Minimize the Ribbon button when the Ribbon is minimized.

②

- Click Home on the Ribbon to display the Home tab (Figure 20).

Office 2010 and Windows 7 Chapter

Q&A

Why would I click the Home tab?

If you want to use a command on a minimized Ribbon, click the main tab to display the groups for that tab. After you select a command on the Ribbon, the groups will be hidden once again. If you decide not to use a command on the Ribbon, you can hide the groups by clicking the same main tab or clicking in the program window.

Figure 20

③

- Click Home on the Ribbon to hide the groups again (shown in Figure 19).

- Click the Expand the Ribbon button on the Ribbon (shown in Figure 19) to restore the Ribbon.

Other Ways
1. Double-click Home on the Ribbon
2. Press CTRL+F1

To Display and Use a Shortcut Menu

When you right-click certain areas of the Excel and other program windows, a shortcut menu will appear. A **shortcut menu** is a list of frequently used commands that relate to the right-clicked object. When you right-click a scroll bar, for example, a shortcut menu appears with commands related to the scroll bar. When you right-click the Quick Access Toolbar, a shortcut menu appears with commands related to the Quick Access Toolbar. You can use shortcut menus to access common commands quickly. The following steps use a shortcut menu to move the Quick Access Toolbar, which by default is located on the title bar.

①

- Right-click the Quick Access Toolbar to display a shortcut menu that presents a list of commands related to the Quick Access Toolbar (Figure 21).

Figure 21

②

- Click Show Quick Access Toolbar Below the Ribbon on the shortcut menu to display the Quick Access Toolbar below the Ribbon (Figure 22).

Figure 22

❸

- Right-click the Quick Access Toolbar to display a shortcut menu (Figure 23).

❹

- Click Show Quick Access Toolbar Above the Ribbon on the shortcut menu to return the Quick Access Toolbar to its original position (shown in Figure 21 on the previous page).

Figure 23

To Customize the Quick Access Toolbar

The Quick Access Toolbar provides easy access to some of the more frequently used commands in Office programs. By default, the Quick Access Toolbar contains buttons for the Save, Undo, and Redo commands. You can customize the Quick Access Toolbar by changing its location in the window, as shown in the previous steps, and by adding more buttons to reflect commands you would like to access easily. The following steps add the Quick Print button to the Quick Access Toolbar in the Excel window.

❶

- Click the Customize Quick Access Toolbar button to display the Customize Quick Access Toolbar menu (Figure 24).

Q&A Which commands are listed on the Customize Quick Access Toolbar menu?

It lists commands that commonly are added to the Quick Access Toolbar.

Q&A What do the check marks next to some commands signify?

Check marks appear next to commands that already are on the Quick Access Toolbar. When you add a button to the Quick Access Toolbar, a check mark will be displayed next to its command name.

Figure 24

❷

- Click Quick Print on the Customize Quick Access Toolbar menu to add the Quick Print button to the Quick Access Toolbar (Figure 25).

Q&A How would I remove a button from the Quick Access Toolbar?

You would right-click the button you wish to remove and then click Remove from Quick Access Toolbar on the shortcut menu. If you want your screens to match the screens in the remaining chapters in this book, you would remove the Quick Print button from the Quick Access Toolbar.

Figure 25

To Enter Text in a Workbook

To enter data into a cell, you first must select it. The easiest way to select a cell (make it active) is to use the mouse to move the block plus sign mouse pointer to the cell and then click. An alternative method is to use the arrow keys that are located just to the right of the typewriter keys on the keyboard. An arrow key selects the cell adjacent to the active cell in the direction of the arrow on the key.

In Excel, any set of characters containing a letter, hyphen (as in a telephone number), or space is considered text. **Text** is used to place titles, such as worksheet titles, column titles, and row titles, on the worksheet. The following steps enter the worksheet title in cell A1.

1

- If it is not already the active cell, click cell A1 to make it the active cell (Figure 26).

Q&A What if I make an error while typing?

You can press the BACKSPACE key until you have deleted the text in error and then retype the text correctly.

Figure 26

2

- Type `Brain Busters Book Rentals` in cell A1.

- Press the ENTER key to complete the entry and enter the worksheet title (Figure 27).

Figure 27

Saving and Organizing Files

While you are creating a workbook, the computer stores it in memory. When you save a workbook, the computer places it on a storage medium such as a hard disk, USB flash drive, or optical disc. A saved workbook is referred to as a file. A **file name** is the name assigned to a file when it is saved. It is important to save a workbook frequently for the following reasons:

- The workbook in memory might be lost if the computer is turned off or you lose electrical power while a program is running.

- If you run out of time before completing a project, you may finish it at a future time without starting over.

When saving files, you should organize them so that you easily can find them later. Windows 7 provides tools to help you organize files.

Organizing Files and Folders

A file contains data. This data can range from an inventory report to an accounting spreadsheet to an expense report. You should organize and store these files in folders to avoid misplacing a file and to help you find a file quickly.

If you are a freshman taking an introductory computer class (CIS 101, for example), you may want to design a series of folders for the different subjects covered in the class. To accomplish this, you can arrange the folders in a hierarchy for the class, as shown in Figure 28.

Figure 28

The hierarchy contains three levels. The first level contains the storage device, in this case a USB flash drive. Windows 7 identifies the storage device with a letter, and, in some cases, a name. In Figure 28, the USB flash drive is identified as REMOVABLE (E:). The second level contains the class folder (CIS 101, in this case), and the third level contains seven folders, one each for a different Office program that will be covered in the class (Word, PowerPoint, Excel, Access, Outlook, Publisher, and OneNote).

When the hierarchy in Figure 28 is created, the USB flash drive is said to contain the CIS 101 folder, and the CIS 101 folder is said to contain the separate Office folders (i.e., Word, PowerPoint, Excel, etc.). In addition, this hierarchy easily can be expanded to include folders from other classes taken during additional semesters.

The vertical and horizontal lines in Figure 28 form a pathway that allows you to navigate to a drive or folder on a computer or network. A **path** consists of a drive letter (preceded by a drive name when necessary) and colon, to identify the storage device, and one or more folder names. Each drive or folder in the hierarchy has a corresponding path.

Table 3 shows examples of paths and their corresponding drives and folders.

Table 3 Paths and Corresponding Drives and Folders	
Path	**Drive and Folder**
Computer ▶ REMOVABLE (E:)	Drive E (REMOVABLE (E:))
Computer ▶ REMOVABLE (E:) ▶ CIS 101	CIS 101 folder on drive E
Computer ▶ REMOVABLE (E:) ▶ CIS 101 ▶ Excel	Excel folder in CIS 101 folder on drive E

BTW

Saving Online
Instead of saving files on a USB flash drive, some people prefer to save them online so that they can access the files from any computer with an Internet connection. For more information, read Appendix C.

The following pages illustrate the steps to organize folders for a class and save a file in a folder:

1. Create a folder identifying your class.
2. Create an Excel folder in the folder identifying your class.
3. Save a file in the Excel folder.
4. Verify the location of the saved file.

To Create a Folder

When you create a folder, such as the CIS 101 folder shown in Figure 28, you must name the folder. A folder name should describe the folder and its contents. A folder name can contain spaces and any uppercase or lowercase characters, except a backslash (\), slash (/), colon (:), asterisk (*), question mark (?), quotation marks ("), less than symbol (<), greater than symbol (>), or vertical bar (|). Folder names cannot be CON, AUX, COM1, COM2, COM3, COM4, LPT1, LPT2, LPT3, PRN, or NUL. The same rules for naming folders also apply to naming files.

To store files and folders on a USB flash drive, you must connect the USB flash drive to an available USB port on a computer. The following steps create your class folder (CIS 101, in this case) on a USB flash drive.

1

- Connect the USB flash drive to an available USB port on the computer to open the AutoPlay window (Figure 29). (You may need to click the Windows Explorer program button on the taskbar to make the AutoPlay window visible.)

Q&A Why does the AutoPlay window not open?

Some computers are not configured to open an AutoPlay window. Instead, they might display the contents of the USB flash drive automatically, or you might need to access contents of the USB flash drive using the Computer window. To use the Computer window to display the USB flash drive's contents, click the Start button, click Computer on the Start menu, and then click the icon representing the USB flash drive and then proceed to Step 3 on the next page.

Q&A Why does the AutoPlay window look different from the one in Figure 29?

The AutoPlay window that opens on your computer might display different options. The type of USB flash drive, its contents, and the next available drive letter on your computer all will determine which options are displayed in the AutoPlay window.

Figure 29

2

- Click the 'Open folder to view files' link in the AutoPlay window to open the USB flash drive window (Figure 30).

Q&A Why does Figure 30 show REMOVABLE (E:) for the USB flash drive?

REMOVABLE is the name of the USB flash drive used to illustrate these steps. The (E:) refers to the drive letter assigned by Windows 7 to the USB flash drive. The name and drive letter of your USB flash drive probably will be different.

Figure 30

3

- Click the New folder button on the toolbar to display a new folder icon with the name, New folder, selected in a text box.

- Type CIS 101 (or your class code) in the text box to name the folder.

- Press the ENTER key to create a folder identifying your class on the selected drive (Figure 31). If the CIS 101 folder does not appear in the navigation pane, double-click REMOVABLE (E:) in the navigation pane to display the folder just added.

Q&A

What happens when I press the ENTER key?

The class folder (CIS 101, in this case) is displayed in the File list, which contains the folder name, date modified, type, and size.

Q&A

Why is the folder icon displayed differently on my computer?

Windows might be configured to display contents differently on your computer.

Figure 31

Folder Windows

The USB flash drive window (shown in Figure 31) is called a folder window. Recall that a folder is a specific named location on a storage medium that contains related files. Most users rely on **folder windows** for finding, viewing, and managing information on their computer. Folder windows have common design elements, including the following (Figure 31).

- The **Address bar** provides quick navigation options. The arrows on the Address bar allow you to visit different locations on the computer.

- The buttons to the left of the Address bar allow you to navigate the contents of the left pane and view recent pages. Other buttons allow you to specify the size of the window.

- The **Previous Locations button** saves the locations you have visited and displays the locations when clicked.

- The **Refresh button** on the right side of the Address bar refreshes the contents of the right pane of the folder window.

- The **search box** to the right of the Address bar contains the dimmed word, Search. You can type a term in the search box for a list of files, folders, shortcuts, and elements containing that term within the location you are searching. A **shortcut** is an icon on the desktop that provides a user with immediate access to a program or file.

- The **Command bar** contains five buttons used to accomplish various tasks on the computer related to organizing and managing the contents of the open window.

- The **navigation pane** on the left contains the Favorites area, Libraries area, Computer area, and Network area.

- The **Favorites area** contains links to your favorite locations. By default, this list contains only links to your Desktop, Downloads, and Recent Places.
- The **Libraries area** shows links to files and folders that have been included in a library.

A **library** helps you manage multiple folders and files stored in various locations on a computer. It does not store the files and folders; rather, it displays links to them so that you can access them quickly. For example, you can save pictures from a digital camera in any folder on any storage location on a computer. Normally, this would make organizing the different folders difficult; however, if you add the folders to a library, you can access all the pictures from one location regardless of where they are stored.

To Create a Folder within a Folder

With the class folder created, you can create folders that will store the files you create using Excel. The following steps create an Excel folder in the CIS 101 folder (or the folder identifying your class).

1
- Double-click the icon or folder name for the CIS 101 folder (or the folder identifying your class) in the File list to open the folder (Figure 32).

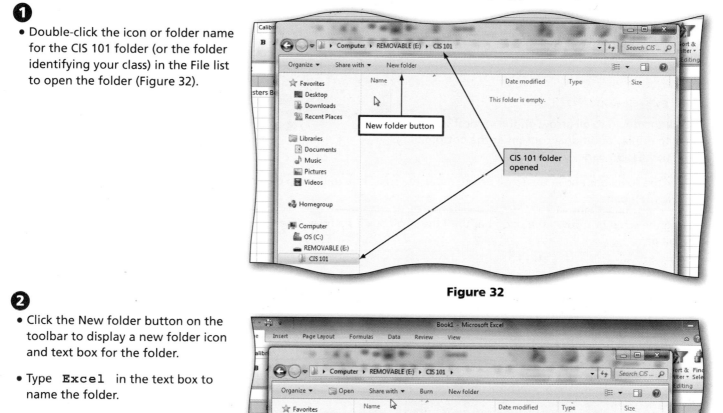

Figure 32

2
- Click the New folder button on the toolbar to display a new folder icon and text box for the folder.

- Type **Excel** in the text box to name the folder.

- Press the ENTER key to create the folder (Figure 33).

Figure 33

To Expand a Folder, Scroll through Folder Contents, and Collapse a Folder

Folder windows display the hierarchy of items and the contents of drives and folders in the right pane. You might want to expand a drive in the navigation pane to view its contents, scroll through its contents, and collapse it when you are finished viewing its contents. When a folder is expanded, it lists all the folders it contains. By contrast, a collapsed folder does not list the folders it contains. The steps on the next page expand, scroll through, and then collapse the folder identifying your class (CIS 101, in this case).

1

● Double-click the folder identifying your class (CIS 101, in this case) in the navigation pane, which expands the folder to display its contents and displays a black arrow to the left of the folder icon (Figure 34).

Q&A Why is the Excel folder indented below the CIS 101 folder in the navigation pane?

It shows that the folder is contained within the CIS 101 folder.

Q&A Why did a scroll bar appear in the navigation pane?

When all contents cannot fit in a window or pane, a scroll bar appears. As described earlier, you can view areas currently not visible by (1) clicking the scroll arrows, (2) clicking above or below the scroll bar, and (3) dragging the scroll box.

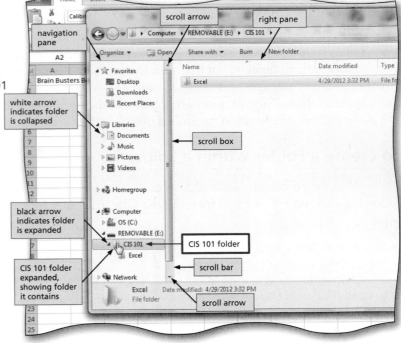

Figure 34

🔑 **Experiment**

● Click the down scroll arrow on the vertical scroll bar to display additional content at the bottom of the navigation pane.

● Click the scroll bar above the scroll box to move the scroll box to the top of the navigation pane.

● Drag the scroll box down the scroll bar until the scroll box is halfway down the scroll bar.

2

● Double-click the folder identifying your class (CIS 101, in this case) in the navigation pane to collapse the folder (Figure 35).

Figure 35

Other Ways	
1. Point in navigation pane to display arrows, click white arrow to expand or click black arrow to collapse	2. Select folder to expand or collapse using arrow keys, press RIGHT ARROW to expand; press LEFT ARROW to collapse

To Switch from One Program to Another

The next step is to save the Excel file containing the worksheet title you typed earlier. Excel, however, currently is not the active window. You can use the program button on the taskbar and live preview to switch to Excel and then save the workbook in the Excel window.

If Windows Aero is active on your computer, Windows displays a live preview window whenever you move your mouse on a button or click a button on the taskbar. If Aero is not supported or enabled on your computer, you will see a window title instead of a live preview. These steps use the Excel program; however, the steps are the same for any active Office program currently displayed as a program button on the taskbar.

The next steps switch to the Excel window.

①

- Point to the Excel program button on the taskbar to see a live preview of the open workbook(s) or the window title(s) of the open workbook(s), depending on your computer's configuration (Figure 36).

②

- Click the program button or the live preview to make the program associated with the program button the active window (shown in Figure 27 on page OFF 19).

Q&A

What if multiple documents are open in a program?

If Aero is enabled on your computer, click the desired live preview. If Aero is not supported or not enabled, click the window title.

Figure 36

To Save a File in a Folder

Now that you have created the Excel folder for storing files, you can save the Excel workbook in that folder. The following steps save a file on a USB flash drive in the Excel folder contained in your class folder (CIS 101, in this case) using the file name, Brain Busters.

①

- With a USB flash drive connected to one of the computer's USB ports, click the Save button on the Quick Access Toolbar to display the Save As dialog box (Figure 37).

Figure 37

2

- Type **Brain Busters** in the File name text box (Save As dialog box) to change the file name. Do not press the ENTER key after typing the file name because you do not want to close the dialog box at this time (Figure 38).

Q&A What characters can I use in a file name?

The only invalid characters are the backslash (\), slash (/), colon (:), asterisk (*), question mark (?), quotation mark ("), less than symbol (<), greater than symbol (>), and vertical bar (|).

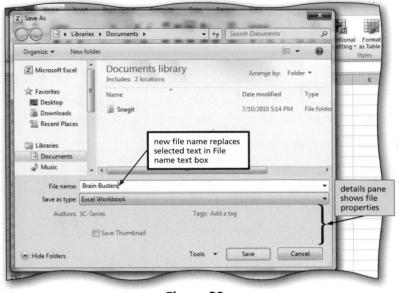

Figure 38

3

- Navigate to the desired save location (in this case, the Excel folder in the CIS 101 folder [or your class folder] on the USB flash drive) by performing the tasks in Steps 3a – 3c.

3a

- If the navigation pane is not displayed in the dialog box, click the Browse Folders button to expand the dialog box.

- If Computer is not displayed in the navigation pane, drag the navigation pane scroll bar until Computer appears.

- If Computer is not expanded in the navigation pane, double-click Computer to display a list of available storage devices in the navigation pane.

- If necessary, scroll through the dialog box until your USB flash drive appears in the list of available storage devices in the navigation pane (Figure 39).

Figure 39

3b

- If your USB flash drive is not expanded, double-click the USB flash drive in the list of available storage devices in the navigation pane to select that drive as the new save location and display its contents in the right pane.

3c

- If your class folder (CIS 101, in this case) is not expanded, double-click the CIS 101 folder to select the folder and display its contents in the right pane.

Q&A What if I do not want to save in a folder?

Although storing files in folders is an effective technique for organizing files, some users prefer not to store files in folders. If you prefer not to save this file in a folder, skip all instructions in Step 3c and proceed to Step 4.

- Click the Excel folder to select the folder and display its contents in the right pane (Figure 40).

Figure 40

4

- Click the Save button (Save As dialog box) to save the workbook in the selected folder on the selected drive with the entered file name (Figure 41).

Q&A

How do I know that the file is saved?

While an Office program such as Excel is saving a file, it briefly displays a message on the status bar indicating the amount of the file saved. In addition, the USB flash drive may have a light that flashes during the save process.

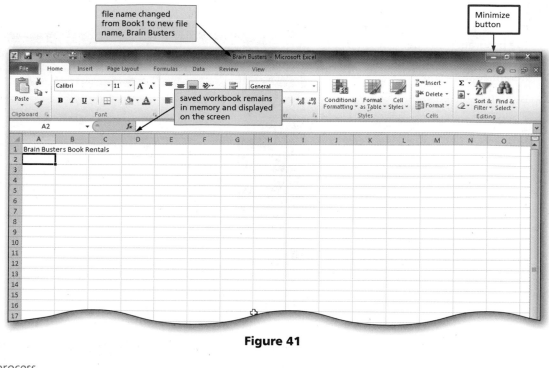

file name changed from Book1 to new file name, Brain Busters

saved workbook remains in memory and displayed on the screen

Minimize button

Figure 41

Other Ways
1. Click File on Ribbon, click Save, type file name, navigate to desired save location, click Save button   2. Press CTRL+S or press SHIFT+F12, type file name, navigate to desired save location, click Save button

Navigating in Dialog Boxes

Navigating is the process of finding a location on a storage device. While saving the Brain Busters file, for example, Steps 3a – 3c in the previous set of steps navigated to the Excel folder located in the CIS 101 folder. When performing certain functions in Windows programs, such as saving a file, opening a file, or inserting a picture in an existing file, you most likely will have to navigate to the location where you want to save the file or to the folder containing the file you want to open or insert. Most dialog boxes in Windows programs requiring navigation follow a similar procedure; that is, the way you navigate to a folder in one dialog box, such as the Save As dialog box, is similar to how you might navigate in another dialog box, such as the Open dialog box. If you chose to navigate to a specific location in a dialog box, you would follow the instructions in Steps 3a – 3c on page OFF 26.

BTW

File Type
Depending on your Windows 7 settings, the file type .xlsx may be displayed immediately to the right of the file name after you save the file. The file type .xlsx is an Excel 2010 workbook.

To Minimize and Restore a Window

Before continuing, you can verify that the Excel file was saved properly. To do this, you will minimize the Excel window and then open the USB flash drive window so that you can verify the file is stored on the USB flash drive. A **minimized window** is an open window hidden from view but that can be displayed quickly by clicking the window's program button on the taskbar.

In the following example, Excel is used to illustrate minimizing and restoring windows; however, you would follow the same steps regardless of the Office program you are using.

The steps on the next page minimize the Excel window, verify that the file is saved, and then restore the minimized window.

1

- Click the Minimize button on the program's title bar (shown in Figure 41 on the previous page) to minimize the window.

Q&A Is the minimized window still available?

The minimized window, Excel in this case, remains available but no longer is the active window. It is minimized as a program button on the taskbar.

- If necessary, click the Windows Explorer program button on the taskbar to open the USB flash drive window (Figure 42).

2

- Double-click the Excel folder to select the folder and display its contents (Figure 43).

Q&A Why does the Windows Explorer button on the taskbar change?

The button changes to reflect the status of the folder window (in this case, the USB flash drive window). A selected button indicates that the folder window is active on the screen. When the button is not selected, the window is open but not active.

3

- After viewing the contents of the selected folder, click the Excel program button on the taskbar to restore the minimized window (as shown in Figure 41 on the previous page).

Other Ways

1. Right-click title bar, click Minimize on shortcut menu, click taskbar button in taskbar button area

2. Press WINDOWS+M, press WINDOWS+SHIFT+M

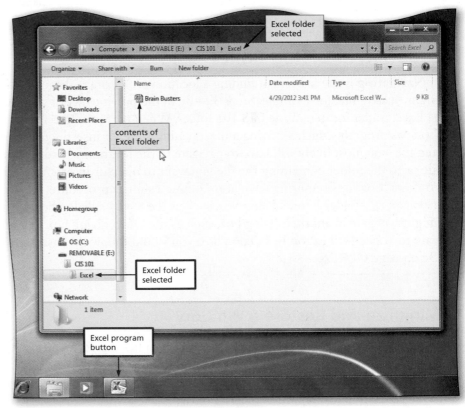

Figure 42

Figure 43

Screen Resolution

Screen resolution indicates the number of pixels (dots) that the computer uses to display the letters, numbers, graphics, and background you see on the screen. When you increase the screen resolution, Windows displays more information on the screen, but the information decreases in size. The reverse also is true: as you decrease the screen resolution, Windows displays less information on the screen, but the information increases in size.

Screen resolution usually is stated as the product of two numbers, such as 1024×768 (pronounced "ten twenty-four by seven sixty-eight"). A 1024×768 screen resolution results in a display of 1,024 distinct pixels on each of 768 lines, or about 786,432 pixels. Changing the screen resolution affects how the Ribbon appears in Office programs. Figure 44, for example, shows the Excel Ribbon at screen resolutions of 1024×768 and 1280×800. All of the same commands are available regardless of screen resolution. Excel, however, makes changes to the groups and the buttons within the groups to accommodate the various screen resolutions. The result is that certain commands may need to be accessed differently depending on the resolution chosen. A command that is visible on the Ribbon and available by clicking a button at one resolution may not be visible and may need to be accessed using its Dialog Box Launcher at a different resolution.

Comparing the two Ribbons in Figure 44, notice the changes in content and layout of the groups and galleries. In some cases, the content of a group is the same in each resolution, but the layout of the group differs. For example, the same gallery and buttons appear in the Cells groups in the two resolutions, but the layouts differ. In other cases, the content and layout are the same across the resolution, but the level of detail differs with the resolution. In the Clipboard group, when the resolution increases to 1280×800, the names of all the buttons in the group appear in addition to the buttons themselves. At the lower resolution, only the buttons appear.

Figure 44 (a) Ribbon at resolution of 1024 x 768

Figure 44 (b) Ribbon at resolution of 1280 x 800

To Change the Screen Resolution

If you are using a computer to step through the chapters in this book and you want your screen to match the figures, you may need to change your screen's resolution. The figures in this book use a screen resolution of 1024×768. The following steps change the screen resolution to 1024×768. Your computer already may be set to 1024×768 or some other resolution. Keep in mind that many computer labs prevent users from changing the screen resolution; in that case, read the following steps for illustration purposes.

1
- Click the Show desktop button on the taskbar to display the Windows 7 desktop.

- Right-click an empty area on the Windows 7 desktop to display a shortcut menu that displays a list of commands related to the desktop (Figure 45).

Q&A

Why does my shortcut menu display different commands?

Depending on your computer's hardware and configuration, different commands might appear on the shortcut menu.

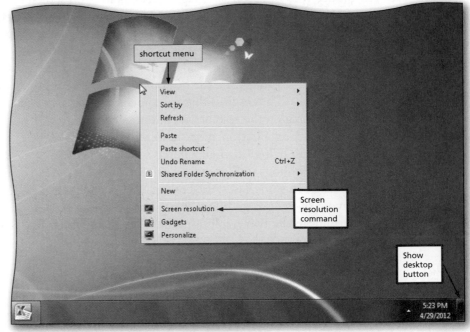

Figure 45

2
- Click Screen resolution on the shortcut menu to open the Screen Resolution window (Figure 46).

Figure 46

3

- Click the Resolution button in the Screen Resolution window to display the resolution slider.

Q&A What is a slider?

A **slider** is an object that allows users to choose from multiple predetermined options. In most cases, these options represent some type of numeric value. In most cases, one end of the slider (usually the left or bottom) represents the lowest of available values, and the opposite end (usually the right or top) represents the highest available value.

- If necessary, drag the resolution slider until the desired screen resolution (in this case, 1024 × 768) is selected (Figure 47).

Q&A What if my computer does not support the 1024 × 768 resolution?

Some computers do not support the 1024 × 768 resolution. In this case, select a resolution that is close to the 1024 × 768 resolution.

Figure 47

4

- Click an empty area of the Screen Resolution window to close the resolution slider.

- Click the OK button to change the screen resolution and display the Display Settings dialog box (Figure 48).

5

- Click the Keep changes button (Display Settings dialog box) to accept the new screen resolution.

Figure 48

Q&A Why is a message displayed stating that the image quality can be improved?

Some computer monitors are designed to display contents better at a certain screen resolution, sometimes referred to as an optimal resolution.

To Quit a Program with One File Open

When you quit an Office program, such as Excel, if you have made changes to a file since the last time the file was saved, the Office program displays a dialog box asking if you want save the changes you made to the file before it closes the program window. The dialog box contains three buttons with these resulting actions: the Save button saves the changes and then quits the Office program, the Don't Save button quits the Office program without saving changes, and the Cancel button closes the dialog box and redisplays the file without saving the changes.

If no changes have been made to an open file since the last time the file was saved, the Office program will close the window without displaying a dialog box.

The following steps quit Excel. You would follow similar steps in other Office programs.

1

- If necessary, click the Excel program button on the taskbar to display the Excel window on the desktop.

- Point to the Close button on the right side of the program's title bar, Excel in this case (Figure 49).

Figure 49

2

- Click the Close button to close the workbook and quit Excel.

Q&A What if I have more than one workbook open in Excel?

You would click the Close button for each open workbook. When you click the last open workbook's Close button, Excel also quits. As an alternative, you could click File on the Ribbon to open the Backstage view and then click Exit in the Backstage view to close all open workbooks and quit Excel.

Q&A What is the Backstage view?

The **Backstage view** contains a set of commands that enable you to manage files and data about the files. The Backstage view is discussed in more depth later in this chapter.

- If a Microsoft Excel dialog box appears, click the Save button to save any changes made to the workbook since the last save.

> **Other Ways**
>
> 1. Right-click the Office program button on Windows 7 taskbar, click Close window or 'Close all windows' on shortcut menu
> 2. Press ALT+F4

Break Point: If you wish to take a break, this is a good place to do so. To resume at a later time, continue to follow the steps from this location forward.

Additional Common Features of Office Programs

The previous section used Excel to illustrate common features of Office and some basic elements unique to Excel. The following sections continue to use Excel to present additional common features of Office.

In the following pages, you will learn how to do the following:

1. Start an Office program (Excel) using the search box.
2. Open a file in an Office program (Excel).
3. Save and close the file.
4. Reopen the file just closed.
5. Create a blank Office file from Windows Explorer and then open the file.
6. Save an Office file with a new file name.

To Start a Program Using the Search Box

The next steps, which assume Windows 7 is running, use the search box to start Excel based on a typical installation; however, you would follow similar steps to start any program. You may need to ask your instructor how to start programs for your computer.

1

- Click the Start button on the Windows 7 taskbar to display the Start menu.

- Type **Microsoft Excel** as the search text in the 'Search programs and files' text box and watch the search results appear on the Start menu (Figure 50).

Q&A

Do I need to type the complete program name or correct capitalization?

No, just enough of it for the program name to appear on the Start menu. For example, you may be able to type Excel or excel, instead of Microsoft Excel.

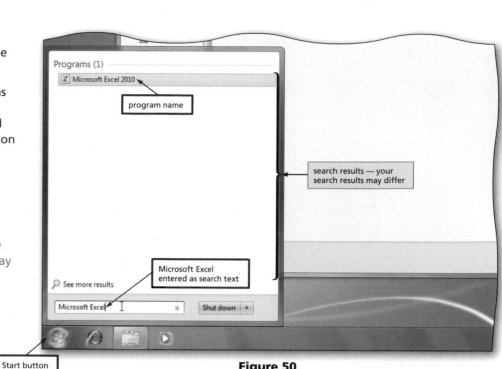

Figure 50

2

- Click the program name, Microsoft Excel 2010 in this case, in the search results on the Start menu to start Excel and display a new blank workbook in the Excel window.

- If the program window is not maximized, click the Maximize button on its title bar to maximize the window (Figure 51).

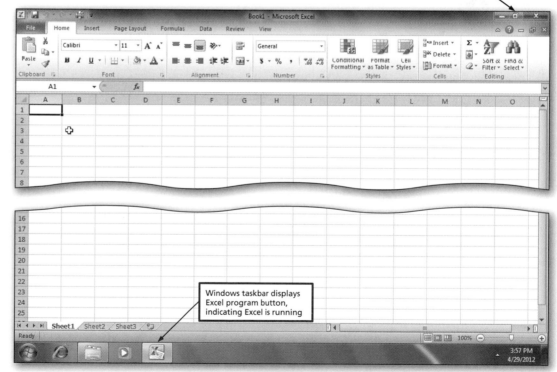

Figure 51

To Open an Existing File from the Backstage View

As discussed earlier, the Backstage view provides data about files and contains a set of commands that assist you with managing files. From the Backstage view in Excel, for example, you can create, open, print, and save workbooks. You also can share workbooks, manage versions, set permissions, and modify workbook properties.

Assume you wish to continue working on an existing file, that is, a file you previously saved. The following steps use the Backstage view to open a saved file, specifically the Brain Busters file, from the USB flash drive.

1

- With your USB flash drive connected to one of the computer's USB ports, if necessary, click File on the Ribbon to open the Backstage view (Figure 52).

Q&A What is the purpose of the File tab?

The File tab is used to display the Backstage view for each Office program.

Figure 52

2

- Click Open in the Backstage view to display the Open dialog box (Figure 53).

3

- Navigate to the location of the file to be opened (in this case, the USB flash drive, then to the CIS 101 folder [or your class folder], and then to the Excel folder). For detailed steps about navigating, see Steps 3a – 3c on page OFF 26.

Q&A What if I did not save my file in a folder?

If you did not save your file in a folder, the file you wish to open should be displayed in the Open dialog box before navigating to any folders.

Figure 53

- Click the file to be opened, Brain Busters in this case, to select the file (Figure 54).

4

- Click the Open button (Open dialog box) to open the selected file and display the opened file in the current program window (shown in Figure 41 on page OFF 27).

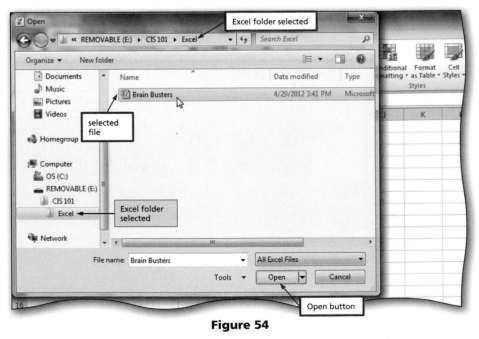

Figure 54

Other Ways

1. Click File on the Ribbon, click Recent in Backstage view, double-click file
2. Press CTRL+O
3. Navigate to file in Windows Explorer, double-click file

To Create a New Workbook from the Backstage View

You can create multiple files at the same time in an Office program, such as Excel. The following steps create a file, a blank workbook in this case, from the Backstage view.

1

- Click File on the Ribbon to open the Backstage view.

- Click the New tab in the Backstage view to display the New gallery (Figure 55).

Q&A

Can I create files through the Backstage view in other Office programs?

Yes. If the Office program has a New tab in the Backstage view, the New gallery displays various options for creating a new file.

Figure 55

2

- Click the Create button in the New gallery to create a new workbook (Figure 56).

Figure 56

Other Ways
1. Press CTRL+N

To Enter Text in a Workbook

The next Excel workbook identifies the names of the Brain Busters sponsors. The following steps enter text in a workbook.

1

Type **List of Current Sponsors for the Brain Busters Event** and then press the ENTER key to enter the text and make cell A2 the active cell (Figure 57).

Figure 57

BTW

Customizing the Ribbon

In addition to customizing the Quick Access Toolbar, you can add items to and remove items from the Ribbon. To customize the Ribbon, click File on the Ribbon to open the Backstage view, click Options in the Backstage view, and then click Customize Ribbon in the left pane of the Options dialog box. More information about customizing the Ribbon is presented in a later chapter.

To Save a File in a Folder

The following steps save the second file in the Excel folder in the class folder (CIS 101, in this case) on a USB flash drive using the file name, Brain Busters Sponsors.

1 With a USB flash drive connected to one of the computer's USB ports, click the Save button on the Quick Access Toolbar to display the Save As dialog box.

2 Type **Brain Busters Sponsors** in the File name text box to change the file name. Do not press the ENTER key after typing the file name because you do not want to close the dialog box at this time.

3 If necessary, navigate to the desired save location (in this case, the Excel folder in the CIS 101 folder [or your class folder] on the USB flash drive).

4 Click the Save button (Save As dialog box) to save the file in the selected folder on the selected drive with the entered file name.

To Close a File Using the Backstage View

Sometimes, you may want to close an Office file, such as an Excel workbook, entirely and start over with a new file. You also may want to close a file when you are finished working with it so that you can begin a new file. The following steps close the current active Excel file (that is, the Brain Busters Sponsors workbook) without quitting the active program (Excel in this case).

1
- Click File on the Ribbon to open the Backstage view (Figure 58).

2
- Click Close in the Backstage view to close the open file (Brain Busters Sponsors, in this case) without quitting the active program.

Q&A What if Excel displays a dialog box about saving?

Click the Save button if you want to save the changes, click the Don't Save button if you want to ignore the changes since the last time you saved, and click the Cancel button if you do not want to close the file.

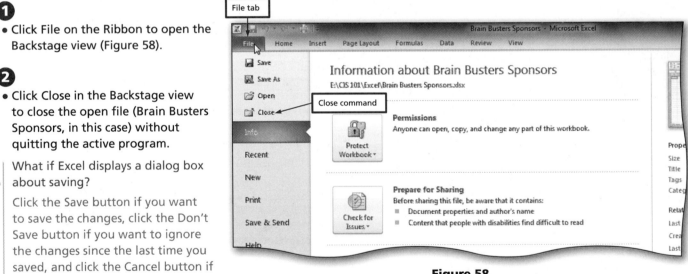

Figure 58

Q&A Can I use the Backstage view to close an open file in other Office programs, such as Word and PowerPoint?

Yes.

To Open a Recent File Using the Backstage View

You sometimes need to open a file that you recently modified. You may have more changes to make such as adding more content or correcting errors. The Backstage view allows you to access recent files easily. The next steps reopen the Brain Busters Sponsors file just closed.

1

- Click File on the Ribbon to open the Backstage view.

- Click the Recent tab in the Backstage view to display the Recent gallery (Figure 59).

2

- Click the desired file name in the Recent gallery, Brain Busters Sponsors in this case, to open the file (shown in Figure 57 on page OFF 35).

Q&A

Can I use the Backstage view to open a recent file when I am working in other Office programs, such as Word and PowerPoint?

Yes, as long as the file name appears in the list of recent files in the Recent gallery.

Figure 59

Other Ways

1. Click Start button, point to program name, click file name on submenu

2. Click File on Ribbon, click Open in Backstage view, navigate to file (Open dialog box), click Open button

To Create a New Blank Workbook from Windows Explorer

Windows Explorer provides a means to create a blank Office file without ever starting an Office program. The following steps use Windows Explorer to create a blank Excel workbook.

1

- Click the Windows Explorer program button on the taskbar to make the folder window the active window in Windows Explorer.

- If necessary, navigate to the desired location for the new file (in this case, the Excel folder in the CIS 101 folder [or your class folder] on the USB flash drive).

- With the Excel folder selected, right-click an open area in the right pane to display a shortcut menu.

- Point to New on the shortcut menu to display the New submenu (Figure 60).

Figure 60

2

- Click Microsoft Excel Worksheet on the New submenu to display an icon and text box for a new file in the current folder window (Figure 61).

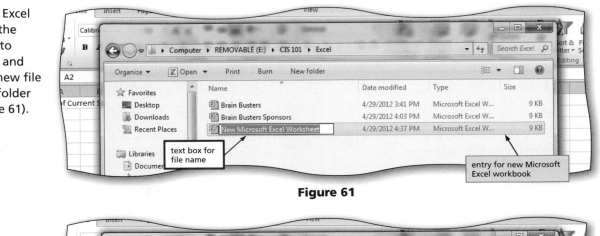

text box for file name

entry for new Microsoft Excel workbook

Figure 61

3

- Type **Brain Busters Staff** in the text box and then press the ENTER key to assign a name to the new file in the current folder (Figure 62).

name assigned to new file

Brain Busters Staff workbook icon

Figure 62

To Start a Program from Windows Explorer and Open a File

Previously, you learned how to start an Office program (Excel) using the Start menu and the search box. Another way to start an Office program is to open an existing file from Windows Explorer, which causes the program in which the file was created to start and then open the selected file. The following steps, which assume Windows 7 is running, use Windows Explorer to start Excel based on a typical installation. You may need to ask your instructor how to start Excel for your computer.

1

- If necessary, display the file to open in the folder window in Windows Explorer (shown in Figure 62).

- Right-click the file icon or file name (Brain Busters Staff, in this case) to display a shortcut menu (Figure 63).

Open command

file to be opened

shortcut menu

Figure 63

❷

- Click Open on the shortcut menu to open the selected file in the program used to create the file, Microsoft Excel in this case.

- If the program window is not maximized, click the Maximize button on the title bar to maximize the window (Figure 64).

Figure 64

To Enter Text in a Workbook

The next step is to enter text in this blank Excel workbook. The following step enters text in a cell.

❶ Type **Brain Busters Staff** and then press the ENTER key to enter the text and make cell A2 the active cell (shown in Figure 65).

To Save an Existing File with the Same File Name

Saving frequently cannot be overemphasized. You have made modifications to the file (workbook) since you created it. Thus, you should save again. Similarly, you should continue saving files frequently so that you do not lose your changes since the time you last saved the file. You can use the same file name, such as Brain Busters Staff, to save the changes made to the file. The following step saves a file again.

❶

- Click the Save button on the Quick Access Toolbar to overwrite the previously saved file (Brain Busters Staff, in this case) on the USB flash drive (Figure 65).

Q&A

Why did the Save As dialog box not appear?

Office programs, including Excel, overwrite the file using the setting specified the first time you saved the file.

Figure 65

Other Ways
1. Press CTRL+S or press SHIFT+F12

To Use Save As to Change the Name of a File

You might want to save a file with a different name and even to a different location. For example, you might start a homework assignment with a data file and then save it with a final file name for submitting to your instructor, saving it to a location designated by your instructor. The following steps save a file with a different file name.

❶ With your USB flash drive connected to one of the computer's USB ports, click File on the Ribbon to open the Backstage view.

2 Click Save As in the Backstage view to display the Save As dialog box.

3 Type **Brain Busters Event Staff** in the File name text box (Save As dialog box) to change the file name. Do not press the ENTER key after typing the file name because you do not want to close the dialog box at this time.

4 If necessary, navigate to the desired save location (the Excel folder in the CIS 101 folder [or your class folder] on the USB flash drive, in this case).

5 Click the Save button (Save As dialog box) to save the file in the selected folder on the selected drive with the new file name.

To Quit an Office Program

You are finished using Excel. The following steps quit Excel. You would use similar steps to quit other Office programs.

1 Because you have multiple Excel workbooks open, click File on the Ribbon to open the Backstage view and then click Exit in the Backstage view to close all open workbooks and quit Excel.

2 If a dialog box appears, click the Save button to save any changes made to the file since the last save.

Moving, Renaming, and Deleting Files

Earlier in this chapter, you learned how to organize files in folders, which is part of a process known as **file management**. The following sections cover additional file management topics including renaming, moving, and deleting files.

To Rename a File

In some circumstances, you may want to change the name of, or rename, a file or a folder. For example, you may want to distinguish a file in one folder or drive from a copy of a similar file, or you may decide to rename a file to better identify its contents. The Excel folder shown in Figure 66 contains the Excel workbook, Brain Busters. The following steps change the name of the Brain Busters file in the Excel folder to Brain Busters Information.

1

- If necessary, click the Windows Explorer program button on the taskbar to display the folder window in Windows Explorer.

- If necessary, navigate to the location of the file to be renamed (in this case, the Excel folder in the CIS 101 [or your class folder] folder on the USB flash drive) to display the file(s) it contains in the right pane.

- Right-click the Brain Busters icon or file name in the right pane to select the Brain Busters file and display a shortcut menu that presents a list of commands related to files (Figure 66).

Figure 66

2

- Click Rename on the shortcut menu to place the current file name in a text box.

- Type **Brain Busters Information** in the text box and then press the ENTER key (Figure 67).

Are any risks involved in renaming files that are located on a hard disk?

If you inadvertently rename a file that is associated with certain programs, the programs may not be able to find the file and, therefore, may not execute properly. Always use caution when renaming files.

Can I rename a file when it is open?

No, a file must be closed to change the file name.

Figure 67

Other Ways

1. Select file, press F2, type new file name, press ENTER

To Move a File

At some time, you may want to move a file from one folder, called the source folder, to another, called the destination. When you move a file, it no longer appears in the original folder. If the destination and the source folders are on the same disk drive, you can move a file by dragging it. If the folders are on different disk drives, then you will need to right-drag the file. The following step moves the Brain Busters Staff file from the Excel folder to the CIS 101 folder.

1

- In Windows Explorer, if necessary, navigate to the location of the file to be moved (in this case, the Excel folder in the CIS 101 folder [or your class folder] on the USB flash drive).

- If necessary, click the Excel folder in the navigation pane to display the files it contains in the right pane.

- Drag the Brain Busters Staff file in the right pane to the CIS 101 folder in the navigation pane and notice the ScreenTip as you drag the mouse (Figure 68).

Figure 68

Other Ways

1. Right-click file, drag file to destination folder, click Move here
2. Right-click file to copy, click Cut on shortcut menu, right-click destination

folder, click Paste on shortcut menu
3. Select file to copy, press CTRL+X, select destination folder, press CTRL+V

To Delete a File

A final task you may want to perform is to delete a file. Exercise extreme caution when deleting a file or files. When you delete a file from a hard disk, the deleted file is stored in the Recycle Bin where you can recover it until you empty the Recycle Bin. If you delete a file from removable media, such as a USB flash drive, the file is deleted permanently. The next steps delete the Brain Busters Staff file from the CIS 101 folder.

1

- In Windows Explorer, navigate to the location of the file to be deleted (in this case, the CIS 101 folder [or your class folder] on the USB flash drive).

- If necessary, click the CIS 101 folder in the navigation pane to display the files it contains in the right pane.

- Right-click the Brain Busters Staff icon or file name in the right pane to select the file and display a shortcut menu (Figure 69).

Figure 69

2

- Click Delete on the shortcut menu to display the Delete File dialog box (Figure 70).

3

- Click the Yes button (Delete File dialog box) to delete the selected file.

Q&A

Can I use this same technique to delete a folder?

Yes. Right-click the folder and then click Delete on the shortcut menu. When you delete a folder, all of the files and folders contained in the folder you are deleting, together with any files and folders on lower hierarchical levels, are deleted as well.

Figure 70

Other Ways

1. Select icon, press DELETE

Microsoft Office and Windows Help

At any time while you are using one of the Microsoft Office 2010 programs, such as Excel, you can use Office Help to display information about all topics associated with the program. This section illustrates the use of Excel Help. Help in other Office 2010 programs operates in a similar fashion.

In Office 2010, Help is presented in a window that has Web-browser-style navigation buttons. Each Office 2010 program has its own Help home page, which is the starting Help page that is displayed in the Help window. If your computer is connected to the Internet, the contents of the Help page reflect both the local help files installed on the computer and material from Microsoft's Web site.

To Open the Help Window in an Office Program

The following step opens the Excel Help window. The step to open a Help window in other Office programs is similar.

1

- Start Excel.

- Click the Microsoft Excel Help button near the upper-right corner of the program window to open the Excel Help window (Figure 71).

Q&A
What should I do if the Help table of contents is displayed when the Excel Help window opens?

Click the Hide Table of Contents button to close the table of contents.

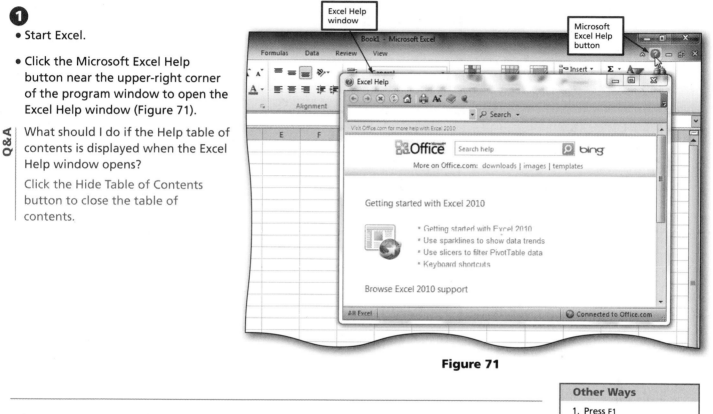

Figure 71

Other Ways

1. Press F1

Moving and Resizing Windows

Up to this point, this chapter has used minimized and maximized windows. At times, however, it is useful, or even necessary, to have more than one window open and visible on the screen at the same time. You can resize and move these open windows so that you can view different areas of and elements in the window. In the case of the Help window, for example, it could be covering document text in the Excel window that you need to see.

To Move a Window by Dragging

You can move any open window that is not maximized to another location on the desktop by dragging the title bar of the window. The step on the next page drags the Excel Help window to the top left of the desktop.

1

- Drag the window title bar (the Excel Help window title bar, in this case) so that the window moves to the top left of the desktop, as shown in Figure 72.

Figure 72

To Resize a Window by Dragging

Sometimes, information is not visible completely in a window. A method used to change the size of the window is to drag the window borders. The following step changes the size of the Excel Help window by dragging its borders.

1

- Point to the lower-right corner of the window (the Excel Help window, in this case) until the mouse pointer changes to a two-headed arrow.

- Drag the bottom border downward to display more of the active window (Figure 73).

Q&A Can I drag other borders on the window to enlarge or shrink the window?

Yes, you can drag the left, right, and top borders and any window corner to resize a window.

Q&A Will Windows 7 remember the new size of the window after I close it?

Yes. When you reopen the window, Windows 7 will display it at the same size it was when you closed it.

Figure 73

Using Office Help

Once an Office program's Help window is open, several methods exist for navigating Help. You can search for help by using any of the three following methods from the Help window:

1. Enter search text in the 'Type words to search for' text box.
2. Click the links in the Help window.
3. Use the Table of Contents.

To Obtain Help Using the 'Type words to search for' Text Box

Assume for the following example that you want to know more about the Backstage view. The following steps use the 'Type words to search for' text box to obtain useful information about the Backstage view by entering the word, Backstage, as search text.

①

- Type **Backstage** in the 'Type words to search for' text box at the top of the Excel Help window to enter the search text.

- Click the Search button arrow to display the Search menu (Figure 74).

②

- If it is not selected already, click All Excel on the Search menu, so that Help performs the most complete search of the current program (Excel, in this case). If All Excel already is selected, click the Search button arrow again to close the Search menu.

Q&A

Why select All Excel on the Search menu?

Selecting All Excel on the Search menu ensures that Excel Help will search all possible sources for information about your search term. It will produce the most complete search results.

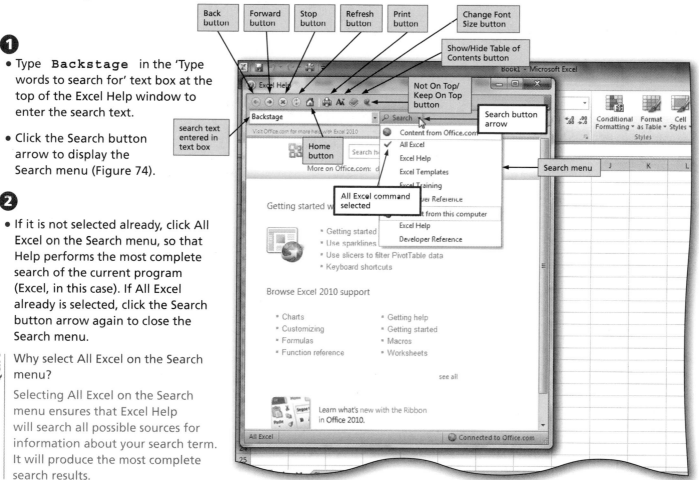

Figure 74

- Click the Search button to display the search results (Figure 75).

Q&A Why do my search results differ?

If you do not have an Internet connection, your results will reflect only the content of the Help files on your computer. When searching for help online, results also can change as material is added, deleted, and updated on the online Help Web pages maintained by Microsoft.

Q&A Why were my search results not very helpful?

When initiating a search, be sure to check the spelling of the search text; also, keep your search specific, with fewer than seven words, to return the most accurate results.

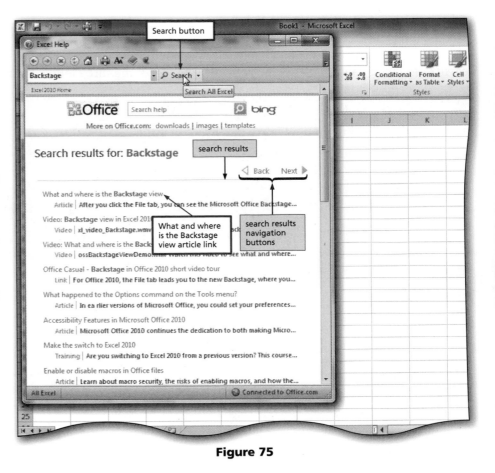

Figure 75

❸

- Click the What and where is the Backstage view link to open the Help document associated with the selected topic (Figure 76).

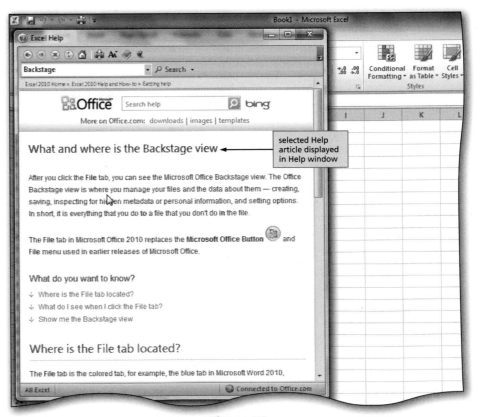

Figure 76

4

• Click the Home button on the toolbar to clear the search results and redisplay the Help home page (Figure 77).

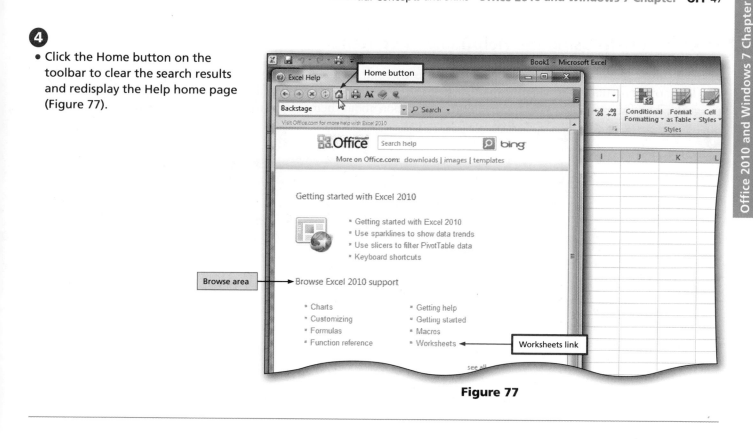

Figure 77

To Obtain Help Using the Help Links

If your topic of interest is listed in the Browse area of the Help window, you can click the link to begin browsing the Help categories instead of entering search text. You browse Help just as you would browse a Web site. If you know which category contains your Help information, you may wish to use these links. The following step finds the Worksheets Help information using the category links from the Excel Help home page.

1

• Click the Worksheets link on the Help home page (shown in Figure 77) to display the Worksheets page (Figure 78).

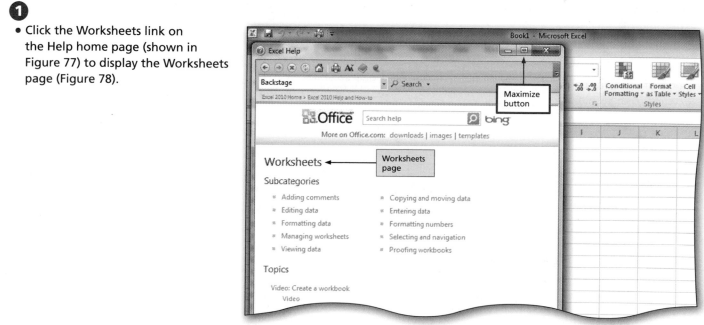

Figure 78

To Obtain Help Using the Help Table of Contents

A third way to find Help in Office programs is through the Help Table of Contents. You can browse through the Table of Contents to display information about a particular topic or to familiarize yourself with an Office program. The following steps access the Help information about themes by browsing through the Table of Contents.

1

- Click the Home button on the toolbar to display the Help home page.

- Click the Show Table of Contents button on the toolbar to display the Table of Contents pane on the left side of the Help window. If necessary, click the Maximize button on the Help title bar to maximize the window (Figure 79).

Figure 79

Q&A Why does the appearance of the Show Table of Contents button change?

When the Table of Contents is displayed in the Help window, the Hide Table of Contents button replaces the Show Table of Contents button.

2

- Click the Charts link in the Table of Contents pane to view a list of Help subtopics.

- Click the Creating charts link in the Table of Contents pane to expand the topic.

- Click the 'Create a chart from start to finish' link to view the selected Help document in the right pane (Figure 80).

Figure 80

3

- After reviewing the page, click the Close button to quit Help.

- Click Excel's Close button to quit Excel.

Q&A How do I remove the Table of Contents pane when I am finished with it?

The Show Table of Contents button acts as a toggle. When the Table of Contents pane is visible, the button changes to Hide Table of Contents. Clicking it hides the Table of Contents pane and changes the button to Show Table of Contents.

Obtaining Help while Working in an Office Program

Help in Office programs, such as Excel, provides you with the ability to obtain help directly, without the need to open the Help window and initiate a search. For example, you may be unsure about how a particular command works, or you may be presented with a dialog box that you are not sure how to use.

Figure 81 shows one option for obtaining help while working in Excel. If you want to learn more about a command, point to the command button and wait for the Enhanced ScreenTip to appear. If the Help icon appears in the Enhanced ScreenTip, press the F1 key while pointing to the command to open the Help window associated with that command.

Figure 82 shows a dialog box that contains a Help button. Pressing the F1 key while the dialog box is displayed opens a Help window. The Help window contains help about that dialog box, if available. If no help file is available for that particular dialog box, then the main Help window opens.

Figure 81

Using Windows Help and Support

One of the more powerful Windows 7 features is Windows Help and Support. **Windows Help and Support** is available when using Windows 7 or when using any Microsoft program running under Windows 7. This feature is designed to assist you in using Windows 7 or the various programs. Table 4 describes the content found in the Help and Support Center. The same methods used for searching Microsoft Office Help can be used in Windows Help and Support. The difference is that Windows Help and Support displays help for Windows 7, instead of for Microsoft Office.

Figure 82

Table 4 Windows Help and Support Center Content Areas	
Area	**Function**
Find an answer quickly	This area contains instructions about how to do a quick search using the search box.
Not sure where to start?	This area displays three topics to help guide a user: How to get started with your computer, Learn about Windows Basics, and Browse Help topics. Clicking one of the options navigates to corresponding Help and Support pages.
More on the Windows Website	This area contains links to online content from the Windows Web site. Clicking the links navigates to the corresponding Web pages on the Web site.

To Start Windows Help and Support

The steps on the next page start Windows Help and Support and display the Windows Help and Support window, containing links to more information about Windows 7.

1

- Click the Start button on the taskbar to display the Start menu (Figure 83).

Q&A

Why are the programs that are displayed on the Start menu different?

Windows adds the programs you have used recently to the left pane on the Start menu. You have started Excel while performing the steps in this chapter, so that program now is displayed on the Start menu.

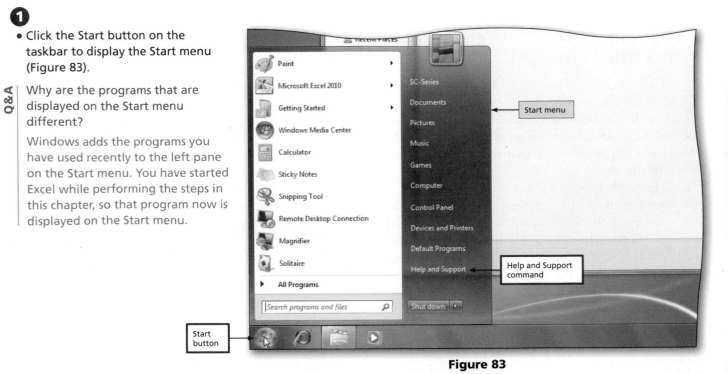

Figure 83

2

- Click Help and Support on the Start menu to open the Windows Help and Support window (Figure 84).

3

- After reviewing the Windows Help and Support window, click the Close button to quit Windows Help and Support.

Other Ways

1. Press CTRL+ESC, press RIGHT ARROW, press UP ARROW, press ENTER
2. Press WINDOWS+F1

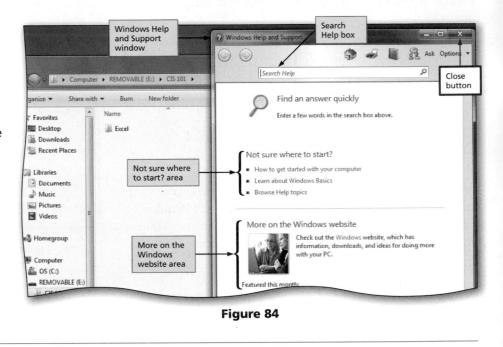

Figure 84

Chapter Summary

In this chapter, you learned about the Windows 7 interface. You started Windows 7, were introduced to the components of the desktop, and learned several mouse operations. You opened, closed, moved, resized, minimized, maximized, and scrolled a window. You used folder windows to expand and collapse drives and folders, display drive and folder contents, create folders, and rename and then delete a file.

You also learned some basic features of Microsoft Excel 2010. As part of this learning process, you discovered the common elements that exist among Microsoft Office programs.

Microsoft Office Help was demonstrated using Excel, and you learned how to use the Excel Help window. You were introduced to the Windows 7 Help and Support Center and learned how to use it to obtain more information about Windows 7.

The items listed below include all of the new Windows 7 and Excel 2010 skills you have learned in this chapter.

1. Log On to the Computer (OFF 6)
2. Start a Program Using the Start Menu (OFF 10)
3. Maximize a Window (OFF 12)
4. Display a Different Tab on the Ribbon (OFF 16)
5. Minimize, Display, and Restore the Ribbon (OFF 16)
6. Display and Use a Shortcut Menu (OFF 17)
7. Customize the Quick Access Toolbar (OFF 18)
8. Enter Text in a Workbook (OFF 19)
9. Create a Folder (OFF 20)
10. Create a Folder within a Folder (OFF 23)
11. Expand a Folder, Scroll through Folder Contents, and Collapse a Folder (OFF 23)
12. Switch from One Program to Another (OFF 24)
13. Save a File in a Folder (OFF 25)
14. Minimize and Restore a Window (OFF 27)
15. Change the Screen Resolution (OFF 30)
16. Quit a Program with One File Open (OFF 31)
17. Start a Program Using the Search Box (OFF 32)
18. Open an Existing File from the Backstage View (OFF 33)
19. Create a New Workbook from the Backstage View (OFF 35)
20. Close a File Using the Backstage View (OFF 36)
21. Open a Recent File Using the Backstage View (OFF 36)
22. Create a New Blank Workbook from Windows Explorer (OFF 37)
23. Start a Program from Windows Explorer and Open a File (OFF 38)
24. Save an Existing File with the Same File Name (OFF 39)
25. Rename a File (OFF 40)
26. Move a File (OFF 41)
27. Delete a File (OFF 42)
28. Open the Help Window in an Office Program (OFF 43)
29. Move a Window by Dragging (OFF 43)
30. Resize a Window by Dragging (OFF 44)
31. Obtain Help Using the 'Type words to search for' Text Box (OFF 45)
32. Obtain Help Using the Help Links (OFF 47)
33. Obtain Help Using the Help Table of Contents (OFF 48)
34. Start Windows Help and Support (OFF 49)

If you have a SAM 2010 user profile, your instructor may have assigned an autogradable version of this assignment. If so, log into the SAM 2010 Web site at www.cengage.com/sam2010 to download the instruction and start files.

Learn It Online

Test your knowledge of chapter content and key terms.

Instructions: To complete the Learn It Online exercises, start your browser, click the Address bar, and then enter the Web address **scsite.com/ex2010/learn**. When the Office 2010 Learn It Online page is displayed, click the link for the exercise you want to complete and then read the instructions.

Chapter Reinforcement TF, MC, and SA

A series of true/false, multiple choice, and short answer questions that test your knowledge of the chapter content.

Flash Cards

An interactive learning environment where you identify chapter key terms associated with displayed definitions.

Practice Test

A series of multiple choice questions that test your knowledge of chapter content and key terms.

Who Wants To Be a Computer Genius?

An interactive game that challenges your knowledge of chapter content in the style of a television quiz show.

Wheel of Terms

An interactive game that challenges your knowledge of chapter key terms in the style of the television show *Wheel of Fortune*.

Crossword Puzzle Challenge

A crossword puzzle that challenges your knowledge of key terms presented in the chapter.

Apply Your Knowledge

Reinforce the skills and apply the concepts you learned in this chapter.

Creating a Folder and a Document

Instructions: You will create an Excel folder and then create an Excel workbook and save it in the folder.

Perform the following tasks:

1. Connect a USB flash drive to an available USB port and then open the USB flash drive window.

2. Click the New folder button on the toolbar to display a new folder icon and text box for the folder name.

3. Type **Excel** in the text box to name the folder. Press the ENTER key to create the folder on the USB flash drive.

4. Start Excel.

5. Enter the text shown in Figure 85.

6. Click the Save button on the Quick Access Toolbar. Navigate to the Excel folder on the USB flash drive and then save the document using the file name, Apply 1 Class List.

7. If your Quick Access Toolbar does not show the Quick Print button, add the Quick Print button to the Quick Access Toolbar. Print the document using the Quick Print button on the Quick Access Toolbar. When you are finished printing, remove the Quick Print button from the Quick Access Toolbar.

8. Submit the printout to your instructor.

9. Quit Excel.

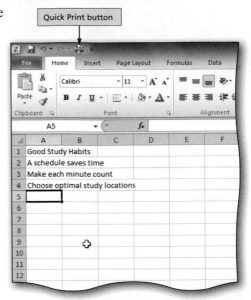

Figure 85

Extend Your Knowledge

Extend the skills you learned in this chapter and experiment with new skills. You will use Help to complete the assignment.

Using Help

Instructions: Use Excel Help to perform the following tasks.

Perform the following tasks:

1. Start Excel.

2. Click the Microsoft Excel Help button to open the Excel Help window (Figure 86).

Figure 86

3. Search Excel Help to answer the following questions.

   a. What are three features new to Excel 2010?

   b. What training videos are available through Help?

   c. What are the steps to add a new group to the Ribbon?

   d. What are sparklines?

   e. What is a relative cell reference?

   f. What is a template?

   g. How do you print a workbook?

   h. What is a SmartArt graphic?

   i. What are five available chart types?

   j. What is the purpose of the Merge & Center command?

4. Submit the answers from your searches in the format specified by your instructor.

5. Quit Excel.

Make It Right

Analyze a file structure and correct all errors and/or improve the design.

Organizing Vacation Photos

Note: To complete this assignment, you will be required to use the Data Files for Students. See the inside back cover of this book for instructions on downloading the Data Files for Students, or contact your instructor for information about accessing the required files.

Instructions: Traditionally, you have stored photos from past vacations together in one folder. The photos are becoming difficult to manage, and you now want to store them in appropriate folders. You will create the folder structure shown in Figure 87. You then will move the photos to the folders so that they will be organized properly.

1. Connect a USB flash drive to an available USB port to open the USB flash drive window.

2. Create the hierarchical folder structure shown in Figure 87.

3. Move one photo to each folder in the folder structure you created in Step 2. The five photos are available on the Data Files for Students.

4. Submit your work in the format specified by your instructor.

Figure 87

In the Lab

Use the guidelines, concepts, and skills presented in this chapter to increase your knowledge of Windows 7 and Excel 2010. Labs are listed in order of increasing difficulty.

Lab 1: Using Windows Help and Support

Problem: You have a few questions about using Windows 7 and would like to answer these questions using Windows Help and Support.

Instructions: Use Windows Help and Support to perform the following tasks:

1. Display the Start menu and then click Help and Support to start Windows Help and Support.

2. Use the Help and Support Content page to answer the following questions.

   a. How do you reduce computer screen flicker?

   b. Which dialog box do you use to change the appearance of the mouse pointer?

   c. How do you minimize all windows?

   d. What is a VPN?

3. Use the Search Help text box in Windows Help and Support to answer the following questions.

   a. How can you minimize all open windows on the desktop?

   b. How do you start a program using the Run command?

   c. What are the steps to add a toolbar to the taskbar?

   d. What wizard do you use to remove unwanted desktop icons?

4. The tools to solve a problem while using Windows 7 are called **troubleshooters**. Use Windows Help and Support to find the list of troubleshooters (Figure 88), and answer the following questions.

   a. What problems does the HomeGroup troubleshooter allow you to resolve?

   b. List five Windows 7 troubleshooters that are not listed in Figure 88.

5. Use Windows Help and Support to obtain information about software licensing and product activation, and answer the following questions.

   a. What is genuine Windows?

   b. What is activation?

   c. What steps are required to activate Windows?

   d. What steps are required to read the Microsoft Software License Terms?

   e. Can you legally make a second copy of Windows 7 for use at home, work, or on a mobile computer or device?

   f. What is registration?

6. Close the Windows Help and Support window.

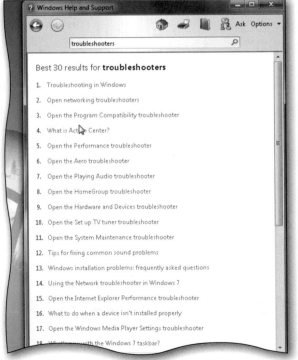

Figure 88

In the Lab

Lab 2: Creating Folders for a Pet Supply Store

Problem: Your friend works for Pete's Pet Supplies. He would like to organize his files in relation to the types of pets available in the store. He has five main categories: dogs, cats, fish, birds, and exotic. You are to create a folder structure similar to Figure 89.

Instructions: Perform the following tasks:

1. Connect a USB flash drive to an available USB port and then open the USB flash drive window.

2. Create the main folder for Pete's Pet Supplies.

3. Navigate to the Pete's Pet Supplies folder.

4. Within the Pete's Pet Supplies folder, create a folder for each of the following: Dogs, Cats, Fish, Birds, and Exotic.

5. Within the Exotic folder, create two additional folders, one for Primates and the second for Reptiles.

6. Submit the assignment in the format specified by your instructor.

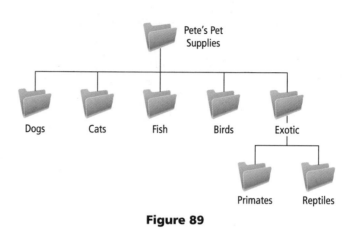

Figure 89

In the Lab

Lab 3: Creating Excel Workbooks and Saving Them in Appropriate Folders

Problem: You are taking a class that requires you to complete three Excel chapters. You will save the work completed in each chapter in a different folder (Figure 90).

Instructions: Create the folders shown in Figure 90. Then, using Excel, create three small files to save in each folder.

1. Connect a USB flash drive to an available USB port and then open the USB flash drive window.

2. Create the folder structure shown in Figure 90.

3. Navigate to the Chapter 1 folder.

4. Create an Excel Workbook containing the text, My Chapter 1 Excel Workbook, and then save it in the Chapter 1 folder using the file name, Excel Chapter 1 Workbook.

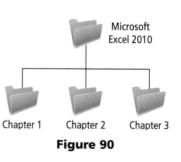

Figure 90

5. Navigate to the Chapter 2 folder.

6. Create another Excel workbook containing the text, My Chapter 2 Excel Workbook, and then save it in the Chapter 2 folder using the file name, Excel Chapter 2 Workbook.

7. Navigate to the Chapter 3 folder.

8. Create another Excel workbook containing the text, My Chapter 3 Excel Workbook, and then save it in the Chapter 3 folder using the file name, Excel Chapter 3 Workbook.

9. Quit Excel.

10. Submit the assignment in the format specified by your instructor.

Cases and Places

Apply your creative thinking and problem solving skills to design and implement a solution.

Note: To complete these assignments, you may be required to use the Data Files for Students. See the inside back cover of this book for instructions on downloading the Data Files for Students, or contact your instructor for information about accessing the required files.

1: Creating Beginning Files for Classes

Academic

You are taking the following classes: Introduction to Engineering, Beginning Psychology, Introduction to Biology, and Accounting. Create folders for each of the classes. Use the following folder names: Engineering, Psychology, Biology, and Accounting, when creating the folder structure. In the Engineering folder, use Excel to create a workbook with the name of the class and the class meeting location and time (MW 10:30 – 11:45, Room 317). In the Psychology folder, use Excel to create a workbook containing the text, Behavioral Observations. In the Biology folder, use Excel to create a workbook with the title Research in the Biology folder. In the Accounting folder, create an Excel workbook with the text, Tax Information. Use the concepts and techniques presented in this chapter to create the folders and files.

2: Using Help

Personal

Your parents enjoy working and playing games on their home computers. Your mother uses a notebook computer downstairs, and your father uses a desktop computer upstairs. They expressed interest in sharing files between their computers and sharing a single printer, so you offered to research various home networking options. Start Windows Help and Support, and search Help using the keywords, home networking. Use the link for installing a printer on a home network. Start Excel and then type the main steps for installing a printer. Use the link for setting up a HomeGroup and then type the main steps for creating a HomeGroup in the Excel workbook. Use the concepts and techniques presented in this chapter to use Help and create the Excel workbook.

3: Creating Folders

Professional

Your boss at the bookstore where you work part-time has asked for help with organizing her files. After looking through the files, you decided upon a file structure for her to use, including the following folders: books, magazines, tapes, DVDs, and general merchandise. Within the books folder, create folders for hardback and paperback books. Within magazines, create folders for special issues and periodicals. In the tapes folder, create folders for celebrity and major release. In the DVDs folder, create a folder for book to DVD. In the general merchandise folder, create folders for novelties, posters, and games. Use the concepts and techniques presented in this chapter to create the folders.

1 | Creating a Worksheet and an Embedded Chart

Objectives

You will have mastered the material in this chapter when you can:

- Describe the Excel worksheet
- Enter text and numbers
- Use the Sum button to sum a range of cells
- Copy the contents of a cell to a range of cells using the fill handle
- Apply cell styles
- Format cells in a worksheet

- Create a Clustered Cylinder chart
- Change a worksheet name and worksheet tab color
- Change document properties
- Preview and print a worksheet
- Use the AutoCalculate area to display statistics
- Correct errors on a worksheet

1 | Creating a Worksheet and an Embedded Chart

Introduction

Almost any organization collects vast amounts of data. Often, data is consolidated into a summary so that people in the organization better understand the meaning of the data. An Excel worksheet allows data easily to be summarized and charted. A chart conveys a visual representation of data. In this chapter, you will create a worksheet that includes a chart. The data in the worksheet and chart includes data for donations made to a not-for-profit organization that operates in several cities.

Project Planning Guidelines

> The process of developing a worksheet that communicates specific information requires careful analysis and planning. As a starting point, establish why the worksheet is needed. Once the purpose is determined, analyze the intended users of the worksheet and their unique needs. Then, gather information about the topic and decide what to include in the worksheet. Finally, determine the worksheet design and style that will be most successful at delivering the message. Details of these guidelines are provided in Appendix A. In addition, each project developed in this book provides practical applications of these planning considerations.

Project — Worksheet with an Embedded Chart

The project in this chapter follows proper design guidelines and uses Excel to create the worksheet shown in Figure 1–1. The worksheet contains fundraising data for the Save Sable River Foundation. The Save Sable River Foundation raises funds to care for the environment and preserve the usability of a river that flows through six cities. The foundation raises funds by using five different fundraising activities. Through a concentrated marketing campaign and providing visible results to the communities, the Save Sable River Foundation quickly became a popular local institution. After several years of successful fundraising, senior management requested an easy-to-read worksheet that shows lifetime fundraising amounts for each fundraising technique by city. In addition, they asked for a chart showing lifetime fundraising amounts because the president of the foundation likes to have a graphical representation that allows him quickly to identify stronger and weaker fundraising activities by city.

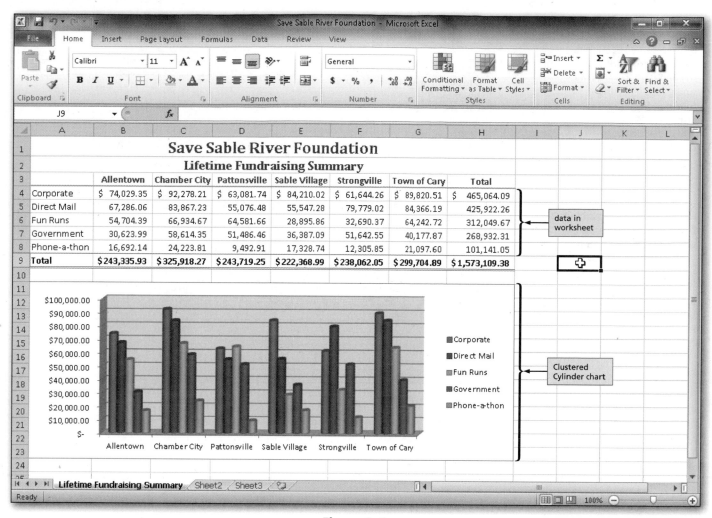

Figure 1-1

The first step in creating an effective worksheet is to make sure you understand what is required. The person or persons requesting the worksheet should supply their requirements in a requirements document. A **requirements document** includes a needs statement, a source of data, a summary of calculations, and any other special requirements for the worksheet, such as charting and Web support. Figure 1-2 on the following page shows the requirements document for the new workbook to be created in this chapter.

Excel 2010 Features
With its what-if analysis tools, research capabilities, collaboration tools, streamlined user interface, smart tags, charting features, Web capabilities, hundreds of functions, and enhanced formatting capabilities, Excel 2010 is one of the easier and more powerful spreadsheet programs available. Its dynamic analytical features make it possible to answer complicated what-if questions and its Web capabilities allow you to create, publish, view, share, and analyze data on an intranet or the World Wide Web.

requirements document →

Worksheet Development Cycle
Spreadsheet specialists do not sit down and start entering text, formulas, and data into a blank Excel worksheet as soon as they have a spreadsheet assignment. Instead, they follow an organized plan, or methodology, that breaks the development cycle into a series of tasks. The recommended methodology for creating worksheets includes: (1) analyze requirements (supplied in a requirements document); (2) design solution; (3) validate design; (4) implement design; (5) test solution; and (6) document solution.

REQUEST FOR NEW WORKBOOK	
Date Submitted:	March 22, 2012
Submitted By:	Kevin Li
Worksheet Title:	Save Sable River Foundation Lifetime Fundraising Summary
Needs:	An easy-to-read worksheet that shows a summary of the Save Sable River Foundation's lifetime fundraising efforts for each city in which we operate (Allentown, Chamber City, Pattonsville, Sable Village, Strongville, and the Town of Cary). The worksheet also should include total funds raised for each city, total funds raised for each fundraising activity, and total lifetime funds raised.
Source of Data:	The data for the worksheet is available from the chief financial officer (CFO) of the Save Sable River Foundation.
Calculations:	The following calculations must be made for the worksheet: (a) total lifetime funds raised for each of the six cities; (b) total lifetime funds raised for each of the five fundraising activities; and (c) total lifetime funds raised for the organization.
Chart Requirements:	Below the data in the worksheet, construct a Clustered Cylinder chart that compares the total funds raised for each city within each type of fundraising activity.

Approvals

Approval Status:	X	Approved
		Rejected
Approved By:	Marsha Davis	
Date:	March 29, 2012	
Assigned To:	J. Quasney, Spreadsheet Specialist	

Figure 1–2

Overview

As you read this chapter, you will learn how to create the worksheet shown in Figure 1–1 on the previous page by performing these general tasks:

- Enter text in the worksheet
- Total data in the worksheet
- Format the text in the worksheet
- Insert a chart into the worksheet
- Identify the worksheet with a worksheet name
- Preview and print the worksheet

Plan Ahead

BTWs
For a complete list of the BTWs found in the margins of this book, visit the Excel 2010 BTW Web page (scsite.com/ex2010/btw).

General Project Guidelines
While creating an Excel worksheet, you need to make several decisions that will determine the appearance and characteristics of the finished worksheet. As you create the worksheet shown in Figure 1–1, you should follow these general guidelines:

1. **Select titles and subtitles for the worksheet.** Follow the *less is more* guideline. The less text in the titles and subtitles, the more impact the titles and subtitles will have. Use the fewest words possible to specify the information presented in the worksheet to the intended audience.

(continued)

(continued)

2. **Determine the contents for rows and columns.** Rows typically contain information that is analogous to items in a list, such as the fundraising techniques used by an organization. Columns typically contain descriptive information about items in rows or contain information that helps to group the data in the worksheet, such as the locations in which the organization operates. Row headings and column headings are usually placed in alphabetical sequence, unless an alternative order is recommended in the requirements document.

3. **Determine the calculations that are needed.** You can decide to total data in a variety of ways, such as across rows or in columns. You also can include a grand total.

4. **Determine where to save the workbook.** You can store a workbook permanently, or **save** it, on a variety of storage media including a hard disk, USB flash drive, CD, or DVD. You also can indicate a specific location on the storage media for saving the workbook.

5. **Identify how to format various elements of the worksheet.** The overall appearance of a worksheet significantly affects its ability to communicate clearly. Examples of how you can modify the appearance, or format, of text include changing its shape, size, color, and position on the worksheet.

6. **Decide on the type of chart needed.** Excel can create many different types of charts, such as cylinder charts and pie charts. Each type of chart relays a different message about the data in the worksheet. Choose a type of chart that relays the message that you want to convey.

7. **Establish where to position and how to format the chart.** The position and format of the chart should command the attention of the intended audience. If possible, position the chart so that it prints with the worksheet data on a single page.

8. **Choose a name for the worksheet.** Each worksheet in a workbook should be named to clarify its purpose. A good worksheet name is succinct, unique to the workbook, and meaningful to any user of the workbook

9. **Determine the best method for distributing the workbook.** Workbooks and worksheets can be distributed on paper or electronically. The decision regarding how to distribute workbooks and worksheets greatly depends on your intended audience. For example, a worksheet may be printed for inclusion in a report, or a workbook may be distributed using e-mail if the recipient intends to update the workbook.

When necessary, more specific details concerning the above guidelines are presented at appropriate points in the chapter. The chapter also will identify the actions performed and decisions made regarding these guidelines during the creation of the worksheet shown in Figure 1–1 on page EX 3.

Plan Ahead

BTW

Worksheet Development
The key to developing a useful worksheet is careful planning. Careful planning can reduce your effort significantly and result in a worksheet that is accurate, easy to read, flexible, and useful. When analyzing a problem and designing a worksheet solution, you should follow these steps: (1) define the problem, including need, source of data, calculations, charting, and Web or special requirements; (2) design the worksheet; (3) enter the data and formulas; and (4) test the worksheet.

After carefully reviewing the requirements document (Figure 1–2) and making the necessary decisions, the next step is to design a solution or draw a sketch of the worksheet based on the requirements, including titles, column and row headings, the location of data values, and the Clustered Cylinder chart, as shown in Figure 1–3 on the following page. The dollar signs, 9s, and commas that you see in the sketch of the worksheet indicate formatted numeric values.

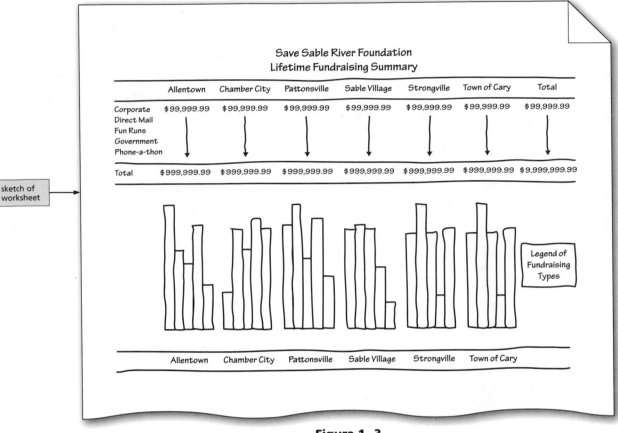

sketch of worksheet

Figure 1–3

For an introduction to Windows 7 and instruction about how to perform basic Windows 7 tasks, read the Office 2010 and Windows 7 chapter at the beginning of this book, where you can learn how to resize windows, change screen resolution, create folders, move and rename files, use Windows Help, and much more.

BTW

The Ribbon and Screen Resolution
Excel may change how the groups and buttons within the groups appear on the Ribbon, depending on the computer's screen resolution. Thus, your Ribbon may look different from the ones in this book if you are using a screen resolution other than 1024 × 768.

With a good understanding of the requirements document, an understanding of the necessary decisions, and a sketch of the worksheet, the next step is to use Excel to create the worksheet and chart.

To Start Excel

If you are using a computer to step through the project in this chapter and you want your screens to match the figures in this book, you should change your screen's resolution to 1024 × 768. For information about how to change a computer's resolution, refer to the Office 2010 and Windows 7 chapter at the beginning of this book.

The following steps, which assume Windows 7 is running, start Excel based on a typical installation. You may need to ask your instructor how to start Excel for your computer. For a detailed example of the procedure summarized below, refer to the Office 2010 and Windows 7 chapter.

1 Click the Start button on the Windows 7 taskbar to display the Start menu.

2 Type **Microsoft Excel** as the search text in the 'Search programs and files' text box and watch the search results appear on the Start menu.

3 Click Microsoft Excel 2010 in the search results on the Start menu to start Excel and display a new blank workbook in the Excel window.

4 If the Excel window is not maximized, click the Maximize button next to the Close button on its title bar to maximize the window.

Selecting a Cell

To enter data into a cell, you first must select it. The easiest way **to select a cell** (make it active) is to use the mouse to move the block plus sign mouse pointer to the cell and then click.

An alternative method is to use the arrow keys that are located just to the right of the alphanumeric keys on a standard keyboard. An arrow key selects the cell adjacent to the active cell in the direction of the arrow on the key.

You know a cell is selected, or active, when a heavy border surrounds the cell and the active cell reference appears in the Name box on the left side of the formula bar. Excel also changes the active cell's column heading and row heading to a gold color.

Entering Text

In Excel, any set of characters containing a letter, hyphen (as in a telephone number), or space is considered text. **Text** is used to place titles, such as worksheet titles, column titles, and row titles, on the worksheet.

Select titles and subtitles for the worksheet.
Worksheet titles and subtitles should be as brief and meaningful as possible. A worksheet title could include the name of the organization, department, or a description of the content of the worksheet. A worksheet subtitle, if included, could include a more detailed description of the content of the worksheet. Examples of worksheet titles are December 2010 Payroll and Year 2011 Projected Budget, and examples of subtitles are Marketing Department and Rent and Utilities, respectively.

Determine the contents of rows and columns.
As shown in Figure 1–4, data in a worksheet often is identified by row and column titles so that the user of a worksheet easily can identify the meaning of the data. Rows typically contain information that is similar to items in a list. Columns typically contain descriptive information about items in rows or contain information that helps to group the data in the worksheet. Examples of row titles are Product and Total, and examples of column titles are Name and Address.

Plan Ahead

Plan Ahead

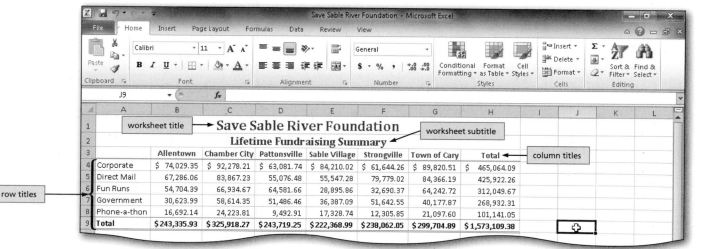

Figure 1–4

To Enter the Worksheet Titles

As shown in Figure 1–4 on the previous page, the worksheet title, Save Sable River Foundation, identifies the organization for which the worksheet is being created in Chapter 1. The worksheet subtitle, Lifetime Fundraising Summary, identifies the type of report.

The following steps enter the worksheet titles in cells A1 and A2. Later in this chapter, the worksheet titles will be formatted so they appear as shown in Figure 1–4.

1

- If necessary, click cell A1 to make cell A1 the active cell (Figure 1–5).

Q&A

What if I make a mistake while typing?

If you type the wrong letter and notice the error before clicking the Enter box or pressing the ENTER key, use the BACKSPACE key to delete all the characters back to and including the incorrect letter. To cancel the entire entry before entering it into the cell, click the Cancel box in the formula bar or press the ESC key. If you see an error in a cell after entering the text, select the cell and retype the entry.

Figure 1–5

2

- Type **Save Sable River Foundation** in cell A1 and then point to the Enter box in the formula bar to prepare to enter text in the active cell (Figure 1–6).

Q&A

Why did the appearance of the formula bar change?

Excel displays the title in the formula bar and in cell A1. When you begin typing a cell entry, Excel displays two additional boxes in the formula bar: the Cancel box and the Enter box. Clicking the **Enter box** completes an entry. Clicking the **Cancel box** cancels an entry.

Figure 1–6

Q&A

What is the vertical line in cell A1?

The text in cell A1 is followed by the insertion point. The **insertion point** is a blinking vertical line that indicates where the next typed character will appear.

3

- Click the Enter box to complete the entry and enter a worksheet title (Figure 1–7).

Q&A

Why does the entered text appear in three cells?

When the text is longer than the width of a column, Excel displays the overflow characters in adjacent cells to the right as long as those adjacent cells contain no data. If the adjacent cells contain data, Excel would hide the overflow characters. Excel displays the overflow characters in the formula bar whenever that cell is the active cell.

Figure 1–7

4

- Click cell A2 to select it.

- Type **Lifetime Fundraising Summary** as the cell entry.

- Click the Enter box to complete the entry and enter a worksheet subtitle (Figure 1–8).

Q&A

What happens when I click the Enter box?

When you complete an entry by clicking the Enter box, the insertion point disappears and the cell in which the text is entered remains the active cell.

Figure 1–8

Other Ways

1. To complete entry, click any cell other than active cell

2. To complete entry, press ENTER

3. To complete entry, press HOME, PAGE UP, PAGE DOWN, or END

4. To complete entry, press UP ARROW, DOWN ARROW, LEFT ARROW, or RIGHT ARROW.

AutoCorrect

The **AutoCorrect feature** of Excel works behind the scenes, correcting common mistakes when you complete a text entry in a cell. AutoCorrect makes three types of corrections for you:

1. Corrects two initial capital letters by changing the second letter to lowercase.

2. Capitalizes the first letter in the names of days.

3. Replaces commonly misspelled words with their correct spelling. For example, it will change the misspelled word *recieve* to *receive* when you complete the entry. AutoCorrect will correct the spelling of hundreds of commonly misspelled words automatically.

BTW

Q&As
For a complete list of the Q&As found in many of the step-by-step sequences in this book, visit the Excel 2010 Q&A Web page (scsite.com/ex2010/qa).

To Enter Column Titles

The column titles in row 3 (Allentown, Chamber City, Pattonsville, Sable Village, Strongville, Town of Cary, and Total) identify the numbers in each column. In the case of the Save the Sable River Foundation data, the cities identify the funds raised using each fundraising type. The cities, therefore, are placed in columns. To enter the column titles in row 3, select the appropriate cell and then enter the text. The following steps enter the column titles in row 3.

1
- Click cell B3 to make it the active cell (Figure 1–9).

Figure 1–9

2
- Type **Allentown** to begin entry of a column title in the active cell (Figure 1–10).

Figure 1–10

3

- Press the RIGHT ARROW key to enter a column title and make the cell to the right the active cell (Figure 1–11).

Q&A

Why is the RIGHT ARROW key used to complete the entry in the cell?

If the next entry you want to enter is in an adjacent cell, use the arrow keys to complete the entry in a cell. When you press an arrow key to complete an entry, the adjacent cell in the direction of the arrow (up, down, left, or right) becomes the active cell. If the next entry is in a nonadjacent cell, complete the current entry by clicking the next cell in which you plan to enter data. You also can click the Enter box or press the ENTER key and then click the appropriate cell for the next entry.

Figure 1–11

4

- Repeat Steps 2 and 3 to enter the remaining column titles; that is, enter **Chamber City** in cell C3, **Pattonsville** in cell D3, **Sable Village** in cell E3, **Strongville** in cell F3, **Town of Cary** in cell G3, and **Total** in cell H3 (complete the last entry in cell H3 by clicking the Enter box in the formula bar) (Figure 1–12).

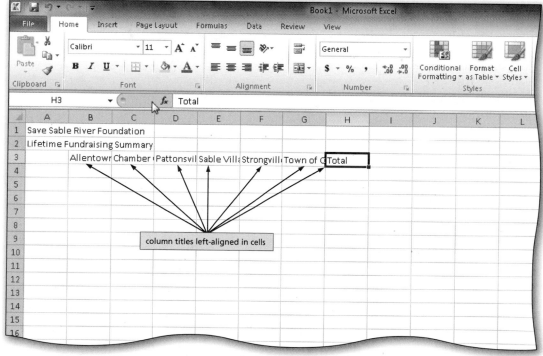

Figure 1–12

To Enter Row Titles

The next step in developing the worksheet for this project is to enter the row titles in column A. For the Save Sable River Foundation data, the list of fundraising activities meets the criterion that information that identifies columns be in a list. It is more likely that in the future, the organization will add more fundraising activities as opposed to more cities. Each fundraising activity, therefore, should be placed in its own row. The row titles in column A (Corporate, Direct Mail, Fun Runs, Government, Phone-a-thon, and Total) identify the numbers in each row.

This process for entering row titles is similar to the process for entering column titles. The following steps enter the row titles in the worksheet.

1
- Click cell A4 to select it.

- Type **Corporate** and then press the DOWN ARROW key to enter a row title and to make the cell below the current cell the active cell (Figure 1–13).

Figure 1–13

2
- Repeat Step 1 to enter the remaining row titles in column A; that is, enter **Direct Mail** in cell A5, **Fun Runs** in cell A6, **Government** in cell A7, **Phone-a-thon** in cell A8, and **Total** in cell A9 (Figure 1–14).

Why is the text left-aligned in the cells?

When you enter text, Excel automatically left-aligns the text in the cell. Excel treats any combination of numbers, spaces, and nonnumeric characters as text. For example, Excel recognizes the following entries as text:

401AX21, 921–231, 619 321, 883XTY

You can change the text alignment in a cell by realigning it. Other alignment techniques are discussed later in this chapter.

Figure 1–14

Entering Numbers

In Excel, you can enter numbers into cells to represent amounts. A **number** can contain only the following characters:

0 1 2 3 4 5 6 7 8 9 + - ( ) , / . $ % E e

If a cell entry contains any other keyboard character (including spaces), Excel interprets the entry as text and treats it accordingly. The use of the special characters is explained when they are used in this book.

BTW

Numeric Limitations
In Excel, a number can be between approximately -1×308^{10} and 1×308^{10}. This means it can be between a negative 1 followed by 308 zeros and a positive 1 followed by 308 zeros. To enter a number such as 6,000,000,000,000,000, you can type 6,000,000,000,000,000, or you can type 6E15, which translates to 6×1015.

To Enter Numbers

The Save Sable River Foundation Lifetime Fundraising Summary numbers used in Chapter 1 are summarized in Table 1–1. These numbers, which represent lifetime fundraising amounts for each of the fundraising activities and cities, must be entered in rows 4, 5, 6, 7, and 8.

Table 1–1 Save Sable River Foundation Lifetime Fundraising Summary						
	Allentown	**Chamber City**	**Pattonsville**	**Sable Village**	**Strongville**	**Town of Cary**
Corporate	74029.35	92278.21	63081.74	84210.02	61644.26	89820.51
Direct Mail	67286.06	83867.23	55076.48	55547.28	79779.02	84366.19
Fun Runs	54704.39	66934.67	64581.66	28895.86	32690.37	64242.72
Government	30623.99	58614.35	51486.46	36387.09	51642.55	40177.87
Phone-a-thon	16692.14	24223.81	9492.91	17328.74	12305.85	21097.60

The following steps enter the numbers in Table 1–1 one row at a time.

1
- Click cell B4 to select it.

- Type 74029.35 and then press the RIGHT ARROW key to enter the data in the selected cell and make the cell to the right the active cell (Figure 1–15).

Figure 1–15

Q&A

Do I need to enter dollar signs, commas, or trailing zeros for the fundraising summary amounts?

You are not required to type dollar signs, commas, or trailing zeros. When you enter a dollar value that has cents, however, you must add the decimal point and the numbers representing the cents. Later in this chapter, the numbers will be formatted to use dollar signs, commas, and trailing zeros to improve the appearance and readability of the numbers.

2

- Enter 92278.21 in cell C4, 63081.74 in cell D4, 84210.02 in cell E4, 61644.26 in cell F4, and 89820.51 in cell G4 to complete the first row of numbers in the worksheet (Figure 1–16).

Q&A

Why are the numbers right-aligned?

When you enter numeric data in a cell, Excel recognizes the values as numbers and right-aligns the values in order to properly vertically align decimal and integer values. For example, values entered below those entered in this step automatically will be right-aligned as well so that the decimals of the values properly align.

Figure 1–16

3

- Click cell B5 to select it and complete the entry in the previously selected cell.

- Enter the remaining lifetime fundraising summary numbers provided in Table 1–1 on page EX 13 for each of the four remaining fundraising activities in rows 5, 6, 7, and 8 to finish entering numbers in the worksheet (Figure 1–17).

Q&A

Why did clicking cell B5 complete the entry in cell G4?

Selecting another cell completes the entry in the previously selected cell in the same way as pressing the ENTER key, pressing an arrow key, or clicking the Enter box on the formula bar. In the next set of steps, the entry of the number in cell G4 will be completed by selecting another cell.

Figure 1–17

Calculating a Sum

The next step in creating the worksheet is to perform any necessary calculations, such as calculating the column and row totals.

To Sum a Column of Numbers

As stated in the requirements document in Figure 1–2 on page EX 4, totals are required for each city, each fundraising activity, and the organization. The first calculation is to determine the fundraising total for the fundraising activities in the city of Allentown in column B. To calculate this value in cell B9, Excel must add, or sum, the numbers in cells B4, B5, B6, B7, and B8. Excel's **SUM function**, which adds all of the numbers in a range of cells, provides a convenient means to accomplish this task.

A **range** is a series of two or more adjacent cells in a column or row or a rectangular group of cells. For example, the group of adjacent cells B4, B5, B6, B7, and B8 is called a range. Many Excel operations, such as summing numbers, take place on a range of cells.

After the total lifetime fundraising amount for the fundraising activities in the city of Allentown in column B is determined, the totals for the remaining cities and totals for each fundraising activity will be determined. The following steps sum the numbers in column B.

1

- Click cell B9 to make it the active cell and complete the entry in the previously selected cell.

- Click the Sum button (Home tab | Editing group) to display a formula in the formula bar and in the active cell (Figure 1–18).

Figure 1–18

How does Excel know which cells to sum?

When you enter the SUM function using the Sum button, Excel automatically selects what it considers to be your choice of the range to sum. When proposing the range to sum, Excel first looks for a range of cells with numbers above the active cell and then to the left. If Excel proposes the wrong range, you can correct it by dragging through the correct range before pressing the ENTER key. You also can enter the correct range by typing the beginning cell reference, a colon (:), and the ending cell reference.

Calculating Sums
Excel calculates sums for a variety of data types. For example, Boolean values, such as TRUE and FALSE, can be summed. Excel treats the value of TRUE as 1 and the value of FALSE as 0. Times also can be summed. For example, Excel treats the sum of 1:15 and 2:45 as 4:00.

❷

- Click the Enter box in the formula bar to enter a sum in the active cell (Figure 1–19).

Q&A

What is the purpose of the Sum button arrow?

If you click the Sum button arrow on the right side of the Sum button (Home tab | Editing group) (Figure 1–19), Excel displays a list of often used functions from which you can choose. The list includes functions

Figure 1–19

that allow you to determine the average, the number of items in the selected range, the maximum value, or the minimum value of a range of numbers.

Other Ways

1. Click Insert Function button in the formula bar, select SUM in Select a function list, click OK button, select range, click OK button

2. Click Sum button arrow (Home tab | Editing group), click More Functions, select SUM (Insert Function dialog box), click OK button, select range, click OK button

3. Type = s in cell, select SUM from list, select range

4. Press ALT + EQUAL SIGN (=) twice

BTW

Entering Numbers as Text
Sometimes, you will want Excel to treat numbers, such as postal codes and telephone numbers, as text. To enter a number as text, start the entry with an apostrophe (').

Using the Fill Handle to Copy a Cell to Adjacent Cells

Excel also must calculate the totals for Chamber City in cell C9, Pattonsville in cell D9, Sable Village in cell E9, Strongville in cell F9, and the Town of Cary in cell G9. Table 1–2 illustrates the similarities between the entry in cell B9 and the entries required to sum the totals in cells C9, D9, E9, F9 and G9.

Table 1–2 Sum Function Entries in Row 9		
Cell	**Sum Function Entries**	**Remark**
B9	=SUM(B4:B8)	Sums cells B4, B5, B6, B7, and B8
C9	=SUM(C4:C8)	Sums cells C4, C5, C6, C7, and C8
D9	=SUM(D4:D8)	Sums cells D4, D5, D6, D7, and D8
E9	=SUM(E4:E8)	Sums cells E4, E5, E6, E7, and E8
F9	=SUM(F4:F8)	Sums cells F4, F5, F6, F7, and F8
G9	=SUM(G4:G8)	Sums cells G4, G5, G6, G7, and G8

To place the SUM functions in cells C9, D9, E9, F9, and G9, you could follow the same steps shown previously in Figures 1–18 on page EX 15 and 1–19. A second, more efficient method, however, is to copy the SUM function from cell B9 to the range C9:G9. The cell being copied is called the **source area** or **copy area**. The range of cells receiving the copy is called the **destination area** or **paste area**.

Although the SUM function entries in Table 1–2 are similar, they are not exact copies. The range in each SUM function entry uses cell references that are one column to the right of the previous column. When you copy formulas that include cell references, Excel automatically adjusts them for each new position, resulting in the SUM function entries illustrated in Table 1–2. Each adjusted cell reference is called a **relative reference**.

To Copy a Cell to Adjacent Cells in a Row

The easiest way to copy the SUM formula from cell B9 to cells C9, D9, E9, F9, and G9 is to use the fill handle. The **fill handle** is the small black square located in the lower-right corner of the heavy border around the active cell. The following steps use the fill handle to copy cell B9 to the adjacent cells C9:G9.

- With cell B9 active, point to the fill handle to activate it (Figure 1–20).

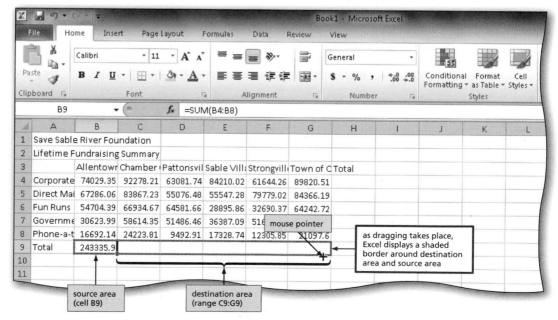

Figure 1–20

- Drag the fill handle to select the destination area, range C9:G9, to display a shaded border around the source area and the destination area (Figure 1–21). Do not release the mouse button.

Figure 1–21

3

- Release the mouse button to copy the SUM function from the active cell to the destination area and calculate the sums (Figure 1–22).

Figure 1–22

Q&A

What is the purpose of the Auto Fill Options button?

When you copy one range to another, Excel displays an Auto Fill Options button (Figure 1–22). The Auto Fill Options button allows you to choose whether you want to copy the values from the source area to the destination area with formatting, do so without formatting, or copy only the format. To view the available fill options, click the Auto Fill Options button. The Auto Fill Options button disappears when you begin another activity in Excel, such as typing data in another cell or applying formatting to a cell or range of cells.

Other Ways		
1. Select source area, click Copy button (Home tab | Clipboard group), select destination area, click Paste button (Home tab | Clipboard group)	2. Right-click source area, click Copy on shortcut menu, right-click destination area, click Paste on shortcut menu	3. Select source area and then point to border of range; while holding down CTRL, drag source area to destination area

To Determine Multiple Totals at the Same Time

The next step in building the worksheet is to determine the lifetime fundraising totals for each fundraising activity and total lifetime fundraising for the organization in column H. To calculate these totals, you can use the SUM function much as it was used to total the lifetime fundraising amounts by city in row 9. In this example, however, Excel will determine totals for all of the rows at the same time. The following steps sum multiple totals at once.

1

- Click cell H4 to make it the active cell (Figure 1–23).

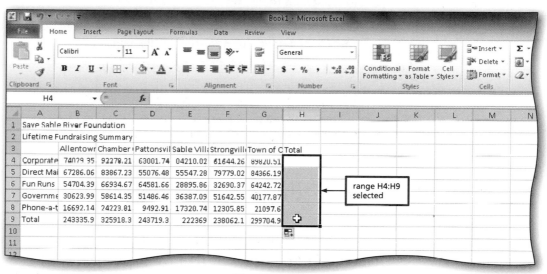

Figure 1–23

2

- With the mouse pointer in cell H4 and in the shape of a block plus sign, drag the mouse pointer down to cell H9 to highlight the range with a transparent view (Figure 1–24).

Figure 1–24

3

- Click the Sum button (Home tab | Editing group) to calculate and display the sums of the corresponding rows (Figure 1–25).

- Select cell A10 to deselect the selected range.

Q&A

How does Excel create unique totals for each row?

If each cell in a selected range is next to a row of numbers, Excel assigns the SUM function to each cell when you click the Sum button.

Figure 1–25

BTW

Organizing Files and Folders
You should organize and store files in folders so that you easily can find the files later. For example, if you are taking an introductory computer class called CIS 101, a good practice would be to save all Excel files in an Excel folder in a CIS 101 folder. For a discussion of folders and detailed examples of creating folders, refer to the Office 2010 and Windows 7 chapter at the beginning of this book.

To Save a Workbook

You have performed many tasks while creating this workbook and do not want to risk losing work completed thus far. Accordingly, you should save the workbook.

The following steps assume you already have created folders for storing your files, for example, a CIS 101 folder (for your class) that contains an Excel folder (for your assignments). Thus, these steps save the workbook in the Excel folder in the CIS 101 folder on a USB flash drive using the file name, Save Sable River Foundation. For a detailed example of the procedure summarized below, refer to the Office 2010 and Windows 7 chapter at the beginning of this book.

1 With a USB flash drive connected to one of the computer's USB ports, click the Save button on the Quick Access Toolbar to display the Save As dialog box.

2 Type `Save Sable River Foundation` in the File name text box to change the file name. Do not press the ENTER key after typing the file name because you do not want to close the dialog box at this time.

3 Navigate to the desired save location (in this case, the Excel folder in the CIS 101 folder [or your class folder] on the USB flash drive).

4 Click the Save button (Save As dialog box) to save the document in the selected folder on the selected drive with the entered file name.

Break Point: If you wish to take a break, this is a good place to do so. You can quit Excel. To resume at a later time, start Excel, open the file called Save Sable River Foundation, and continue following the steps from this location forward.

Formatting the Worksheet

The text, numeric entries, and functions for the worksheet now are complete. The next step is to format the worksheet. You **format** a worksheet to emphasize certain entries and make the worksheet easier to read and understand.

Figure 1–26a shows the worksheet before formatting. Figure 1–26b shows the worksheet after formatting. As you can see from the two figures, a worksheet that is formatted not only is easier to read but also looks more professional.

Plan Ahead

Identify how to format various elements of the worksheet.
By formatting the contents of the worksheet, you can improve its overall appearance. When formatting a worksheet, consider the following formatting suggestions:

- **Increase the font size of cells.** An increased font size gives more impact to the text in a cell. In order to indicate their relative importance, worksheet titles should have the largest font size, followed by worksheet subtitles, and then column and row headings.

- **Change the font color of cells.** Different cell colors help the reader of a worksheet quickly differentiate between the sections of a worksheet. Worksheet titles and subtitles easily should be identifiable from column and row headings. The overuse of too many colors, however, may be distracting to the reader of a worksheet.

- **Center the worksheet titles, subtitles, and column headings.** Centering text in worksheet titles and subtitles over the portion of the worksheet that they represent helps the reader of a worksheet quickly to identify the information that is of interest to them.

(continued)

(continued)

- **Modify column widths to best fit text in cells.** Make certain that text in a cell does not overflow into another cell. A column's width should be adjusted to accommodate the largest amount of text used in a cell in the column. Columns that contain data that is similar in nature to other columns should share the same column width.

- **Change the font style of cells.** Use a bold font style to make worksheet titles, worksheet subtitles, column headings, row heading, and totals stand out. Use italics and underline font styles judiciously, as specific rules of grammar apply to their use.

Figure 1–26 (a) Before Formatting

Figure 1–26 (b) After Formatting

To change the unformatted worksheet in Figure 1–26a on the previous page to the formatted worksheet in Figure 1–26b on the previous page, the following tasks must be completed:

1. Change the font, change the font style to bold, increase the font size, and change the font color of the worksheet titles in cells A1 and A2.
2. Center the worksheet titles in cells A1 and A2 across columns A through H.
3. Format the body of the worksheet. The body of the worksheet, range A3:H9, includes the column titles, row titles, and numbers. Formatting the body of the worksheet changes the numbers to use a dollars-and-cents format, with dollar signs in the first row (row 4) and the total row (row 9); adds underlining that emphasizes portions of the worksheet; and modifies the column widths to fit the text in the columns and make the text and numbers readable.

The remainder of this section explains the process required to format the worksheet. Although the formatting procedures are explained in the order described above, you should be aware that you could make these format changes in any order. Modifying the column widths, however, usually is done last because other formatting changes may affect the size of data in the cells in the column.

Font, Style, Size, and Color

The characters that Excel displays on the screen are a specific font, style, size, and color. The **font**, or font face, defines the appearance and shape of the letters, numbers, and special characters. Examples of fonts include Calibri, Cambria, Times New Roman, Arial, and Courier. **Font style** indicates how the characters are emphasized. Common font styles include regular, bold, underline, and italic. The **font size** specifies the size of the characters on the screen. Font size is gauged by a measurement system called points. A single point is about 1/72 of one inch in height. Thus, a character with a **point size** of 10 is about 10/72 of one inch in height. The **font color** defines the color of the characters. Excel can display characters in a wide variety of colors, including black, red, orange, and blue.

When Excel begins, the preset font for the entire workbook is Calibri, with a font size, font style, and font color of 11–point regular black. Excel allows you to change the font characteristics in a single cell, a range of cells, the entire worksheet, or the entire workbook.

To Change a Cell Style

Excel includes the capability of changing several characteristics of a cell, such the font, font size, and font color, all at once by assigning a predefined cell style to a cell. Using the predefined styles that Excel includes provides a consistent appearance to common portions of your worksheets, such as worksheet titles, worksheet subtitles, column headings, and total rows. The following steps assign the Title cell style to the worksheet title in cell A1.

BTW

Fonts
In general, use no more than two font types in a worksheet because the use of more fonts can make a worksheet difficult to read.

BTW

Fonts and Themes
Excel uses default recommended fonts based on the workbook's theme. A theme is a collection of fonts and color schemes. The default theme is named Office, and the two default fonts for the Office theme are Calibri and Cambria. Excel, however, allows you to apply any font to a cell or range as long as the font is installed on your computer.

1

- Click cell A1 to make cell A1 the active cell.

- Click the Cell Styles button (Home tab | Styles group) to display the Cell Styles gallery (Figure 1–27).

Figure 1–27

2

- Point to the Title cell style in the Titles and Headings area of the Cell Styles gallery to see a live preview of the cell style in the active cell (Figure 1–28).

 Experiment

- Point to several other cell styles in the Cell Styles gallery to see a live preview of other cell styles in cell A1.

Figure 1–28

3

- Click the Title cell style to apply the cell style to the active cell (Figure 1–29).

Q&A

Why do several items in the Font group on the Ribbon change?

The changes to the Font box, Bold button, and Font Size box indicate the font changes applied to the active cell, cell A1, as a result of applying the Title cell style.

Figure 1–29

To Change the Font

Different fonts often are used in a worksheet to make it more appealing to the reader and to relate or distinguish data in the worksheet. The following steps change the worksheet subtitle's fonts from Calibri to Cambria.

1

- Click cell A2 to make it the active cell.

- Click the Font box arrow (Home tab | Font group) to display the Font gallery (Figure 1–30).

Q&A Which fonts are displayed in the Font gallery?

Because many programs supply additional fonts beyond what comes with the Windows 7 operating system, the number of fonts available on your computer will depend on the programs installed. This book uses only fonts that come with the Windows 7 operating system and Microsoft Office 2010.

Figure 1–30

2

- Point to Cambria in the Theme Fonts area of the Font gallery to see a live preview of the selected font in the active cell (Figure 1–31).

Experiment

- Point to several other fonts in the Font gallery to see a live preview of other fonts in the selected cell.

Q&A What is the Theme Fonts area?

Excel applies the same default theme to any new workbook that you start. A **theme** is a collection of cell styles and other styles that have common characteristics, such as a color scheme and font. The default theme for an Excel workbook is the Office theme. The Theme Fonts area of the Font gallery includes the fonts included in the default Office theme. Cambria is recommended for headings and Calibri is recommended by Microsoft for cells in the body of the worksheet (Figure 1–31).

Figure 1–31

3

• Click Cambria in the Theme Fonts area to change the font of the worksheet subtitle to Cambria (Figure 1–32).

font in cell A2

Cambria font assigned to worksheet subtitle in cell A2

Figure 1–32

To Bold a Cell

You **bold** an entry in a cell to emphasize it or make it stand out from the rest of the worksheet. The following step bolds the worksheet subtitle in cell A2.

1

• With cell A2 active, click the Bold button (Home tab | Font group) to change the font style of the active cell to bold (Figure 1–33).

Home tab

Bold button changes to transparent orange background when active cell is bold

Font group

font style of worksheet subtitle in cell A2 changed to bold

Q&A What if a cell already includes a bold style?

If the active cell is already bold, then Excel displays the Bold button with a transparent orange background.

Q&A How do I remove the bold style from a cell?

Clicking the Bold button (Home tab | Font group) a second time removes the bold font style.

Figure 1–33

To Increase the Font Size of a Cell Entry

Increasing the font size is the next step in formatting the worksheet subtitle. You increase the font size of a cell so that the entry stands out and is easier to read. The following steps increase the font size of the worksheet subtitle in cell A2.

1
- With cell A2 selected, click the Font Size box arrow (Home tab | Font group) to display the Font Size list.

- Point to 14 in the Font Size list to see a live preview of the active cell with the selected font size (Figure 1–34).

Experiment
- Point to several other font sizes in the Font Size list to see a live preview of other font sizes in the selected cell.

Figure 1–34

2
- Click 14 in the Font Size list to change the font size in the active cell (Figure 1–35).

Q&A
Can I assign a font size that is not in the Font Size list?

Yes. An alternative to clicking a font size in the Font Size list is to click the Font Size box (Home tab | Font group), type the font size, and then press the ENTER key. This procedure allows you to assign a font size not available in the Font Size list to a selected cell entry.

Figure 1–35

Other Ways

1. Click Increase Font Size button (Home tab | Font group) or Decrease Font Size button (Home tab | Font group)

2. Click Font Size box arrow on Mini toolbar, click desired font size in Font Size gallery

3. Right-click cell, click Format Cells on shortcut menu, click Font tab (Format Cells dialog box), select font size in Size box, click OK button

To Change the Font Color of a Cell Entry

The next step is to change the color of the font in cell A2 from black to dark blue. The following steps change the font color of a cell entry.

1

- With cell A2 selected, click the Font Color button arrow (Home tab | Font group) to display the Font Color gallery.

- Point to Dark Blue, Text 2 (dark blue color in column 4, row 1) in the Theme Colors area of the Font Color gallery to see a live preview of the font color in the active cell (Figure 1–36).

🔍 **Experiment**

- Point to several other colors in the Font Color gallery to see a live preview of other font colors in the active cell.

Q&A Which colors does Excel make available on the Font Color gallery?

You can choose from more than 60 different font colors on the Font Color gallery (Figure 1–36). Your Font Color gallery may have more or fewer colors, depending on color settings of your operating system. The Theme Colors area includes colors that are included in the current workbook's theme.

Figure 1–36

2

- Click Dark Blue, Text 2 (column 4, row 1) on the Font Color gallery to change the font of the worksheet subtitle in the active cell (Figure 1–37).

Q&A Why does the Font Color button change after I select the new font color?

When you choose a color on the Font Color gallery, Excel changes the Font Color button (Home tab | Font group) to the chosen color. Thus, to change the font color of the cell entry in another cell to the same color, you need only to select the cell and then click the Font Color button (Home tab | Font group).

Figure 1–37

Other Ways

1. Click Font Color box arrow on Mini toolbar, click desired font color in the Font Color gallery

2. Right-click cell, click Format Cells on shortcut menu, click Font tab (Format Cells dialog box), select color in Font Color gallery, click OK button

To Center Cell Entries Across Columns by Merging Cells

The final step in formatting the worksheet title and subtitle is to center them across columns A through H. Centering a title across the columns used in the body of the worksheet improves the worksheet's appearance. To do this, the eight cells in the range A1:H1 are combined, or merged, into a single cell that is the width of the columns in the body of the worksheet. The eight cells in the range A2:H2 are merged in a similar manner. **Merging cells** involves creating a single cell by combining two or more selected cells. The following steps center the worksheet title and subtitle across columns by merging cells.

1

- Select cell A1 and then drag to cell H1 to highlight the range to be merged and centered (Figure 1–38).

Q&A

What if a cell in the range B1:H1 contains data?

For the Merge & Center button (Home tab | Alignment group) to work properly, all the cells except the leftmost cell in the selected range must be empty.

Figure 1–38

2

- Click the Merge & Center button (Home tab | Alignment group) to merge cells A1 through H1 and center the contents of the leftmost cell across the selected columns (Figure 1–39).

Q&A

What happened to cells B1 through H1?

After the merge, cells B1 through H1 no longer exist. The new cell A1 now extends across columns A through H.

Figure 1–39

3

- Repeat Steps 1 and 2 to merge and center the worksheet subtitle across cells A2 through H2 (Figure 1–40).

Q&A

Are cells B1 through H1 and B2 through H2 lost forever?

No. The opposite of merging cells is **splitting a merged cell**. After you have merged multiple cells to create one merged cell, you can unmerge, or split, the merged cell to display the original cells on the worksheet. You split a merged cell by selecting it and clicking the Merge & Center button. For example, if you click the Merge & Center button a second time in Step 2, it will split the merged cell A1 into cells A1, B1, C1, D1, E1, F1, G1, and H1.

Figure 1–40

Other Ways

1. Right-click selection, click Merge & Center button on Mini toolbar

2. Right-click selection, click Format Cells on shortcut menu, click Alignment tab (Format Cells dialog box), select Center Across Selection in Horizontal list, click OK button

To Format Column Titles and the Total Row

The next step to format the worksheet is to format the column titles in row 3 and the total values in row 9. Column titles and the total row should be formatted so anyone who views the worksheet quickly can distinguish the column titles and total row from the data in the body of the worksheet. The following steps format the column titles and total row using cell styles in the default worksheet theme.

1

- Click cell A3 and then drag the mouse pointer to cell H3 to select a range (Figure 1–41).

Q&A

Why is cell A3 selected in the range for the column headings?

The style to be applied to the column headings includes an underline that will help to distinguish the column headings from the rest of the worksheet. Including cell A3 in the range ensures that the cell will include the underline, which is visually appealing and further helps to separate the data in the worksheet.

Figure 1–41

2

- Click the Cell Styles button (Home tab | Styles group) to display the Cell Styles gallery.

- Point to the Heading 3 cell style in the Titles and Headings area of the Cell Styles gallery to see a live preview of the cell style in the selected range (Figure 1–42).

Figure 1–42

Experiment

- Point to other cell styles in the Titles and Headings area of the Cell Styles gallery to see a live preview of other cell styles in the selected range, A3:H3.

3

- Click the Heading 3 cell style to apply the cell style to the selected range.

- Click the Center button (Home tab | Alignment group) to center the column headings in the selected range.

- Click cell A9 and then drag the mouse pointer to cell H9 to select a range (Figure 1–43).

Figure 1–43

Q&A

Why should I choose Heading 3 instead of another heading cell style?

Excel includes many types of headings, such as Heading 1 and Heading 2, because worksheets often include many levels of headings above columns. In the case of the worksheet created for this project, the Heading 3 title includes formatting that makes the column titles' font size smaller than the title and subtitle and makes the column titles stand out from the data in the body of the worksheet.

4

- Click the Cell Styles button (Home tab | Styles group) to display the Cell Styles gallery and then click the Total cell style in the Titles and Headings area to apply the selected cell style to the cells in the selected range.

- Click cell A11 to select it (Figure 1–44).

Figure 1–44

To Format Numbers in the Worksheet

As previously noted, the numbers in the worksheet should be formatted to use a dollar-and-cents format, with dollar signs in the first row (row 4) and the total row (row 9). Excel allows you to format numbers in a variety of ways, and these methods are discussed in other chapters in this book. The following steps use buttons on the Ribbon to format the numbers in the worksheet.

1

- Select cell B4 and drag the mouse pointer to cell H4 to select a range (Figure 1–45).

Figure 1–45

2

- Click the Accounting Number Format button (Home tab | Number group) to apply the Accounting Number format to the cells in the selected range.

- Select the range B5:H8 (Figure 1–46).

Figure 1–46

Q&A What effect does the Accounting Number format have on the selected cells?

The Accounting Number format causes the cells to be displayed with two decimal places so that decimal places in cells below the selected cells align vertically. Cell widths are adjusted automatically to accommodate the new formatting.

3

- Click the Comma Style button (Home tab | Number group) to apply the Comma Style format to the selected range.

- Select the range B9:H9 to make it the active range (Figure 1–47).

Figure 1–47

Q&A What effect does the Comma Style format have on the selected cells?

The Comma Style format causes the cells to be displayed with two decimal places and commas as thousands separators.

4

- Click the Accounting Number Format button (Home tab | Number group) to apply the Accounting Number format to the cells in the selected range.

- Select cell A11 (Figure 1–48).

Q&A

Why did the column widths automatically adjust again?

Because the total row contains larger numbers, the Accounting Number format again causes the cell widths automatically to adjust to accommodate the new formatting just as occurred in Step 2.

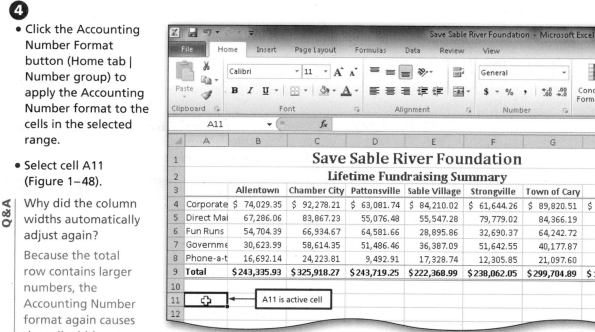

Figure 1–48

Other Ways

1. Click Accounting Number Format or Comma Style button on Mini toolbar

2. Right-click selection, click Format Cells on the shortcut menu, click

Number tab (Format Cells dialog box), select Accounting in Category list or select Number and click Use 1000 Separator, click OK button

---

To Adjust the Column Width

The last step in formatting the worksheet is to adjust the width of column A so that the word Phone-a-thon in cell A8 is shown in its entirety in the cell. Excel includes several methods for adjusting cell widths and row heights, and these methods are discussed later in this book. The following steps adjust the width of column A so that the contents of cell A8 are displayed in the cell.

1

- Point to the boundary on the right side of the column A heading above row 1 to change the mouse pointer to a split double arrow (Figure 1–49).

Figure 1–49

2

• Double-click on the boundary to adjust the width of the column to the width of the largest item in the column (Figure 1–50).

Q&A

What if none of the items in column A extends through the entire width of the column?

If all of the items in column A were shorter in length than the width of the column when you double-click the right side of the column A heading, then Excel still would adjust the column width to the largest item in the column. That is, Excel would reduce the width of the column to the largest item.

Figure 1–50

Using the Name Box to Select a Cell

The next step is to chart the lifetime fundraising amounts for the five fundraising activities used by the organization. To create the chart, you first must select the cell in the upper-left corner of the range to chart (cell A3). Rather than clicking cell A3 to select it, the next section describes how to use the Name box to select the cell.

To Use the Name Box to Select a Cell

The Name box is located on the left side of the formula bar. To select any cell, click the Name box and enter the cell reference of the cell you want to select. The following steps select cell A3 using the Name box.

1

• Click the Name box in the formula bar and then type **a3** as the cell you wish to select (Figure 1–51).

Q&A

Why is cell A11 still selected?

Even though cell A11 is the active cell, Excel displays the typed cell reference a3 in the Name box until you press the ENTER key.

Figure 1–51

2

● Press the ENTER key to change the active cell in the Name box (Figure 1–52).

Figure 1–52

Other Ways to Select Cells

As you will see in later chapters, in addition to using the Name box to select any cell in a worksheet, you also can use it to assign names to a cell or range of cells. Excel supports several additional ways to select a cell, as summarized in Table 1–3.

Table 1–3 Selecting Cells in Excel	
Key, Box, or Command	**Function**
ALT+PAGE DOWN	Selects the cell one worksheet window to the right and moves the worksheet window accordingly.
ALT+PAGE UP	Selects the cell one worksheet window to the left and moves the worksheet window accordingly.
ARROW	Selects the adjacent cell in the direction of the arrow on the key.
CTRL+ARROW	Selects the border cell of the worksheet in combination with the arrow keys and moves the worksheet window accordingly. For example, to select the rightmost cell in the row that contains the active cell, press CTRL+RIGHT ARROW. You also can press the END key, release it, and then press the appropriate arrow key to accomplish the same task.
CTRL+HOME	Selects cell A1 or the cell one column and one row below and to the right of frozen titles and moves the worksheet window accordingly.
Find command on Find and Select menu or SHIFT+F5	Finds and selects a cell that contains specific contents that you enter in the Find and Replace dialog box. If necessary, Excel moves the worksheet window to display the cell. You also can press CTRL+F to display the Find dialog box.
Go To command on Find and Select menu or F5	Selects the cell that corresponds to the cell reference you enter in the Go To dialog box and moves the worksheet window accordingly. You also can press CTRL+G to display the Go To dialog box.
HOME	Selects the cell at the beginning of the row that contains the active cell and moves the worksheet window accordingly.
Name box	Selects the cell in the workbook that corresponds to the cell reference you enter in the Name box.
PAGE DOWN	Selects the cell down one worksheet window from the active cell and moves the worksheet window accordingly.
PAGE UP	Selects the cell up one worksheet window from the active cell and moves the worksheet window accordingly.

Break Point: If you wish to take a break, this is a good place to do so. Be sure to save the Save Sable River Foundation file again and then you can quit Excel. To resume at a later time, start Excel, open the file called Save Sable River Foundation, and continue following the steps from this location forward.

Adding a Clustered Cylinder Chart to the Worksheet

As outlined in the requirements document in Figure 1–2 on page EX 4, the worksheet should include a Clustered Cylinder chart to graphically represent the lifetime fundraising for each fundraising activity in which the organization engages. The Clustered Cylinder chart shown in Figure 1–53 is called an **embedded chart** because it is drawn on the same worksheet as the data.

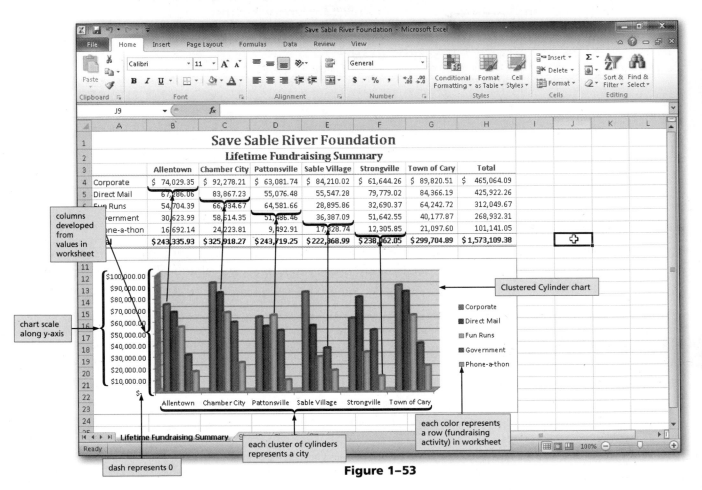

Figure 1–53

	Plan Ahead	**Decide on the type of chart needed.**

Decide on the type of chart needed.
Excel includes 11 chart types from which you can choose, including column, line, pie, bar, area, X Y (scatter), stock, surface, doughnut, bubble, and radar. The type of chart you choose depends on the type of data that you have, how much data you have, and the message you want to convey.

A line chart often is used to illustrate changes in data over time. Pie charts show the contribution of each piece of data to the whole, or total, of the data. Area charts, like line charts, illustrate changes over time, but often are used to compare more than one set of data and the area under the lines is filled in with a different color for each set of data. An X Y (scatter) chart is used much line a line chart, but each piece of data is represented by a dot and is not connected with a line. A stock chart provides a number of methods commonly

(continued)

(continued)

used in the financial industry to show stock market data. A surface chart compares data from three columns and/or rows in a three-dimensional manner. A doughnut chart is much like a pie chart, but a doughnut chart allows for comparing more than one set of data, resulting in a chart that looks like a doughnut, with each subsequent set of data surrounding the previous set. A bubble chart is much like an X Y (scatter) chart, but a third set of data results indicates how large each individual dot, or bubble, is on the chart. A radar chart can compare several sets of data in a manner that resembles a radar screen, with each set of data represented by a different color. A column or cylinder chart is a good way to compare values side by side. A Clustered Cylinder chart can go even further in comparing values across categories.

Establish where to position and how to format the chart.

- When possible, try to position charts so that both the data and chart appear on the screen on the worksheet together and so that the data and chart can be printed in the most readable manner possible.

- When choosing/selecting colors for a chart, consider the color scheme of the rest of the worksheet. The chart should not present colors that are in stark contrast to the rest of the worksheet. If the chart will be printed in color, minimize the amount of dark colors on the chart so that the chart both prints quickly and conserves ink.

Plan Ahead

BTW

Cell Values and Charting
When you change a cell value on which a chart is dependent, Excel redraws the chart instantaneously, unless automatic recalculation is disabled. If automatic recalculation is disabled, then you must press the F9 key to redraw the chart. To enable or disable automatic recalculation, click the Calculations Options button (Formulas tab | Calculation group).

In the case of the Save Sable River Foundation Lifetime Fundraising Summary, comparisons of fundraising activities within each city can be made side by side with a Clustered Cylinder chart. The chart uses differently colored cylinders to represent amounts raised for different fundraising activities. Each city uses the same color scheme for identifying fundraising activities, which allows for easy identification and comparison.

- For the city of Allentown, for example, the dark blue cylinder representing Corporate donations shows lifetime donations of $74,029.35

- For Chamber City, the maroon cylinder representing Direct Mail donations shows lifetime donations of $83,867.23

- For the city of Pattonsville, the lime green cylinder representing donations for Fun Runs shows lifetime donations of $64,581.66

- For Sable Village, the purple cylinder representing Government donations shows lifetime donations of $36,387.09

- For the city of Strongville, the light blue cylinder representing Phone-a-thon donations shows lifetime donations of $12,305.85

Because the same color scheme is used in each city to represent the five fundraising activities, you easily can compare funds raised by each fundraising activity among the cities. The totals from the worksheet are not represented, because the totals are not in the range specified for charting.

Excel derives the chart scale based on the values in the worksheet and then displays the scale along the vertical axis (also called the **y-axis** or **value axis**) of the chart. For example, no value in the range B4:G8 is less than 0 or greater than $100,000.00, so the scale ranges from 0 to $100,000.00. Excel also determines the $10,000.00 increments of the scale automatically. For the numbers along the y-axis, Excel uses a format that includes representing the 0 value with a dash (Figure 1–53).

To Add a Clustered Cylinder Chart to the Worksheet

The area on the worksheet where the chart appears is called the chart location. As shown in Figure 1–53 on page EX 36, the chart location in this worksheet is the range A11:G23; this range is immediately below the worksheet data. Placing the chart below the data on the Save Sable River Foundation Lifetime Fundraising Summary worksheet makes it easier to read the chart along with the data, and the chart and data easily can be printed on one sheet of paper.

The following steps draw a Clustered Cylinder chart that compares the funds raised by fundraising activity for the six cities.

1

- Click cell A3 and then drag the mouse pointer to cell G8 to select the range to be charted (Figure 1–54).

Figure 1–54

2

- Click Insert on the Ribbon to display the Insert tab (Figure 1–55).

Q&A

What tasks can I perform with the Insert tab?

The Insert tab includes commands that allow you to insert various objects, such as shapes, tables, illustrations, and charts, into a worksheet. These objects will be discussed as they are used throughout this book.

Figure 1–55

3

- Click the Column button (Insert tab | Charts group) to display the Column gallery (Figure 1–56).

Figure 1–56

4

- Click the Clustered Cylinder chart type in the Cylinder area of the Column gallery to add the selected chart type to the middle of the worksheet in a selection rectangle.

- Press and hold down the mouse button while pointing to the upper-right edge of the selection rectangle to change the mouse pointer to a double two-headed arrow (Figure 1–57).

Q&A

Why is a new tab displayed on the Ribbon?

When you select objects such as shapes or charts, Excel displays contextual tabs that include special commands that are used to work

Figure 1–57

with the type of object selected. Because a chart is selected, Excel displays the Chart Tools contextual tab. The three tabs below the Chart Tools contextual tab, Design, Layout, and Format, are tabs that include commands to work with charts.

5

- Drag the chart down and to the left to position the upper-left corner of the dotted line rectangle over the upper-left corner of cell A11.

- Press and hold down the mouse button while pointing to the middle sizing handle on the right edge of the chart (Figure 1–58).

Q&A

How does Excel know which data to use to create the chart?

Excel automatically selects the entries in the topmost row of the chart range (row 3) as the titles for the horizontal axis (also called the **x-axis** or **category axis**) and draws a column for each of the 30 cells in the range containing numbers.

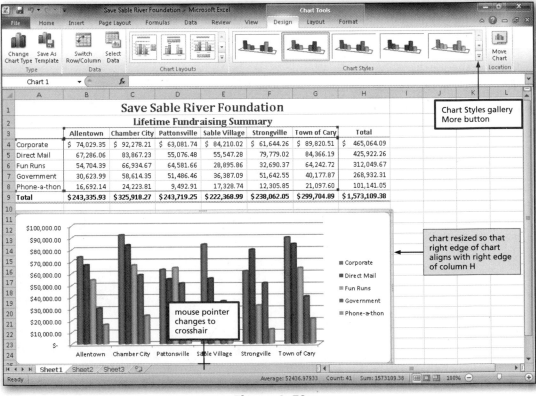

Figure 1–58

6

- While continuing to hold down the mouse button, press the ALT key and drag the right edge of the chart to the right edge of column H and then release the mouse button to resize the chart.

- Press and hold down the mouse button while pointing to the middle sizing handle on the bottom edge of the selection rectangle and do not release the mouse button (Figure 1–59).

Q&A

Why should I hold the ALT key down while I resize a chart?

Holding down the ALT key while you drag a chart **snaps** (aligns) the edge of the chart area to the worksheet gridlines. If you do not hold down the ALT key, then you can place an edge of a chart in the middle of a column or row.

Figure 1–59

7

- While continuing to hold down the mouse button, press the ALT key and drag the bottom edge of the chart up to the bottom edge of row 23 and then release the mouse button to resize the chart.

- If necessary, scroll the worksheet so that row 1 displays at the top of the worksheet.

- Click the More button in the Chart Styles gallery (Chart Tools Design tab | Chart Styles group) to expand the gallery (Figure 1–60).

Figure 1–60

8

- Click Style 34 in the Chart Styles gallery (column 2, row 5) to apply the chart style to the chart.

- Click cell J9 to deselect the chart and complete the worksheet (Figure 1–61).

Q&A

What is the purpose of the items on the right side of the chart?

The items to the right of the column chart in Figure 1–61 are the **legend**, which identifies the colors assigned to each bar in the chart. Excel automatically selects the entries in the leftmost column of the chart range (column A) as titles within the legend.

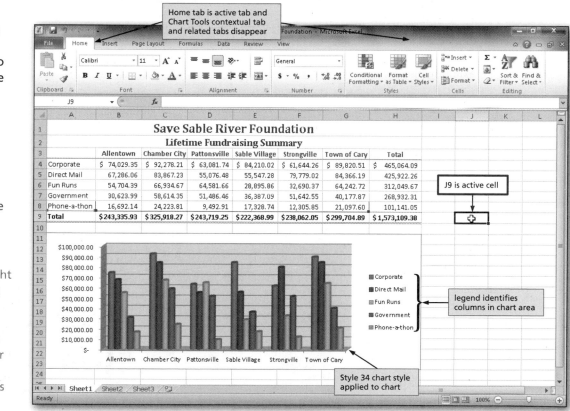

Figure 1–61

Changing the Worksheet Names

The sheet tabs at the bottom of the window allow you to view any worksheet in the workbook. You click the sheet tab of the worksheet you want to view in the Excel window. By default, Excel presets the names of the worksheets to Sheet1, Sheet2, and so on. The worksheet names become increasingly important as you move toward more sophisticated workbooks, especially workbooks in which you reference cells between worksheets.

Plan Ahead

Choose a name for the worksheet.
Use simple, meaningful names for each worksheet. Worksheet names often match the worksheet title. If a worksheet includes multiple titles in multiple sections of the worksheet, use a name that encompasses the meaning of all of the sections.

To Change the Worksheet Names

Lifetime Fundraising Summary is a meaningful name for the Save Sable River Foundation Lifetime Fundraising Summary worksheet. The following steps rename worksheets by double-clicking the sheet tabs.

1

- Double-click the sheet tab labeled Sheet1 in the lower-left corner of the window.

- Type **Lifetime Fundraising Summary** as the worksheet name and then press the ENTER key to display the new worksheet name on the sheet tab (Figure 1–62).

Q&A What is the maximum length for a worksheet tab?

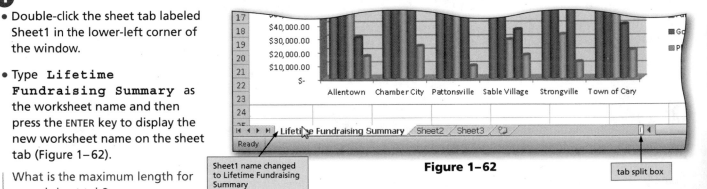

Figure 1–62

Worksheet names can be up to 31 characters (including spaces) in length. Longer worksheet names, however, mean that fewer sheet tabs will show. To view more sheet tabs, you can drag the tab split box (Figure 1–62) to the right. This will reduce the size of the scroll bar at the bottom of the screen. Double-click the tab split box to reset it to its normal position.

2

- Right-click the sheet tab labeled Lifetime Fundraising Summary in the lower-left corner of the window to display a shortcut menu.

- Point to Tab Color on the shortcut menu to display the color gallery (Figure 1–63).

Q&A How can I quickly move between worksheet tabs?

You can use the tab scrolling buttons to the left of the sheet tabs (Figure 1–63) to move between worksheets. The leftmost and rightmost scroll buttons move to the first or last worksheet in the workbook. The two middle scroll buttons move one worksheet to the left or right.

Figure 1–63

3
- Click Red, Accent 2 (column 6, row 1) in the Theme Colors area to change the color of the tab (Figure 1–64)

4
- If necessary, click Home on the Ribbon to display the Home tab.

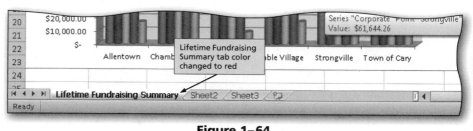

Figure 1–64

Changing Document Properties

Excel helps you organize and identify your files by using **document properties**, which are the details about a file. Document properties, also known as **metadata**, can include information such as the project author, title, subject, and keywords. A **keyword** is a word or phrase that further describes the document. For example, a class name or document topic can describe the file's purpose or content.

Document properties are valuable for a variety of reasons:

- Users can save time locating a particular file because they can view a document's properties without opening the document.

- By creating consistent properties for files having similar content, users can better organize their documents.

- Some organizations require Excel users to add document properties so that other employees can view details about these files.

Five different types of document properties exist, but the more common ones used in this book are standard and automatically updated properties. **Standard properties** are associated with all Microsoft Office documents and include author, title, and subject. **Automatically updated properties** include file system properties, such as the date you create or change a file, and statistics, such as the file size.

To Change Document Properties

The **Document Information Panel** contains areas where you can view and enter document properties. You can view and change information in this panel at any time while you are creating a workbook. Before saving the workbook again, you want to add your name and course information as document properties. The following steps use the Document Information Panel to change document properties.

1
- Click File on the Ribbon to open the Backstage view. If necessary, click the Info tab in the Backstage view to display the Info gallery (Figure 1–65).

Q&A

How do I close the Backstage view?

Click File on the Ribbon or click the preview of the document in the Info gallery to return to the Excel document window.

Figure 1–65

2

- Click the Properties button in the right pane of the Info gallery to display the Properties menu (Figure 1–66).

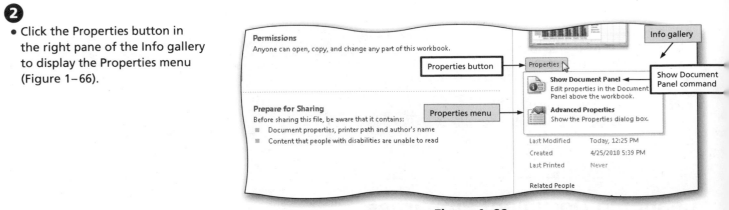

Figure 1–66

3

- Click Show Document Panel on the Properties menu to close the Backstage view and display the Document Information Panel in the Excel workbook window (Figure 1–67).

Q&A

Why are some of the document properties in my Document Information Panel already filled in?

The person who installed Microsoft Office 2010 on your computer or network may have set or customized the properties.

Figure 1–67

4

- Click the Author text box, if necessary, and then type your name as the Author property. If a name already is displayed in the Author text box, delete it before typing your name.

- Click the Subject text box, if necessary delete any existing text, and then type your course and section as the Subject property.

- If an AutoComplete dialog box appears, click its Yes button.

- Click the Keywords text box, if necessary delete any existing text, and then type **Lifetime Fundraising Summary** as the Keywords property (Figure 1–68).

Figure 1–68

Q&A

What types of document properties does Excel collect automatically?

Excel records details such as time spent editing a workbook, the number of times a workbook has been revised, and the fonts and themes used in a workbook.

5

- Click the Close the Document Information Panel button so that the Document Information Panel no longer is displayed. If a dialog box is displayed, click the No button to close it.

Other Ways

1. Click File on Ribbon, click Info in the Backstage view, if necessary click Show All Properties link in Info gallery, click property to change and type new information, close the Backstage view

To Save an Existing Workbook with the Same File Name

You have made several modifications to the workbook since you last saved it. Thus, you should save it again. The following step saves the workbook again. For an example of the step listed below, refer to the Introduction to Office 2010 and Windows 7 chapter at the beginning of this book.

1 Click the Save button on the Quick Access Toolbar to overwrite the previously saved file.

Previewing and Printing a Worksheet

After creating a worksheet, you may want to print it. Printing a worksheet enables you to distribute the worksheet to others in a form that can be read or viewed but typically not edited. It is a good practice to save a workbook before printing a worksheet, in the event you experience difficulties printing.

Determine the best method for distributing the worksheet.
The traditional method of distributing a worksheet uses a printer to produce a hard copy. A **hardcopy or printout** is information that exists on a physical medium such as paper. For users that can receive fax documents, you can elect to print a hard copy on a remote fax machine. Hard copies can be useful for the following reasons:

* Many people prefer proofreading a hard copy of a worksheet rather than viewing it on the screen to check for errors and readability.

* Hard copies can serve as reference material if your storage medium is lost or becomes corrupted and you need to re-create the worksheet.

Instead of distributing a hard copy of a worksheet, users can choose to distribute the worksheet as an electronic image that mirrors the original worksheet's appearance. The electronic image of the worksheet can be e-mailed, posted on a Web site, or copied to a portable storage medium such as a USB flash drive. Two popular electronic image formats, sometimes called fixed formats, are PDF by Adobe Systems and XPS by Microsoft. In Excel, you can create electronic image files through the Print tab in the Backstage view, the Save & Send tab in the Backstage view, and the Save As dialog box. Electronic images of worksheets, such as PDF and XPS, can be useful for the following reasons:

* Users can view electronic images of worksheets without the software that created the original worksheet (e.g., Excel). Specifically, to view a PDF file, you use a program called Acrobat Reader, which can be downloaded free from Adobe's Web site. Similarly, to view an XPS file, you use a program called an XPS Viewer, which is included in the latest versions of Windows and Internet Explorer.

* Sending electronic documents saves paper and printer supplies. Society encourages users to contribute to **green computing**, which involves reducing the environmental waste generated when using a computer.

BTW

Printing Document Properties
To print document properties, click File on the Ribbon to open the Backstage view, click the Print tab in the Backstage view to display the Print gallery, click the first button in the Settings area to display a list of options specifying what you can print, click Document Properties in the list to specify you want to print the document properties instead of the actual document, and then click the Print button in the Print gallery to print the document properties on the currently selected printer.

Plan Ahead

BTW

Conserving Ink and Toner
If you want to conserve ink or toner, you can instruct Excel to print draft quality documents by clicking File on the Ribbon to open the Backstage view, clicking Options in the Backstage view to display the Excel Options dialog box, clicking Advanced in the left pane (Excel Options dialog box), scrolling to the Print area in the right pane, placing a check mark in the 'Use draft quality' check box, and then clicking the OK button. Then, use the Backstage view to print the document as usual.

To Preview and Print a Worksheet in Landscape Orientation

With the completed workbook saved, you may want to print it. Because the worksheet is included in a report, you will print a hard copy on a printer. The following steps print a hard copy of the contents of the Save Sable River Foundation Lifetime Fundraising Summary worksheet.

1

- Click File on the Ribbon to open the Backstage view.

- Click the Print tab in the Backstage view to display the Print gallery (Figure 1–69).

Q&A

How can I print multiple copies of my worksheet?

Increase the number in the Copies box in the Print gallery.

Q&A

What if I decide not to print the worksheet at this time?

Click File on the Ribbon to close the Backstage view and return to the Excel workbook window.

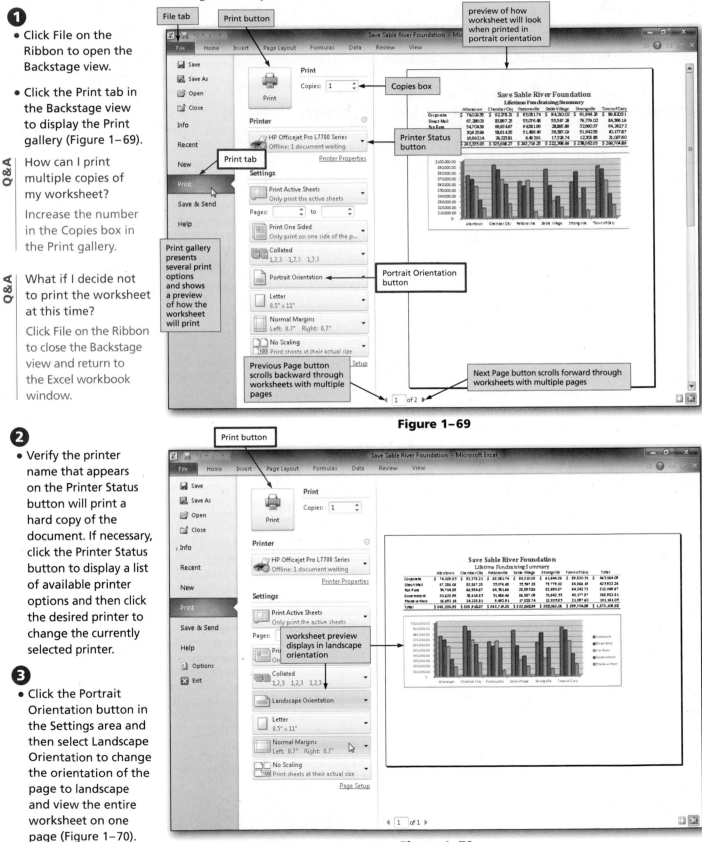

Figure 1–69

2

- Verify the printer name that appears on the Printer Status button will print a hard copy of the document. If necessary, click the Printer Status button to display a list of available printer options and then click the desired printer to change the currently selected printer.

3

- Click the Portrait Orientation button in the Settings area and then select Landscape Orientation to change the orientation of the page to landscape and view the entire worksheet on one page (Figure 1–70).

Figure 1–70

- Click the Print button in the Print gallery to print the worksheet in landscape orientation on the currently selected printer.

- When the printer stops, retrieve the hard copy (Figure 1–71).

Q&A Do I have to wait until my worksheet is complete to print it?

No, you can follow these steps to print a document at any time while you are creating it.

Q&A What if I want to print an electronic image of a worksheet instead of a hard copy?

You would click the Printer Status button in the Print gallery and then select the desired electronic image option such as a Microsoft XPS Document Writer, which would create an XPS file.

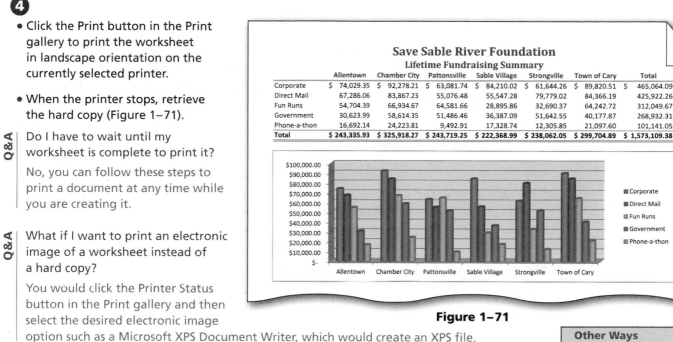

Figure 1–71

Other Ways
1. Press CTRL+P, press ENTER

To Quit Excel

This Save Sable River Foundation workbook now is complete. The following steps quit Excel if only one workbook is open. For a detailed example of the procedure summarized below, refer to the Office 2010 and Windows 7 chapter at the beginning of this book.

1 If you have one Excel workbook open, click the Close button on the right side of the title bar to close the document and quit Excel; or if you have multiple Excel workbooks open, click File on the Ribbon to open the Backstage view and then click the Exit button to close all open workbooks and quit Excel.

2 If a Microsoft Office Excel dialog box appears, click the Save button to save any changes made to the workbook since the last save.

Starting Excel and Opening a Workbook

Once you have created and saved a workbook, you may need to retrieve it from your storage medium. For example, you might want to revise a worksheet or reprint it. Opening a workbook requires that Excel is running on your computer.

To Start Excel

1 Click the Start button on the Windows 7 taskbar to display the Start menu.

2 Type `Microsoft Excel` as the search text in the 'Search programs and files' text box and watch the search results appear on the Start menu.

3 Click Microsoft Excel 2010 in the search results on the Start menu to start Excel and display a new blank workbook in the Excel window.

4 If the Excel window is not maximized, click the Maximize button next to the Close button on its title bar to maximize the window.

To Open a Workbook from Excel

Earlier in this chapter you saved your project on a USB flash drive using the file name, Save Sable River Foundation. The following steps open the Save Sable River Foundation file from the Excel folder in the CIS 101 folder on the USB flash drive. For a detailed example of the procedure summarized below, refer to the Office 2010 and Windows 7 chapter at the beginning of this book.

1 With your USB flash drive connected to one of the computer's USB ports, click File on the Ribbon to open the Backstage view.

2 Click Open in the Backstage view to display the Open dialog box.

3 Navigate to the location of the file to be opened (in this case, the USB flash drive, then to the CIS 101 folder [or your class folder], and then to the Excel folder). For a detailed example of this procedure, refer to Steps 3a–3c in the To Save a File in a Folder section in the Office 2010 and Windows 7 chapter at the beginning of this book.

4 Click Save Sable River Foundation to select the file to be opened.

5 Click the Open button (Open dialog box) to open the selected file and display the opened workbook in the Excel window.

AutoCalculate

You easily can obtain a total, an average, or other information about the numbers in a range by using the **AutoCalculate area** on the status bar. First, select the range of cells containing the numbers you want to check. Next, right-click the AutoCalculate area to display the Status Bar Configuration shortcut menu (Figure 1–72). The check mark to the left of the active functions (Average, Count, and Sum) indicates that the sum, count, and average of the selected range are displayed in the AutoCalculate area on the status bar. The functions of the AutoCalculate commands on the Status Bar Configuration shortcut menu are described in Table 1–4.

BTW

AutoCalculate
Use the AutoCalculate area on the status bar to check your work as you enter data in a worksheet. If you enter large amounts of data, you select a range of data and then check the AutoCalculate area to provide insight into statistics about the data you entered. Often, you will have an intuitive feel for whether the numbers are accurate or if you may have made a mistake while entering the data.

Table 1–4 AutoCalculate Shortcut Menu Commands	
Command	**Function**
Average	AutoCalculate area displays the average of the numbers in the selected range
Count	AutoCalculate area displays the number of nonblank cells in the selected range
Numerical Count	AutoCalculate area displays the number of cells containing numbers in the selected range
Minimum	AutoCalculate area displays the lowest value in the selected range
Maximum	AutoCalculate area displays the highest value in the selected range
Sum	AutoCalculate area displays the sum of the numbers in the selected range

To Use the AutoCalculate Area to Determine a Maximum

The following steps display the largest amounts of funds raised for any city for the Fun Runs fundraising activity.

1

- Select the range B6:G6 and then right-click the AutoCalculate area on the status bar to display the Customize Status Bar shortcut menu (Figure 1–72).

Q&A

What is displayed on the Customize Status Bar shortcut menu?

This shortcut menu includes several commands that allow you to control the items displayed on the Customize Status Bar shortcut menu. The AutoCalculate area includes six commands as well as the result of the associated calculation on the right side of the menu.

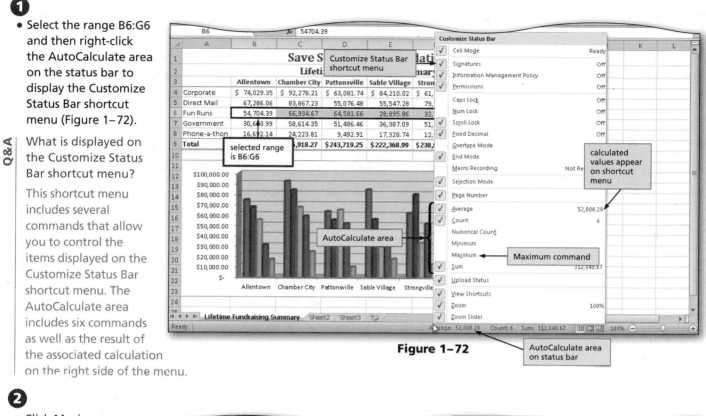

Figure 1–72

2

- Click Maximum on the shortcut menu to display the Maximum value in the range B6:G6 in the AutoCalculate area of the status bar.

Figure 1–73

- Click anywhere on the worksheet to cause the shortcut menu to disappear (Figure 1–73).

3

- Right-click the AutoCalculate area and then click Maximum on the shortcut menu to cause the Maximum value to no longer appear in the AutoCalculate area.

- Click anywhere on the worksheet to cause the shortcut menu to disappear.

Correcting Errors

You can correct errors on a worksheet using one of several methods. The method you choose will depend on the extent of the error and whether you notice it while typing the data or after you have entered the incorrect data into the cell.

Correcting Errors While You Are Typing Data into a Cell

If you notice an error while you are typing data into a cell, press the BACKSPACE key to erase the incorrect characters and then type the correct characters. If the error is a major one, click the Cancel box in the formula bar or press the ESC key to erase the entire entry and then reenter the data from the beginning.

BTW

Quick Reference
For a table that lists how to complete the tasks covered in this book using the mouse, Ribbon, shortcut menu, and keyboard, see the Quick Reference Summary at the back of this book, or visit the Excel 2010 Quick Reference Web page (scsite.com/ex2010/qr).

Correcting Errors After Entering Data into a Cell

If you find an error in the worksheet after entering the data, you can correct the error in one of two ways:

1. If the entry is short, select the cell, retype the entry correctly, and then click the Enter box or press the ENTER key. The new entry will replace the old entry.

2. If the entry in the cell is long and the errors are minor, using Edit mode may be a better choice than retyping the cell entry. Use the Edit mode as described below.

    a. Double-click the cell containing the error to switch Excel to Edit mode. In **Edit mode**, Excel displays the active cell entry in the formula bar and a flashing insertion point in the active cell (Figure 1–74). With Excel in Edit mode, you can edit the contents directly in the cell — a procedure called **in-cell editing**.

    b. Make changes using in-cell editing, as indicated below.

    (1) To insert new characters between two characters, place the insertion point between the two characters and begin typing. Excel inserts the new characters at the location of the insertion point.

    (2) To delete a character in the cell, move the insertion point to the left of the character you want to delete and then press the DELETE key or place the insertion point to the right of the character you want to delete and then press the BACKSPACE key. You also can use the mouse to drag through the character or adjacent characters you want to delete and then press the DELETE key or click the Cut button (Home tab | Clipboard group).

    (3) When you are finished editing an entry, click the Enter box or press the ENTER key.

BTW

In-Cell Editing
An alternative to double-clicking the cell to edit it is to select the cell and then press the F2 key.

Figure 1–74

BTW

Editing the Contents of a Cell
Rather than using in-cell editing, you can select the cell and then click the formula bar to edit the contents.

When Excel enters the Edit mode, the keyboard usually is in Insert mode. In **Insert mode**, as you type a character, Excel inserts the character and moves all characters to the right of the typed character one position to the right. You can change to Overtype mode by pressing the INSERT key. In **Overtype mode**, Excel overtypes, or replaces, the character to the right of the insertion point. The INSERT key toggles the keyboard between Insert mode and Overtype mode.

While in Edit mode, you may have reason to move the insertion point to various points in the cell, select portions of the data in the cell, or switch from inserting characters to overtyping characters. Table 1–5 summarizes the more common tasks performed during in-cell editing.

Table 1–5 Summary of In-Cell Editing Tasks

	Task	Mouse	Keyboard
1	Move the insertion point to the beginning of data in a cell.	Point to the left of the first character and click.	Press HOME
2	Move the insertion point to the end of data in a cell.	Point to the right of the last character and click.	Press END
3	Move the insertion point anywhere in a cell.	Point to the appropriate position and click the character.	Press RIGHT ARROW or LEFT ARROW
4	Highlight one or more adjacent characters.	Drag the mouse pointer through adjacent characters.	Press SHIFT+RIGHT ARROW or SHIFT+LEFT ARROW
5	Select all data in a cell.	Double-click the cell with the insertion point in the cell if there are no spaces in the data in the cell.	
6	Delete selected characters.	Click the Cut button (Home tab | Clipboard group)	Press DELETE
7	Delete characters to the left of the insertion point.		Press BACKSPACE
8	Delete characters to the right of the insertion point.		Press DELETE
9	Toggle between Insert and Overtype modes.		Press INSERT

BTW

Excel Help
At any time while using Excel, you can find answers to questions and display information about various topics through Excel Help. Used properly, this form of assistance can increase your productivity and reduce your frustrations by minimizing the time you spend learning how to use Excel. For instruction about Excel Help and exercises that will help you gain confidence in using it, read the Office 2010 and Windows 7 chapter at the beginning of this book.

Undoing the Last Cell Entry

Excel provides the Undo command on the Quick Access Toolbar (Figure 1–75), which allows you to erase recent cell entries. Thus, if you enter incorrect data in a cell and notice it immediately, click the Undo button and Excel changes the cell entry to what it was prior to the incorrect data entry.

Figure 1–75

Excel remembers the last 100 actions you have completed. Thus, you can undo up to 100 previous actions by clicking the Undo button arrow to display the Undo list and then clicking the action to be undone (Figure 1–75). You can drag through several actions in the Undo list to undo all of them at once. If no actions are available for Excel to undo, then the Undo button is dimmed and inoperative.

The Redo button, next to the Undo button on the Quick Access Toolbar, allows you to repeat previous actions.

Clearing a Cell or Range of Cells

If you enter data into the wrong cell or range of cells, you can erase, or clear, the data using one of the first four methods listed below. The fifth method clears the formatting from the selected cells.

TO CLEAR CELL ENTRIES USING THE FILL HANDLE

1. Select the cell or range of cells and then point to the fill handle so the mouse pointer changes to a crosshair.
2. Drag the fill handle back into the selected cell or range until a shadow covers the cell or cells you want to erase. Release the mouse button.

TO CLEAR CELL ENTRIES USING THE SHORTCUT MENU

1. Select the cell or range of cells to be cleared.
2. Right-click the selection.
3. Click Clear Contents on the shortcut menu.

TO CLEAR CELL ENTRIES USING THE DELETE KEY

1. Select the cell or range of cells to be cleared.
2. Press the DELETE key.

TO CLEAR CELL ENTRIES AND FORMATTING USING THE CLEAR BUTTON

1. Select the cell or range of cells to be cleared.
2. Click the Clear button (Home tab | Editing group) (Figure 1–75 on the previous page).
3. Click Clear Contents on the menu.

TO CLEAR FORMATTING USING THE CELL STYLES BUTTON

1. Select the cell or range of cells from which you want to remove the formatting.
2. Click the Cell Styles button (Home tab | Styles group) and point to Normal.
3. Click Normal in the Cell Styles Gallery.

The Clear button (Home tab | Editing group) is the only command that clears both the cell entry and the cell formatting. As you are clearing cell entries, always remember that you should *never press the* SPACEBAR *to clear a cell*. Pressing the SPACEBAR enters a blank character. A blank character is text and is different from an empty cell, even though the cell may appear empty.

Clearing the Entire Worksheet

If the required worksheet edits are extremely extensive, you may want to clear the entire worksheet and start over. To clear the worksheet or delete an embedded chart, you would use the following steps.

TO CLEAR THE ENTIRE WORKSHEET

1. Click the Select All button on the worksheet (Figure 1–75).
2. Click the Clear button (Home tab | Editing group) and then click Clear All on the Clear menu to delete both the entries and formats.

The Select All button selects the entire worksheet. Instead of clicking the Select All button, you can press CTRL+A. To clear an unsaved workbook, click the workbook's Close Window button or click the Close button in the Backstage view. Click the No button if the Microsoft Excel dialog box asks if you want to save changes. To start a new, blank workbook, click the New button in the Backstage view.

To delete an embedded chart, you would complete the following steps.

TO DELETE AN EMBEDDED CHART

1. Click the chart to select it.
2. Press the DELETE key.

To Quit Excel

The project now is complete. The following steps quit Excel. For a detailed example of the procedure summarized below, refer to the Office 2010 and Windows 7 chapter at the beginning of this book.

1 If you have one Excel workbook open, click the Close button on the right side of the title bar to close the document and quit Excel; or if you have multiple Excel workbooks open, click File on the Ribbon to open the Backstage view and then click Exit in the Backstage view to close all open workbooks and quit Excel.

2 If a Microsoft Office Excel dialog box appears, click the Save button to save any changes made to the document since the last save.

BTW

Quitting Excel
Do not forget to remove your USB flash drive from the USB port after quitting Excel, especially if you are working in a laboratory environment. Nothing can be more frustrating than leaving all of your hard work behind on a USB flash drive for the next user.

Chapter Summary

In this chapter you have learned how to enter text and numbers to create a worksheet, how to select a range, how to use the Sum button, format cells, insert a chart, and preview and print a worksheet. The items listed below include all the new Excel skills you have learned in this chapter.

1. To Start Excel (EX 6)
2. Enter the Worksheet Titles (EX 8)
3. Enter Column Titles (EX 10)
4. Enter Row Titles (EX 12)
5. Enter Numbers (EX 13)
6. Sum a Column of Numbers (EX 15)
7. Copy a Cell to Adjacent Cells in a Row (EX 17)
8. Determine Multiple Totals at the Same Time (EX 18)
9. Save a Workbook (EX 20)
10. Change a Cell Style (EX 22)
11. Change the Font (EX 24)
12. Bold a Cell (EX 25)
13. Increase the Font Size of a Cell Entry (EX 26)
14. Change the Font Color of a Cell Entry (EX 27)
15. Center Cell Entries Across Columns by Merging Cells (EX 28)
16. Format Column Titles and the Total Row (EX 29)
17. Format Numbers in the Worksheet (EX 31)
18. Adjust the Column Width (EX 33)
19. Use the Name Box to Select a Cell (EX 34)
20. Add a Clustered Cylinder Chart to the Worksheet (EX 38)
21. Change the Worksheet Names (EX 42)
22. Change Document Properties (EX 43)
23. Save an Existing Workbook with the Same File Name (EX 45)
24. Preview and Print a Worksheet in Landscape Orientation (EX 46)
25. Quit Excel (EX 47)
26. Start Excel (EX 47)
27. Open a Workbook from Excel (EX 48)
28. Use the AutoCalculate Area to Determine a Maximum (EX 49)
29. Clear Cell Entries Using the Fill Handle (EX 52)
30. Clear Cell Entries Using the Shortcut Menu (EX 52)
31. Clear Cell Entries Using the DELETE Key (EX 52)
32. Clear Cell Entries and Formatting Using the Clear Button (EX 52)
33. Clear Formatting Using the Cell Styles Button (EX 52)
34. Clear the Entire Worksheet (EX 52)
35. Delete an Embedded Chart (EX 53)

If you have a SAM 2010 user profile, your instructor may have assigned an autogradable version of this assignment. If so, log into the SAM 2010 Web site at www.cengage.com/sam2010 to download the instruction and start files.

Learn It Online

Test your knowledge of chapter content and key terms.

Instructions: To complete the Learn It Online exercises, start your browser, click the Address bar, and then enter the Web address **scsite.com/ex2010/learn**. When the Excel 2010 Learn It Online page is displayed, click the link for the exercise you want to complete and then read the instructions.

Chapter Reinforcement TF, MC, and SA
A series of true/false, multiple choice, and short answer questions that test your knowledge of the chapter content.

Flash Cards
An interactive learning environment where you identify chapter key terms associated with displayed definitions.

Practice Test
A series of multiple choice questions that test your knowledge of chapter content and key terms.

Who Wants To Be a Computer Genius?
An interactive game that challenges your knowledge of chapter content in the style of a television quiz show.

Wheel of Terms
An interactive game that challenges your knowledge of chapter key terms in the style of the television show *Wheel of Fortune*.

Crossword Puzzle Challenge
A crossword puzzle that challenges your knowledge of key terms presented in the chapter.

Apply Your Knowledge

Reinforce the skills and apply the concepts you learned in this chapter.

Changing the Values in a Worksheet

Instructions: Start Excel. Open the workbook Apply 1–1 Clothes Campus Third Quarter Expenses (Figure 1–76a). See the inside back cover of this book for instructions for downloading the Data Files for Students, or see your instructor for information on accessing the files required in this book.

1. Make the changes to the worksheet described in Table 1–6 so that the worksheet appears as shown in Figure 1–76b. As you edit the values in the cells containing numeric data, watch the totals in row 7, the totals in column F, and the chart change.

2. Change the worksheet title in cell A1 to the Title cell style and then merge and center it across columns A through F. Use buttons in the Font group on the Home tab on the Ribbon to change the worksheet subtitle in cell A2 to 16-point Cambria red, bold font and then center it across columns A through F. Use the Red, Accent 2 theme color (column 6, row 1 on the Font gallery) for the red font color.

3. Apply the worksheet name, Third Quarter Expenses, to the sheet tab and apply the Red, Accent 2 theme color to the sheet tab.

4. Change the document properties as specified by your instructor. Save the workbook using the file name, Apply 1–1 Clothed for Campus Third Quarter Expenses. Submit the revised workbook as specified by your instructor.

Table 1–6 New Worksheet Data	
Cell	**Change Cell Contents To**
A1	Clothed for Campus
B4	7829.50
C4	19057.83
D5	24217.92
E5	25859.62
E6	35140.84

(a) Before

(b) After

Figure 1–76

Extend Your Knowledge

Extend the skills you learned in this chapter and experiment with new skills. You may need to use Help to complete the assignment.

Formatting a Worksheet and Adding Additional Charts

Instructions: Start Excel. Open the workbook Extend 1–1 Pack Right Moving Supplies. See the inside back cover of this book for instructions for downloading the Data Files for Students, or see your instructor for information on accessing the files required in this book. Perform the following tasks to format cells in the worksheet and to add two charts to the worksheet.

1. Use the commands in the Font group on the Home tab on the Ribbon to change the font of the title in cell A1 to 22-point Arial Black, green, bold, and the subtitle of the worksheet to 14-point Arial, red, bold.

2. Select the range A3:G8, click the Insert tab on the Ribbon, and then click the Dialog Box Launcher in the Charts group on the Ribbon to open the Insert Chart dialog box. If necessary, drag the lower-right corner of the Insert Chart dialog box to expand it (Figure 1–77).

Figure 1–77

3. Insert a Stacked Area in 3-D chart by clicking the Stacked Area in 3-D chart in the gallery and then clicking the OK button. You may need to use the scroll box on the right side of the Insert Chart dialog box to view the Area charts in the gallery. Move the chart either below or to the right of the data in the worksheet. Click the Design tab and apply a chart style of your choice to the chart.

4. Deselect the chart and reselect the range A3:G8, and then follow Step 3 above to insert a Clustered Horizontal Cone chart in the worksheet. Move the chart either below or to the right of the data so that each chart does not overlap the Stacked Area in 3-D chart. Make sure to make the values on the horizontal axis readable by expanding the size of the chart. Choose a different chart style for this chart than the one you selected for the Stacked Area in 3-D chart.

5. Resize each chart so that each snaps to the worksheet gridlines. You may need to scroll the worksheet to resize and view the charts. Preview the worksheet.

6. Apply a worksheet name to the sheet tab and apply a color of your choice to the sheet tab.

7. Change the document properties as specified by your instructor. Save the workbook using the file name, Extend 1–1 Pack Right Moving Supplies Charts. Submit the revised workbook as specified by your instructor.

Make It Right

Analyze a workbook and correct all errors and/or improve the design.

Fixing Formatting Problems and Data Errors in a Worksheet

Instructions: Start Excel. Open the workbook Make It Right 1–1 Pets. See the inside back cover of this book for instructions for downloading the Data Files for Students, or see your instructor for information on accessing the files required for this book. Correct the following formatting problems and data errors (Figure 1–78) in the worksheet, while keeping in mind the guidelines presented in this chapter.

Figure 1–78

1. Merge and center the worksheet title and subtitle appropriately.

2. Format the worksheet title with a cell style appropriate for a worksheet title.

3. Format the subtitle using commands in the Font group on the Home tab on the Ribbon and apply the Red, Accent 2 color to the subtitle.

4. Correct the spelling mistake in cell A1 by changing Quixotic to Exotic. Correct the spelling mistake in cell C3 by changing Clevland to Cleveland.

Continued >

Make It Right *continued*

5. Add a column header for totals in column F and create the necessary totals in row 8.

6. Apply proper formatting to the column headers and total row, including centering the column headers.

7. Adjust the column sizes so that all data in each column is visible.

8. Create the grand total for the annual cost of goods.

9. The SUM function in cell E8 does not sum all of the numbers in the column. Correct this error by editing the range for the SUM function in the cell.

10. Resize and move the chart so that it is below the worksheet data and does not extend past the right edge of the worksheet data. Be certain to snap the chart to the worksheet gridlines by holding down the ALT key as you resize the chart to the right edge of column F and the bottom of row 22.

11. Apply a worksheet name to the sheet tab and apply the Aqua, Accent 5 color to the sheet tab.

12. Change the document properties as specified by your instructor. Save the workbook using the file name, Make It Right 1–1 Exotic Pets Annual Cost of Goods. Submit the revised workbook as specified by your instructor.

In the Lab

Design and/or create a workbook using the guidelines, concepts, and skills presented in this chapter. Labs 1, 2, and 3 are listed in order of increasing difficulty.

Lab 1: Annual Revenue Analysis Worksheet

Problem: You work as a spreadsheet specialist for A Healthy Body Shop, a high-end total fitness center franchise. Your manager has asked you to develop an annual revenue analysis worksheet similar to the one shown in Figure 1–79.

Figure 1–79

Instructions: Perform the following tasks.

1. Start Excel. Enter the worksheet title, A Healthy Body Shop, in cell A1 and the worksheet subtitle, Annual Revenue Analysis, in cell A2. Beginning in row 3, enter the franchise locations, fitness activities, and annual revenues shown in Table 1–7.

Table 1–7 A Healthy Body Shop Annual Revenues

	Atlanta	Boston	New York	Phoenix	Portland
Aquatics	72528.50	53461.85	88367.00	87288.00	65367.37
Cardiovascular	65371.00	92549.86	78345.85	91692.21	58936.63
Dance	53187.96	45493.24	72808.19	57019.34	70114.93
Weight Training	45910.25	85703.71	78719.20	88500.60	47105.30
Yoga & Stretching	58292.50	66884.85	74348.30	76219.00	57390.23

2. Create totals for each franchise location, fitness activity, and company grand total.

3. Format the worksheet title with the Title cell style. Center the title across columns A through G. Do not be concerned if the edges of the worksheet title are not displayed.

4. Format the worksheet subtitle to 14-point Constantia dark blue, bold font, and center it across columns A through G.

5. Use Cell Styles to format the range A3:G3 with the Heading 3 cell style, the range A4:G8 with the 40% - Accent 6 cell style, and the range A9:G9 with the Total cell style. Center the column headers in row 3. Apply the Accounting Number format to the range B4:G4 and the range B9:G9. Apply the Comma Style to the range B5:G8. Adjust any column widths to the widest text entry in each column.

6. Select the range A3:F8 and then insert a Clustered Cylinder chart. Apply the Style 26 chart style to the chart. Move and resize the chart so that it appears in the range A11:G24. If the labels along the horizontal axis (x-axis) do not appear as shown in Figure 1–79, then drag the right side of the chart so that it is displayed in the range A11:G24.

7. Apply the worksheet name, Annual Revenue Analysis, to the sheet tab and apply the Orange, Accent 6, Darker 25% color to the sheet tab. Change the document properties, as specified by your instructor.

8. Save the workbook using the file name Lab 1-1 A Healthy Body Shop Annual Revenue Analysis.

9. Preview and print the worksheet in landscape orientation.

10. Make the following two corrections to the sales amounts: 62,675.45 for New York Weight Training (cell D7), 67,238.56 for Portland Cardiovascular (cell F5). After you enter the corrections, the company totals in cell G8 should equal $1,723,864.05.

11. Preview and print the revised worksheet in landscape orientation. Close the workbook without saving the changes.

12. Submit the assignment as specified by your instructor.

In the Lab

Lab 2: Semiannual Sales Analysis Worksheet

Problem: As the chief accountant for Play 'em Again, a reseller of cell phones, DVDs, electronic games, MP3 players, and accessories, you have been asked by the vice president to create a worksheet to analyze the semiannual sales for the company by products across sales channels (Figure 1–80 on the following page). The sales channels and corresponding revenue by product for the year are shown in Table 1–8.

Continued >

STUDENT ASSIGNMENTS

In the Lab continued

Figure 1–80

Instructions: Perform the following tasks.

1. Create the worksheet shown in Figure 1–80 using the data in Table 1–8.

2. Use the SUM function to determine total revenue for the three sales channels, the totals for each product, and the company total. Add column and row headings for the totals row and totals column, as appropriate.

Table 1–8 Play 'em Again Semiannual Revenue

	Mail	Store	Web
Accessories	378512.09	20380.80	24257.51
Cell Phones	124118.00	366216.77	32333.20
CDs	47055.42	311570.23	427261.96
Controllers	409368.32	118871.41	36140.54
DSs	281443.97	472259.61	431317.79
DVDs	311004.73	109971.82	21209.46
Games	413265.32	112511.16	151722.44
iPods	149327.59	358232.57	37465.90
Other	254398.60	126224.85	298479.20
PlayStation 3s	253917.77	173103.58	293961.01
PSPs	469556.54	136579.71	163465.19
Wiis	495690.83	10169.70	130150.03
XBoxes	456773.97	169627.11	145925.85

3. Format the worksheet title with the Title cell style and center it across columns A through E. Use the Font group on the Ribbon to format the worksheet subtitle to 16-point Cambria red, bold font. Center the title across columns A through E.

4. Format the range B3:E3 with the Heading 3 cell style and center the text in the cells. Format the range A4:E16 with the 20% - Accent 4 cell style, and the range B9:E9 with the Total cell style. Format cells B4:E4 and B17:E17 with the Accounting Number Format and cells B5:E16 with the Comma Style numeric format.

5. Create a pie chart that shows the revenue contributions of each sales channel. Chart the sales channel names (B3:D3) and corresponding totals (B17:D17). That is, select the range B3:D3, and then while holding down the CTRL key, select the range B17:D17. Insert the Pie in 3-D chart, as shown in Figure 1–80, by using the Pie button (Insert tab | Charts group). Use the chart location F3: K17.

6. Apply the worksheet name, Semiannual Revenue, to the sheet tab and apply the Purple, Accent 4, Lighter 80% color to the sheet tab. Change the document properties, as specified by your instructor.

7. Save the workbook using the file name, Lab 1-2 Play 'em Again Semiannual Revenue. Print the worksheet in landscape orientation.

8. Two corrections to the figures were sent in from the accounting department. The correct revenue is $118,124.45 for Cell Phones sold through the mail (cell B5) and $43,573.67 for iPods sold over the Web (cell D11). After you enter the two corrections, the company total in cell E17 should equal $8,723,956.77. Print the revised worksheet in landscape orientation.

9. Use the Undo button to change the worksheet back to the original numbers in Table 1–8. Use the Redo button to change the worksheet back to the revised state.

10. Close Excel without saving the latest changes. Start Excel and open the workbook saved in Step 7. Double-click cell E6 and use in-cell editing to change the PSPs revenue (cell C14) to $128,857.32. Write the company total in cell E17 at the top of the first printout. Click the Undo button.

11. Click cell A1 and then click the Merge & Center button on the Home tab on the Ribbon to split cell A1 into cells A1, B1, C1, D1, and E1. To merge the cells into one again, select the range A1:E1 and then click the Merge & Center button.

12. Close the workbook without saving the changes. Submit the assignment as specified by your instructor.

In the Lab

Lab 3: Projected College Cash Flow Analysis Worksheet

Problem: Attending college is an expensive proposition and your resources are limited. To plan for your four-year college career, you have decided to organize your anticipated resources and expenses in a worksheet. The data required to prepare your worksheet is shown in Table 1–9.

Table 1–9 College Cost and Resources

Resources	Freshman	Sophomore	Junior	Senior
529 Plans	2700.00	2889.00	3091.23	3307.62
Financial Aid	5250.00	5617.50	6010.73	6431.48
Job	3100.00	3317.00	3549.19	3797.63
Parents	3700.00	3959.00	4236.13	4532.66
Savings	4250.00	4547.50	4865.83	5206.43
Other	1100.00	1177.00	1259.39	1347.55
Expenses	**Freshman**	**Sophomore**	**Junior**	**Senior**
Activities Fee	500.00	535.00	572.45	612.52
Books	650.00	695.50	744.19	796.28
Clothes	750.00	802.50	858.68	918.78
Entertainment	1650.00	1765.50	1889.09	2021.32
Room & Board	7200.00	7704.00	8243.28	8820.31
Tuition	8250.00	8827.50	9445.43	10106.60
Miscellaneous	1100.00	1177.00	1259.39	1347.55

Continued >

In the Lab *continued*

Instructions Part 1: Using the numbers in Table 1–9, create the worksheet shown in columns A through F in Figure 1–81. Format the worksheet title as Calibri 24-point bold purple. Merge and center the worksheet title in cell A1 across columns A through F. Format the worksheet subtitles in cells A2 and A11 as Calibri 16-point bold red. Format the ranges A3:F3 and A12:F12 with the Heading 2 cell style and center the text in the cells. Format the ranges A4:F9 and A13:F19 with the 20% - Accent 2 cell style, and the ranges A10:F10 and A20:F20 with the Total cell style.

Change the name of the sheet tab and apply the Purple color from the Standard Colors area to the sheet tab. Update the document properties, including the addition of at least one keyword to the properties, and save the workbook using the file name, Lab 1-3 Part 1 College Resources and Expenses. Print the worksheet. Submit the assignment as specified by your instructor.

Figure 1–81

After reviewing the numbers, you realize you need to increase manually each of the Sophomore-year expenses in column C by $400, except for the Activities Fee. Change the Sophomore-year expenses to reflect this change. Manually change the Parents resources for the Sophomore year by the amount required to cover the increase in costs. The totals in cells F10 and F20 should equal $91,642.87. Print the worksheet. Close the workbook without saving changes.

Instructions Part 2: Open the workbook Lab 1-3 Part 1 College Resources and Expenses and then save the workbook using the file name, Lab 1-3 Part 2 College Resources and Expenses. Insert an Exploded pie in 3-D chart in the range G3:K10 to show the contribution of each category of resources for the Freshman year. Chart the range A4:B9 and apply the Style 26 chart style to the chart. Add the Pie chart title as shown in cell G2 in Figure 1–81. Insert an Exploded pie in 3-D chart in the range G12:K20 to show the contribution of each category of expenses for the Freshman year. Chart the range A13:B19 and apply the Style 26 chart style to the chart. Add the Pie chart title shown in cell G11 in Figure 1–81. Save the workbook. Print the worksheet in landscape orientation. Submit the assignment as specified by your instructor.

Instructions Part 3: Open the workbook Lab 1-3 Part 2 College Resources and Expenses and then save the workbook using the file name, Lab 1-3 Part 3 College Resources and Expenses. A close inspection of Table 1–9 shows that both cost and financial support figures increase 7% each year. Use Excel Help to learn how to enter the data for the last three years using a formula and the Copy and Paste buttons (Home tab | Clipboard group). For example, the formula to enter in cell C4 is =B4*1.07. Enter formulas to replace all the numbers in the range C4:E9 and C13:E19. If necessary, reformat the tables, as described in Part 1. The worksheet should appear as shown in Figure 1–81, except that some of the totals will be off by approximately 0.01 due to rounding errors. Save the workbook. Submit the assignment as specified by your instructor. Close the workbook without saving changes.

Cases and Places

Apply your creative thinking and problem solving skills to design and implement a solution.

1: Analyzing Quarterly Expenses

Academic

To estimate the funds needed by your school's Travel Club to make it through the upcoming quarter, you decide to create a report for the club itemizing the expected quarterly expenses. The anticipated expenses are listed in Table 1–10. Use the concepts and techniques presented in this chapter to create the worksheet and an embedded Clustered Cylinder chart. Be sure to use an appropriate chart style that compares the quarterly cost of each expense. Total each expense item and each quarter. Include a grand total for all of the expenses. Use the AutoCalculate area to determine the average amount spent per quarter on each expense. Manually insert the averages with appropriate titles in an appropriate area on the worksheet.

Table 1–10 Travel Club Quarterly Expenses				
	1st Quarter	**2nd Quarter**	**3rd Quarter**	**4th Quarter**
Copies and Supplies	75	50	80	150
Meeting Room Rent	400	425	400	425
Miscellaneous	150	100	175	70
Refreshments	130	155	150	225
Speaker Fees	200	200	400	500
Travel	450	375	500	375

2: Create an Exploded Pie in 3-D Chart to Summarize Property Values

Personal

Your wealthy Aunt Nicole owns several properties of varying value. She would like to see the values of the properties in a worksheet and chart that helps her to better understand her investments. She has asked you to develop a worksheet totaling the values of the properties and also to include other relevant statistics. The property values are: Property 1, $56,671.99; Property 2, $82,276.58; Property 3, $60,135.45; Property 4, $107,373.39; and Property 5, $87,512.82. Create an Exploded pie in 3-D chart to illustrate the relative property values. Use the AutoCalculate area to find the average, maximum, and minimum property values and manually enter them and their corresponding identifiers in an appropriate area of the worksheet. Use the Sum button to total the property values.

Continued >

Cases and Places *continued*

3: Analyzing Historical Yearly Sales

Business

You are working part-time for Noble's Mobile Services. Your manager has asked you to prepare a worksheet to help her analyze historical yearly sales by type of product (Table 1–11). Use the concepts and techniques presented in this chapter to create the worksheet and an embedded 3-D Clustered Column chart that includes proper numerical formatting, totaling, and formatting of the worksheet.

Table 1–11 Noble's Mobile Services Historical Yearly Sales				
	2008	**2009**	**2010**	**2011**
Camera Phones	92598	10487	136791	176785
Headsets	9035	8909	4886	6512
Music Phones	57942	44923	54590	67696
Other Accessories	27604	38793	24483	33095
Satellite Radios	17161	19293	30763	44367
Standard Mobile Phones	8549	9264	7600	6048
Wireless PDAs	57963	68059	103025	87367

2 Formulas, Functions, and Formatting

Objectives

You will have mastered the material in this chapter when you can:

- Enter formulas using the keyboard
- Enter formulas using Point mode
- Apply the AVERAGE, MAX, and MIN functions
- Verify a formula using Range Finder
- Apply a theme to a workbook
- Apply a date format to a cell or range

- Add conditional formatting to cells
- Change column width and row height
- Check the spelling in a worksheet
- Set margins, headers, and footers in Page Layout view
- Preview and print versions of a worksheet

2 | Formulas, Functions, and Formatting

Introduction

In Chapter 1, you learned how to enter data, sum values, format a worksheet to make it easier to read, and draw a chart. This chapter continues to highlight these topics and presents some new ones.

The new topics covered in this chapter include using formulas and functions to create a worksheet. A **function** is a prewritten formula that is built into Excel. Other new topics include option buttons, verifying formulas, applying a theme to a worksheet, adding borders, formatting numbers and text, using conditional formatting, changing the widths of columns and heights of rows, spell checking, using alternative types of worksheet displays and printouts, and adding page headers and footers to a worksheet. One alternative worksheet display and printout shows the formulas in the worksheet instead of the values. When you display the formulas in the worksheet, you see exactly what text, data, formulas, and functions you have entered into it.

Project — Worksheet with Formulas and Functions

The project in this chapter follows proper design guidelines and uses Excel to create the worksheet shown in Figure 2–1. The Mobile Masses Store opened its doors when consumer demand for mobile devices, such as mobile phones and PDAs, had just begun. The store's owners pay each employee on a biweekly basis. Before the owners pay the employees, they summarize the hours worked, pay rate, and tax information for each employee to ensure that the business properly compensates its employees. This summary includes information such as the employee names, hire dates, number of dependents, hours worked, hourly pay rate, net pay, and tax information. As the complexity of the task of creating the summary increases, the owners want to use Excel to create a biweekly payroll report.

The Mobile Masses Store

Biweekly Payroll Report

Employee	Hire Date	Dependents	Hours Worked	Hourly Pay Rate	Gross Pay	Federal Tax	State Tax	Net Pay	Tax %
Charvat, Emily	3/3/09	1	65.25	$ 20.50	$ 1,337.63	$ 288.93	$ 53.51	$ 995.19	25.60%
Chen, Bin	6/14/10	2	80.00	25.85	2,068.00	444.26	82.72	1,541.02	25.48%
Felski, Noah	10/11/08	0	64.50	12.60	812.70	178.79	32.51	601.40	26.00%
Kersey, Jane	3/4/11	1	68.50	21.45	1,469.33	317.90	58.77	1,092.65	25.64%
Merna, Thomas	1/15/10	3	78.25	22.60	1,768.45	373.01	70.74	1,324.70	25.09%
Pollitt, Sherry	11/15/08	2	49.25	18.25	898.81	187.04	35.95	675.82	24.81%
Prasad, Rao	2/15/08	0	33.50	9.35	313.23	68.91	12.53	231.79	26.00%
Washington, Yolanda	5/11/06	2	79.25	23.75	1,882.19	403.38	75.29	1,403.52	25.43%
Zica, James	4/14/11	1	80.00	19.65	1,572.00	340.49	62.88	1,168.63	25.66%
Totals			**598.50**		**$ 12,122.33**	**$ 2,602.71**	**$ 484.89**	**$ 9,034.73**	**25.47%**
Average		1.333333333	66.50	$19.33	$1,346.93	$289.19	$53.88	$1,003.86	
Highest		3	80.00	$25.85	$2,068.00	$444.26	$82.72	$1,541.02	26.00%
Lowest		0	33.50	$9.35	$313.23	$68.91	$12.53	$231.79	24.81%

Figure 2–1

Recall that the first step in creating an effective worksheet is to make sure you understand what is required. The people who will use the worksheet usually provide the requirements. The requirements document for The Mobile Masses Store Biweekly Payroll Report worksheet includes the following needs: source of data, summary of calculations, and other facts about its development (Figure 2–2 on the following page).

REQUEST FOR NEW WORKSHEET

Date Submitted:	April 16, 2012
Submitted By:	Samuel Snyder
Worksheet Title:	The Mobile Masses Store Biweekly Payroll Report
Needs:	An easy-to-read worksheet that summarizes the company's biweekly payroll (Figure 2-3). For each employee, the worksheet is to include the employee's name, hire date, dependents, hours worked, hourly pay rate, gross pay, federal tax, state tax, net pay, and total tax percent. The worksheet also should include totals and the average, highest value, and lowest value for column of numbers specified below.
Source of Data:	The data supplied by Samuel includes the employee names, hire dates, hours worked, and hourly pay rates. This data is shown in Table 2-1 on page EX 72.
Calculations:	The following calculations must be made for each of the employees: 1. Gross Pay = Hours Worked × Hourly Pay Rate 2. Federal Tax = 0.22 × (Gross Pay − Dependents * 24.32) 3. State Tax = 0.04 × Gross Pay 4. Net Pay = Gross Pay − (Federal Tax + State Tax) 5. Tax % = (Federal Tax + State Tax) / Gross Pay 6. Compute the totals for hours worked, gross pay, federal tax, state tax, and net pay. 7. Compute the total tax percent. 8. Use the AVERAGE function to determine the average for dependents, hours worked, hourly pay rate, gross pay, federal tax, state tax, and net pay. 9. Use the MAX and MIN functions to determine the highest and lowest values for dependents, hours worked, hourly pay rate, gross pay, federal tax, state tax, net pay, and total tax percent.

Approvals

Approval Status:	X	Approved
		Rejected
Approved By:	Julie Adams	
Date:	April 23, 2012	
Assigned To:	J. Quasney, Spreadsheet Specialist	

Figure 2–2

Overview

As you read this chapter, you will learn how to create the worksheet shown in Figure 2–1 by performing these general tasks:

- Enter formulas and apply functions in the worksheet
- Add conditional formatting to the worksheet
- Apply a theme to the worksheet
- Set margins, and add headers and footers to a worksheet
- Work with the worksheet in Page Layout view
- Change margins on the worksheet
- Print a section of the worksheet

General Project Decisions

Plan
Ahead

While creating an Excel worksheet, you need to make several decisions that will determine the appearance and characteristics of the finished worksheet. As you create the worksheet necessary to meet the requirements shown in Figure 2–2, you should follow these general guidelines:

1. **Plan the layout of the worksheet.** Rows typically contain items analogous to items in a list. A name could serve as an item in a list, and, therefore, each name could be placed in a row. As a list grows, such as a list of employees, the number of rows in the worksheet will increase. Information about each item in the list and associated calculations should appear in columns.

2. **Determine the necessary formulas and functions needed.** Calculations result from known values. Formulas for such calculations should be known in advance of creating a worksheet. Values such as the average, highest, and lowest values can be calculated using Excel functions as opposed to relying on complex formulas.

3. **Identify how to format various elements of the worksheet.** The appearance of the worksheet affects its ability to express information clearly. Numeric data should be formatted in generally accepted formats, such as using commas as thousands separators and parentheses for negative values.

4. **Establish rules for conditional formatting.** Conditional formatting allows you to format a cell based on the contents of the cell. Decide under which circumstances you would like a cell to stand out from related cells and determine in what way the cell will stand out.

5. **Specify how the hard copy of a worksheet should appear.** When it is possible that a person will want to create a hard copy of a worksheet, care should be taken in the development of the worksheet to ensure that the contents can be presented in a readable manner. Excel prints worksheets in landscape or portrait orientation, and margins can be adjusted to fit more or less data on each page. Headers and footers add an additional level of customization to the printed page.

When necessary, more specific details concerning the above guidelines are presented at appropriate points in the chapter. The chapter also will identify the actions performed and decisions made regarding these guidelines during the creation of the worksheet shown in Figure 2–1 on page EX 67.

In addition, using a sketch of the worksheet can help you visualize its design. The sketch for The Mobile Masses Store Biweekly Payroll Report worksheet includes a title, a subtitle, column and row headings, and the location of data values (Figure 2–3 on the following page). It also uses specific characters to define the desired formatting for the worksheet, as follows:

1. The row of Xs below the leftmost column defines the cell entries as text, such as employee names.

2. The rows of Zs and 9s with slashes, dollar signs, decimal points, commas, and percent signs in the remaining columns define the cell entries as numbers. The Zs indicate that the selected format should instruct Excel to suppress leading 0s. The 9s indicate that the selected format should instruct Excel to display any digits, including 0s.

3. The decimal point means that a decimal point should appear in the cell entry and indicates the number of decimal places to use.

4. The slashes in the second column identify the cell entry as a date.

5. The dollar signs that are not adjacent to the Zs in the first row below the column headings and in the total row signify a fixed dollar sign. The dollar signs that are adjacent to the Zs below the total row signify a floating dollar sign, or one that appears next to the first significant digit.

BTW

Aesthetics versus Function
The function, or purpose, of a worksheet is to provide a user with direct ways to accomplish tasks. In designing a worksheet, functional considerations should come before visual aesthetics. Avoid the temptation to use flashy or confusing visual elements within the worksheet. One exception to this guideline occurs when you may need to draw the user's attention to an area of a worksheet that will help the user more easily complete a task.

Figure 2–3

6. The commas indicate that the selected format should instruct Excel to display a comma separator only if the number has enough digits to the left of the decimal point.

7. The percent sign (%) in the far-right column indicates a percent sign should appear after the number.

With a good comprehension of the requirements document, an understanding of the necessary decisions, and a sketch of the worksheet, the next step is to use Excel to create the worksheet.

To Start Excel

For an introduction to Windows 7 and instruction about how to perform basic Windows 7 tasks, read the Office 2010 and Windows 7 chapter at the beginning of this book, where you can learn how to resize windows, change screen resolution, create folders, move and rename files, use Windows Help, and much more.

If you are using a computer to step through the project in this chapter and you want your screens to match the figures in this book, you should change your screen's resolution to 1024 × 768. For information about how to change a computer's resolution, refer to the Office 2010 and Windows 7 chapter at the beginning of this book.

The following steps, which assume Windows 7 is running, start Excel based on a typical installation. You may need to ask your instructor how to start Excel for your computer. For a detailed example of the procedure summarized below, refer to the Office 2010 and Windows 7 chapter.

1 Click the Start button on the Windows 7 taskbar to display the Start menu.

2 Type **Microsoft Excel** as the search text in the 'Search programs and files' text box, and watch the search results appear on the Start menu.

3 Click Microsoft Excel 2010 in the search results on the Start menu to start Excel and display a new blank workbook in the Excel window.

4 If the Excel window is not maximized, click the Maximize button next to the Close button on its title bar to maximize the window.

Entering the Titles and Numbers into the Worksheet

The first step in creating the worksheet is to enter the titles and numbers into the worksheet. The following sets of steps enter the worksheet title and subtitle and then the biweekly payroll report data shown in Table 2–1.

To Enter the Worksheet Title and Subtitle

The following steps enter the worksheet title and subtitle into cells A1 and A2.

1 If necessary, select cell A1. Type **The Mobile Masses Store** in the selected cell and then press the DOWN ARROW key to enter the worksheet title.

2 Type **Biweekly Payroll Report** in cell A2 and then press the DOWN ARROW key to enter the worksheet subtitle (Figure 2–4 on page 73).

The employee names and the row titles Totals, Average, Highest, and Lowest in the leftmost column begin in cell A4 and continue down to cell A16. The employee data is entered into rows 4 through 12 of the worksheet. The remainder of this section explains the steps required to enter the column titles, payroll data, and row titles, as shown in Figure 2–4, and then save the workbook.

To Enter the Column Titles

The column titles in row 3 begin in cell A3 and extend through cell J3. Some of the column titles in Figure 2–3 include multiple lines of text, such as Hours Worked in cell D3. To start a new line in a cell, press ALT+ENTER after each line, except for the last line, which is completed by clicking the Enter box, pressing the ENTER key, or pressing one of the arrow keys. When you see ALT+ENTER in a step, press the ENTER key while holding down the ALT key and then release both keys. The following steps enter the column titles.

1 With cell A3 selected, type **Employee** and then press the RIGHT ARROW key to enter the column heading.

2 Type **Hire Date** in cell B3 and then press the RIGHT ARROW key to enter the column heading.

3 Type **Dependents** and then press the RIGHT ARROW key to enter the column heading.

4 In cell D3, type **Hours** and then press ALT+ENTER to enter the first line of the column heading. Type **Worked** and then press the RIGHT ARROW key to enter the column heading.

5 Type **Hourly** and then press ALT+ENTER to begin a new line in the cell. Type **Pay Rate** and then press the RIGHT ARROW key to enter the column heading.

6 Type **Gross Pay** in cell F3 and then press the RIGHT ARROW key to enter the column heading.

7 Type **Federal Tax** in cell G3 and then press the RIGHT ARROW key to enter the column heading.

8 Type **State Tax** in cell H3 and then press the RIGHT ARROW key to enter the column heading.

9 Type **Net Pay** in cell I3 and then press the RIGHT ARROW key to enter the column heading.

10 Type **Tax %** in cell J3 to enter the column heading.

To Enter the Biweekly Payroll Data

The biweekly payroll data in Table 2–1 includes a hire date for each employee. Excel considers a date to be a number and, therefore, it displays the date right-aligned in the cell. The following steps enter the data for each employee: name, hire date, dependents, hours worked, and hourly pay rate.

BTW

Q&As
For a complete list of the Q&As found in many of the step-by-step sequences in this book, visit the Excel 2010 Q&A Web page (scsite.com/ex2010/qa).

1 Select cell A4, type **Charvat, Emily**, and then press the RIGHT ARROW key to enter the employee name.

2 Type **3/3/09** in cell B4 and then press the RIGHT ARROW key to enter a date in the selected cell.

3 Type **1** in cell C4 and then press the RIGHT ARROW key to enter a number in the selected cell.

4 Type **65.25** in cell D4 and then press the RIGHT ARROW key to enter a number in the selected cell.

5 Type **20.50** in cell E4 and then click cell A5 to enter a number in the selected cell.

6 Enter the payroll data in Table 2–1 for the eight remaining employees in rows 5 through 12 (Figure 2–4).

Q&A

In step 2, why did the date that was entered change from 3/3/09 to 3/3/2009?

When Excel recognizes that you entered a date in mm/dd/yy format, it automatically formats the date as mm/dd/yyyy for you. Most professionals prefer to view dates in mm/dd/yyyy format as opposed to mm/dd/yy format because the latter can cause confusion regarding the intended year. For example, a date displayed as 3/3/50 could imply a date of 3/3/1950 or 3/3/2050. The use of a four-digit year eliminates this confusion.

BTW

Two-Digit Years
When you enter a two-digit year value (xx) that is less than 30, Excel changes that value to 20xx; when you enter a value that is 30 or greater (zz), Excel changes the value to 19zz. Use four-digit years, if necessary, to ensure that Excel interprets year values the way you intend.

Table 2–1 The Mobile Masses Store Biweekly Payroll Report Data				
Employee	**Hire Date**	**Dependents**	**Hours Worked**	**Hourly Pay Rate**
Charvat, Emily	3/3/09	1	65.25	20.50
Chen, Bin	6/14/10	2	80.00	25.85
Felski, Noah	10/11/08	0	64.50	12.60
Kersey, Jane	3/4/11	1	68.50	21.45
Merna, Thomas	1/15/10	3	78.25	22.60
Pollitt, Sherry	11/15/08	2	49.25	18.25
Prasad, Rao	2/15/08	0	33.50	9.35
Washington, Yolanda	5/11/06	2	79.25	23.75
Zica, James	4/14/11	1	80.00	19.65

BTW

Wrapping Text
If you have a long text entry, such as a paragraph, you can instruct Excel to wrap the text in a cell. This method is easier than your pressing ALT+ENTER to end each line of text within the paragraph. To wrap text, right-click in the cell, click Format Cells on a shortcut menu, click the Alignment tab, and then click Wrap text. Excel will increase the height of the cell automatically so that the additional lines will fit. If you want to control where each line ends in the cell, rather than letting Excel wrap the text based on the cell width, you must end each line with ALT+ENTER.

To Enter the Row Titles

The following steps add row titles for the rows that will contain the totals, average, highest, and lowest amounts.

1 Select cell A13. Type **Totals** and then press the DOWN ARROW key to enter a row header.

2 Type **Average** in cell A14 and then press the DOWN ARROW key to enter a row header.

3 Type **Highest** in cell A15 and then press the DOWN ARROW key to enter a row header.

4 Type **Lowest** in cell A16 and then press the ENTER key to enter a row header. Select cell F4 to prepare to enter a formula in the cell (Figure 2–4).

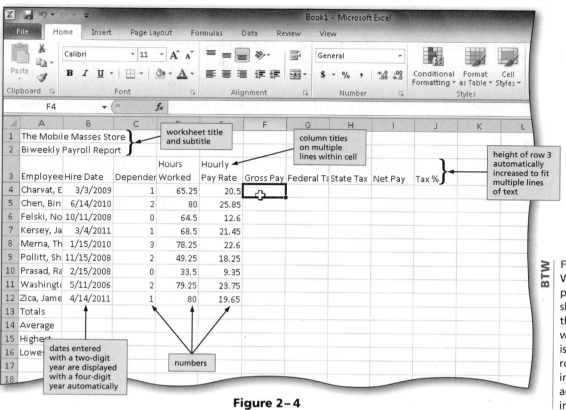

Figure 2–4

BTW

Formatting Worksheets
With early worksheet programs, users often skipped rows to improve the appearance of the worksheet. With Excel it is not necessary to skip rows because you can increase row heights to add white space between information.

To Change Document Properties

As discussed in Chapter 1, the first time you save a workbook, you should change the document properties. The following steps change the document properties.

1 Click File on the Ribbon to open the Backstage view. If necessary, click the Info tab in the Backstage view to display the Info gallery.

2 Click the Properties button in the right pane of the Info gallery to display the Properties menu.

3 Click Show Document Panel on the Properties menu to close the Backstage view and display the Document Information Panel in the Excel workbook window.

4 Click the Author text box, if necessary, and then type your name as the Author property. If a name already is displayed in the Author text box, delete it before typing your name.

5 Click the Subject text box, if necessary delete any existing text, and then type your course and section as the Subject property.

6 If an AutoComplete dialog box appears, click its Yes button.

7 Click the Keywords text box, if necessary delete any existing text, and then type `Biweekly Payroll Report` as the Keywords property.

8 If an AutoComplete dialog box appears, click its Yes button.

9 Click the Close the Document Information Panel button so that the Document Information Panel no longer is displayed.

To Change the Sheet Name and Save the Workbook

The following steps change the sheet name to Biweekly Payroll Report, change the sheet tab color, and save the workbook on a USB flash drive in the Excel folder (for your assignments) using the file name, The Mobile Masses Biweekly Payroll Report.

1 Double-click the Sheet1 tab and then enter `Biweekly Payroll Report` as the sheet name and then press the ENTER key.

2 Right-click the tab to display the shortcut menu and then click Tab Color on the shortcut menu to display the Color gallery. Click Blue, Accent 1, Darker 25% (column 5, row 5) in the Theme Colors area to apply a new color to the sheet tab.

3 With a USB flash drive connected to one of the computer's USB ports, click the Save button on the Quick Access Toolbar to display the Save As dialog box.

4 Type `The Mobile Masses Biweekly Payroll Report` in the File name text box to change the file name. Do not press the ENTER key after typing the file name because you do not want to close the dialog box at this time.

5 Navigate to the desired save location (in this case, the Excel folder in the CIS 101 folder [or your class folder] on the USB flash drive).

6 Click the Save button (Save As dialog box) to save the document in the selected folder on the selected drive with the entered file name.

BTW

Entering Numbers in a Range
An efficient way to enter data into a range of cells is to select a range and then enter the first number in the upper-left cell of the range. Excel responds by accepting the value and moving the active cell selection down one cell. When you enter the last value in the first column, Excel moves the active cell selection to the top of the next column.

Entering Formulas

One of the reasons Excel is such a valuable tool is that you can assign a **formula** to a cell, and Excel will calculate the result. Consider, for example, what would happen if you had to multiply 65.25 by 20.5 and then manually enter the product for Gross Pay, 1,337.625, in cell F4. Every time the values in cells D4 or E4 changed, you would have to recalculate the product and enter the new value in cell F4. By contrast, if you enter a formula in cell F4 to multiply the values in cells D4 and E4, Excel recalculates the product whenever new values are entered into those cells and displays the result in cell F4.

Plan Ahead

> **Determine the formulas and functions needed.**
> As you have learned, formulas and functions simplify the creation and maintenance of worksheets because Excel performs calculations for you. When formulas and functions are used together properly, the amount of data that a user manually must enter in a worksheet greatly can be diminished:
>
> - **Utilize proper algebraic notation.** Most Excel formulas are the result of algebraic calculations. A solid understanding of algebraic operators and the order of operations is important to writing sound formulas.
>
> - **Utilize the fill handle and copy and paste operations to copy formulas.** The fill handle and the Excel copy and paste functionality help to minimize errors caused by retyping formulas. When possible, if a similar formula will be used repeatedly in a worksheet, avoid retyping the formula and instead use the fill handle.
>
> - **Be careful about using invalid and circular cell references.** An invalid reference occurs when Excel does not understand a cell reference used in a formula, resulting in Excel displaying a #REF! error message in the cell.
>
> *(Continued)*

(Continued)

A formula in a cell that contains a reference back to itself is called a **circular reference**. Excel often warns you when you create a circular reference. In almost all cases, circular references are the result of an incorrect formula. A circular reference can be direct or indirect. For example, placing the formula =A1 in cell A1 results in a direct circular reference. An indirect circular reference occurs when a formula in a cell refers to another cell or cells that include a formula that refers back to the original cell.

- **Employ the Excel built-in functions whenever possible.** Excel includes prewritten formulas called **functions** to help you compute a range of values and statistics. A function takes a value or values, performs an operation, and returns a result to the cell. The values that you use with a function are called **arguments**. All functions begin with an equal sign and include the arguments in parentheses after the function name. For example, in the function =AVERAGE(C4:C12), the function name is AVERAGE, and the argument is the range C4:C12. Become familiar with the extensive number of built-in functions. When you have the choice, always use built-in functions instead of writing and typing a formula version of your mathematical expression. Such a practice reduces the possibility of errors and simplifies the formula used in a cell, resulting in improved readability.

Plan Ahead

BTW

Automatic Recalculation
Every time you enter a value into a cell in the worksheet, Excel automatically recalculates all formulas. You can change to manual recalculation by clicking the Calculation Options button (Formulas tab | Calculation group) and then clicking Manual. In manual calculation mode, pressing the F9 key instructs Excel to recalculate all formulas.

To Enter a Formula Using the Keyboard

The formulas needed in the worksheet are noted in the requirements document as follows:

1. Gross Pay (column F) = Hours Worked × Hourly Pay Rate
2. Federal Tax (column G) = 0.22 × (Gross Pay − Dependents × 24.32)
3. State Tax (column H) = 0.04 × Gross Pay
4. Net Pay (column I) = Gross Pay − (Federal Tax + State Tax)
5. Tax% (column J) = (Federal Tax + State Tax) / Gross Pay

The gross pay for each employee, which appears in column F, is equal to hours worked in column D times hourly pay rate in column E. Thus, the gross pay for Emily Charvat in cell F4 is obtained by multiplying 65.25 (cell D4) by 20.50 (cell E4) or =D4*E4. The following steps enter the initial gross pay formula in cell F4 using the keyboard.

1

- With cell F4 selected, type **=d4*e4** in the cell to display the formula in the formula bar and in the current cell and to display colored borders around the cells referenced in the formula (Figure 2–5).

Q&A

What occurs on the worksheet as I enter the formula?

The **equal sign** (=) preceding d4*e4 alerts Excel that you are entering a formula or function and not text. Because the most common error when entering a formula is to reference the wrong cell in a formula mistakenly, Excel colors the borders of the cells referenced in the formula. The coloring helps in the reviewing process to ensure the cell references are correct.

The **asterisk** (*) following d4 is the arithmetic operator that directs Excel to perform the multiplication operation.

Figure 2–5

2

- Press the RIGHT ARROW key to complete the arithmetic operation indicated by the formula, to display the result in the worksheet, and to select the cell to the right (Figure 2–6). The number of decimal places shown in cell F4 may be different, but these values will be adjusted later in this chapter.

Figure 2–6

Arithmetic Operations

Table 2–2 describes multiplication and other valid Excel arithmetic operators.

Table 2–2 Summary of Arithmetic Operators			
Arithmetic Operator	Meaning	Example of Usage	Meaning
–	Negation	–78	Negative 78
%	Percentage	=23%	Multiplies 23 by 0.01
^	Exponentiation	=3 ^ 4	Raises 3 to the fourth power
*	Multiplication	=61.5 * C5	Multiplies the contents of cell C5 by 61.5
/	Division	=H3 / H11	Divides the contents of cell H3 by the contents of cell H11
+	Addition	=11 + 9	Adds 11 and 9
–	Subtraction	=22 – F15	Subtracts the contents of cell F15 from 22

Order of Operations

When more than one arithmetic operator is involved in a formula, Excel follows the same basic order of operations that you use in algebra. Moving from left to right in a formula, the **order of operations** is as follows: first negation (−), then all percentages (%), then all exponentiations (^), then all multiplications (*) and divisions (/), and finally, all additions (+) and subtractions (−).

As in algebra, you can use parentheses to override the order of operations. For example, if Excel follows the order of operations, 8 * 3 + 2 equals 26. If you use parentheses, however, to change the formula to 8 * (3 + 2), the result is 40, because the parentheses instruct Excel to add 3 and 2 before multiplying by 8. Table 2–3 illustrates several examples of valid Excel formulas and explains the order of operations.

BTW

Troubling Formulas
If Excel does not accept a formula, remove the equal sign from the left side and complete the entry as text. Later, after you have entered additional data in the cells reliant on the formula or determined the error, reinsert the equal sign to change the text back to a formula and edit the formula as needed.

Table 2–3 Examples of Excel Formulas

Formula	Meaning
=G15	Assigns the value in cell G15 to the active cell.
=2^4 + 7	Assigns the sum of 16 + 7 (or 23) to the active cell.
=100 + D2 or =D2 +100 or =(100 + D2)	Assigns 100 plus the contents of cell D2 to the active cell.
=25% * 40	Assigns the product of 0.25 times 40 (or 10) to the active cell.
− (K15 * X45)	Assigns the negative value of the product of the values contained in cells K15 and X45 to the active cell. You do not need to type an equal sign before an expression that begins with minus signs, which indicates a negation.
=(U8 − B8) * 6	Assigns the product of the difference between the values contained in cells U8 and B8 times 6 to the active cell.
=J7 / A5 + G9 * M6 − Z2 ^ L7	Completes the following operations, from left to right: exponentiation (Z2 ^ L7), then division (J7 / A5), then multiplication (G9 * M6), then addition (J7 / A5) + (G9 * M6), and finally subtraction (J7 / A5 + G9 * M6) − (Z2 ^ L7). If cells A5 = 6, G9 = 2, J7 = 6, L7 = 4, M6 = 5, and Z2 = 2, then Excel assigns the active cell the value −5; that is, 6 / 6 + 2 * 5 − 2 ^ 4 = −5.

To Enter Formulas Using Point Mode

The sketch of the worksheet in Figure 2–3 on page EX 70 calls for the federal tax, state tax, net pay, and tax % for each employee to appear in columns G, H, I, and J, respectively. All four of these values are calculated using formulas in row 4:

Federal Tax (cell G4) = 0.22 × (Gross Pay − Dependents × 24.32) or =0.22*(F4–C4*24.32)
State Tax (cell H4) = 0.04 × Gross Pay or = 0.04* F4
Net Pay (cell I4) = Gross Pay − (Federal Tax + State Tax) or =F4-(G4+H4)
Tax % (cell J4) = (Federal Tax + State Tax) / Gross Pay or =(G4+H4)/F4

An alternative to entering the formulas in cells G4, H4, I4, and J4 using the keyboard is to enter the formulas using the mouse and Point mode. **Point mode** allows you to select cells for use in a formula by using the mouse. The steps on the following pages enter formulas using Point mode.

1

- With cell G4 selected type =0.22*(to begin the formula and then click cell F4 to add a cell reference in the formula (Figure 2–7).

Note: To help you locate screen elements that are referenced in the step instructions, such as buttons and commands, this book uses red boxes to point to these screen elements.

=0.22*(F4

	A	B	C	D	E	F	G	H
1	The Mobile Masses Store							
2	Biweekly Payroll Report							
3	Employee	Hire Date	Depender	Hours Worked	Hourly Pay Rate	Gross Pay	Federal Ta	State Tax	Net Pay	Tax %
4	Charvat, E	3/3/2009	1	65.25	20.5	337.625	=0.22*(F4	
5	Chen, Bin	6/14/2010	2	80	25.85			
6	Felski, No	10/11/2008	0	64.5	12.6			
7	Kersey, Ja	3/4/2011	1	68.5				
8	Merna, Th	1/15/2010	3	78.25				
9	Pollitt, Sh	11/15/2008	2	49.25	18.25			
10	Prasad, Ra	2/15/2008	0	33.5	9.35			
11	Washingto	5/11/2006	2	79.25	23.75			
12	Zica, Jame	4/14/2011	1	80	19.65			
13	Totals							
14	Average							
15	Highest							
16	Lowest							
17								

cell reference F4 appended to formula

marquee surrounds selected cell F4

Figure 2–7

2

- Type – (minus sign) and then click cell C4 to add a subtraction operator and a reference to another cell to the formula.

- Type *24.32) to complete the formula (Figure 2–8).

formula appears in formula bar

=0.22*(F4-C4*24.32)

	A	B	C	D	E	F	G	H	I	J	K	L
1	The Mobile Masses Store											
2	Biweekly Payroll Report											
3	Employee	Hire Date	Depender	Hours Worked	Hourly Pay Rate	Gross Pay	Federal Ta	State Tax	Net Pay	Tax %		
4	Charvat, E	3/3/2009	1	65.25	20.5	1337.625	=0.22*(F4-C4*24.32)					
5	Chen, Bin	6/14/2010	2	80	25.85							
6	Felski, No	10/11/2008	0	64.5	12.6							
7	Kersey, Ja	3/4/2011	1	68.5	21.45							
8	Merna, Th	1/15/2010	3	78.25	22.6							
9	Pollitt, Sh	11/15/2008	2	49.2								
10	Prasad, Ra	2/15/2008	0	33.								
11	Washingto	5/11/2006	2	79.2								
12	Zica, Jame	4/14/2011	1	80	19.65							
13	Totals											
14	Average											
15	Highest											
16	Lowest											
17												
18												
19												

cell reference C4 added to formula

border of cell and its cell reference in formulas are colored green

Figure 2–8

3

- Click the Enter box in the formula bar and then select cell H4 to prepare to enter the next formula.

- Type **=0.04*** and then click cell F4 to add a cell reference to the formula (Figure 2–9).

Figure 2–9

Q&A

Why should I use Point mode to enter formulas?

Using Point mode to enter formulas often is faster and more accurate than using the keyboard to type the entire formula when the cell you want to select does not require you to scroll. In many instances, as in these steps, you may want to use both the keyboard and mouse when entering a formula in a cell. You can use the keyboard to begin the formula, for example, and then use the mouse to select a range of cells.

4

- Click the Enter box in the formula bar and then select cell I4 to prepare to enter the next formula.

- Type **=** (equal sign) and then click cell F4 to begin the formula and add a cell reference to the formula.

- Type **−(** (minus sign followed by an open parenthesis) and then click cell G4 to add a subtraction operator, open parenthesis, and cell reference to the formula.

Figure 2–10

- Type **+** (plus sign) and then click cell H4 to add an addition operator and cell reference to the formula.

- Type **)** (close parenthesis) to complete the formula (Figure 2–10).

5

- Click the Enter box in the formula bar to enter the formula in cell I4.

- Select cell J4. Type = ((equal sign followed by an open parenthesis) and then click cell G4 to add a reference to the formula.

- Type + (plus sign) and then click cell H4 to add a cell reference to the formula.

- Type) / (close parenthesis followed by a forward slash), and then click cell F4 to add a cell reference to the formula.

- Click the Enter box in the formula bar to enter the formula in cell J4 (Figure 2–11).

Figure 2–11

Q&A

Why do three decimal places show in cell J4?

The actual value assigned by Excel to cell J4 from the division operation in step 5 is 0.256000075. While not all the decimal places appear in Figure 2–11, Excel maintains all of them for computational purposes. Thus, if referencing cell J4 in a formula, the value used for computational purposes is 0.256000075, not 0.256. The cell formatting is set to display six digits after the decimal point, but the formatting also suppresses trailing zeroes. If the cell formatting were set to display six digits and show trailing zeroes, then Excel would display 0.256000 in cell J4. If you change the cell formatting of column J to display nine digits after the decimal point, then Excel displays the true value 0.256000075.

To Copy Formulas Using the Fill Handle

The five formulas for Emily Charvat in cells F4, G4, H4, I4, and J4 now are complete. You could enter the same five formulas one at a time for the eight remaining employees. A much easier method of entering the formulas, however, is to select the formulas in row 4 and then use the fill handle to copy them through row 12. When performing copying operations in Excel, the source area is the cell, or range, from which data or formulas are being copied. When a range is used as a source, sometimes it is called the source range. The destination area is the cell, or range, to which data or formulas are being copied. When a range is used as a destination, sometimes it is called the destination range. Recall from Chapter 1 that the fill handle is a small rectangle in the lower-right corner of the active cell or active range. The following steps copy the formulas using the fill handle.

1

- Select the source range, F4:J4 in this case, and then point to the fill handle.

- Drag the fill handle down through cell J12 and continue to hold the mouse button to select the destination range (Figure 2–12).

initial location of fill handle

range F4:J4 selected as source area

fill handle dragged through cell J12

Figure 2–12

2

- Release the mouse button to copy the formulas to the destination range (Figure 2–13).

Q&A

How does Excel adjust the cell references in the formulas in the destination area?

Recall that when you copy a formula, Excel adjusts the cell references so that the new formulas

gross pay, federal tax, state tax, net pay, and tax % formulas in range F4:J4 copied to range F5:J12

Auto Fill Options button appears after copying the range F4:J4 to range F5:J12

Figure 2–13

contain references corresponding to the new location and perform calculations using the appropriate values. Thus, if you copy downward, Excel adjusts the row portion of cell references. If you copy across, then Excel adjusts the column portion of cell references. These cell references are called **relative cell references**.

Other Ways
1. Select source area, click Copy button (Home tab | Clipboard group), select destination area, click Paste button (Home tab | Clipboard group)   2. Right-click source area, click Copy on shortcut menu, right-click destination area, click Paste icon on shortcut menu   3. Select source area and then point to border of range; while holding down CTRL, drag source area to destination area

Option Buttons

Excel displays Option buttons in a workbook while you are working on it to indicate that you can complete an operation using automatic features such as AutoCorrect, Auto Fill, error checking, and others. For example, the Auto Fill Options button shown in Figure 2–13 appears after a fill operation, such as dragging the fill handle. When an error occurs in a formula in a cell, Excel displays the Trace Error button next to the cell and identifies the cell with the error by placing a green triangle in the upper left of the cell.

Table 2–4 summarizes the Option buttons available in Excel. When one of these buttons appears on your worksheet, click the button arrow to produce the list of options for modifying the operation or to obtain additional information.

Table 2–4 Options Buttons in Excel		
Button	**Name**	**Menu Function**
	Auto Fill Options	Gives options for how to fill cells following a fill operation, such as dragging the fill handle.
	AutoCorrect Options	Undoes an automatic correction, stops future automatic corrections of this type, or causes Excel to display the AutoCorrect Options dialog box.
	Insert Options	Lists formatting options following an insertion of cells, rows, or columns.
(Ctrl) ▾	Paste Options	Specifies how moved or pasted items should appear (for example, with original formatting, without formatting, or with different formatting).
	Trace Error	Lists error-checking options following the assignment of an invalid formula to a cell.

To Determine Totals Using the Sum Button

The next step is to determine the totals in row 13 for the hours worked in column D, gross pay in column F, federal tax in column G, state tax in column H, and net pay in column I. To determine the total hours worked in column D, the values in the range D4 through D12 must be summed. To do so, enter the function =sum(d4:d12) in cell D13 or select cell D13, click the Sum button (Home tab | Editing group), and then press the ENTER key. Recall that a function is a prewritten formula that is built into Excel. Similar SUM functions can be used in cells F13, G13, H13, and I13 to total gross pay, federal tax, state tax, and net pay, respectively. The following steps determine totals in cell D13 and the range F13:I13.

1 Select cell to contain the sum, cell D13 in this case. Click the Sum button (Home tab | Editing group) to sum the contents of the range D4:D12 in cell D13 and then click the Enter box to display a total in the selected cell.

2 Select the range to contain the sums, range F13:I13 in this case. Click the Sum button (Home tab | Editing group) to display totals in the selected range (Figure 2–14).

Figure 2–14

To Determine the Total Tax %

With the totals in row 13 determined, the next step is to copy the tax % formula in cell J12 to cell J13 as performed in the following steps.

1 Select the cell to be copied, J12 in this case, and then point to the fill handle.

2 Drag the fill handle down through cell J13 to copy the formula (Figure 2–15).

Q&A Why was the formula I13/F13 not copied to cell J13 earlier?

The formula, I13/F13, was not copied to cell J13 when cell J4 was copied to the range J5:J12 because both cells involved in the computation (I13 and F13) were blank, or zero, at the time. A **blank cell** in Excel has a numerical value of zero, which would have resulted in an error message in cell J13. Once the totals were determined, both cells I13 and F13 (especially F13, because it is the divisor) had nonzero numerical values.

Figure 2–15

Using the AVERAGE, MAX, and MIN Functions

The next step in creating The Mobile Masses Biweekly Payroll Report worksheet is to compute the average, highest value, and lowest value for the number of dependents listed in the range C4:C12 using the AVERAGE, MAX, and MIN functions in the range C14:C16. Once the values are determined for column C, the entries can be copied across to the other columns.

With Excel, you can enter functions using one of five methods: (1) the keyboard or mouse, (2) the Insert Function box in the formula bar, (3) the Sum menu, (4) the Sum command (Formulas tab | Function Library group), and (5) the Name box area in the formula bar (Figure 2–16). The method you choose will depend on your typing skills and whether you can recall the function name and required arguments.

In the following pages, each of the first three methods will be used. The keyboard and mouse method will be used to determine the average number of dependents (cell C14). The Insert Function button in the formula bar method will be used to determine the highest number of dependents (cell C15). The Sum menu method will be used to determine the lowest number of dependents (cell C16).

Statistical Functions
Excel usually considers a blank cell to be equal to 0. The statistical functions, however, ignore blank cells. Excel thus calculates the average of three cells with values of 10, blank, and 8 to be 9 [(10 + 8) / 2] and not 6 [(10 + 0 + 8) / 3].

To Determine the Average of a Range of Numbers Using the Keyboard and Mouse

The **AVERAGE function** sums the numbers in the specified range and then divides the sum by the number of cells with numeric values in the range. The following steps use the AVERAGE function to determine the average of the numbers in the range C4:C12.

1

- Select the cell to contain the average, cell C14 in this case.

- Type **=av** in the cell to display the Formula AutoComplete list. Press the DOWN ARROW key to highlight the required formula (Figure 2–16).

What is happening as I type?

As you type the equal sign followed by the characters in the name of a function, Excel displays the Formula AutoComplete list. This list contains those functions that alphabetically match the letters you have typed. Because you typed =av, Excel displays all the functions that begin with the letters av.

Figure 2–16

2

- Double-click AVERAGE in the Formula AutoComplete list to select the function.

- Select the range to be averaged, C4:C12 in this case, to insert the range as the argument to the function (Figure 2–17).

Q&A
As I drag, why does the function in cell C14 change?

When you click cell C4, Excel appends cell C4 to the left parenthesis in the formula bar and surrounds cell C4 with a marquee. When you begin dragging, Excel appends to the argument a colon (:) and the cell reference of the cell where the mouse pointer is located.

Figure 2–17

3

- Click the Enter box to compute the average of the numbers in the selected range and display the result in the selected cell (Figure 2–18).

Q&A
Can I use the arrow keys to complete the entry instead?

No. When you use Point mode you cannot use the arrow keys to complete the entry. While in Point mode, the arrow keys change the selected cell reference in the range you are selecting.

Q&A
What is the purpose of the parentheses in the function?

The AVERAGE function requires that the argument (in this case, the range C4:C12) be included within parentheses following the function name. Excel automatically appends the right parenthesis to complete the AVERAGE function when you click the Enter box or press the ENTER key.

Figure 2–18

Other Ways

1. Click Insert Function box in the formula bar, click AVERAGE

2. Click Sum button arrow (Home tab | Editing group), click Average

3. Click Sum button arrow (Formulas tab | Function Library group), click Average

To Determine the Highest Number in a Range of Numbers Using the Insert Function Box

The next step is to select cell C15 and determine the highest (maximum) number in the range C4:C12. Excel includes a function called the **MAX function** that displays the highest value in a range. Although you could enter the MAX function using the keyboard and Point mode as described in the previous steps, an alternative method to entering the function is to use the Insert Function box in the formula bar. The following steps use the Insert Function box in the formula bar to enter the MAX function.

1

- Select the cell to contain the maximum number, cell C15 in this case.

- Click the Insert Function box in the formula bar to display the Insert Function dialog box.

- Click MAX in the 'Select a function' list (Insert Function dialog box) to select it (Figure 2–19). If the MAX function is not displayed in the 'Select a function' list, scroll the list until the function is displayed.

Figure 2–19

2

- Click the OK button (Insert Function dialog box) to display the Function Arguments dialog box.

- Type c4:c12 in the Number1 box (Function Arguments dialog box) to enter the first argument of the function (Figure 2–20).

Q&A

Why did numbers appear in the Function Arguments dialog box?

As shown in Figure 2–20, Excel displays the value the MAX function will return to cell C15 in the Function Arguments dialog box. It also lists the first few numbers in the selected range, next to the Number1 box.

Figure 2–20

3

- Click the OK button (Function Arguments dialog box) to display the highest value in the chosen range in the selected cell (Figure 2–21).

Q&A

Why should I not just enter the highest value that I see in the range C4:C12 in cell C15?

In this example, rather than entering the MAX function, you visually could scan the range C4:C12,

Figure 2–21

determine that the highest number of dependents is 3, and manually enter the number 3 as a constant in cell C15. Excel would display the number the same as in Figure 2–21. Because it contains a constant, however, Excel will continue to display 3 in cell C15, even if the values in the range C4:C12 change. If you use the MAX function, Excel will recalculate the highest value in the range C4:C12 each time a new value is entered into the worksheet.

Other Ways

1. Click Sum button arrow (Home tab | Editing group), click Max

2. Click Sum button arrow (Formulas tab | Function Library group), click Max

3. Type **=MAX** in cell

To Determine the Lowest Number in a Range of Numbers Using the Sum Menu

The next step is to enter the **MIN function** in cell C16 to determine the lowest (minimum) number in the range C4:C12. Although you can enter the MIN function using either of the methods used to enter the AVERAGE and MAX functions, the following steps perform an alternative using the Sum button (Home tab | Editing group).

1

- Select cell C16 to prepare to enter the next function.

- Click the Sum button arrow (Home tab | Editing group) to display the Sum button menu (Figure 2–22).

Q&A

Why should I use the Sum button menu?

Using the Sum button menu allows you to enter one of five often-used functions easily into a cell, without having to memorize its name or the required arguments.

Figure 2–22

2

- Click Min to display the MIN function in the formula bar and in the active cell (Figure 2–23).

Q&A

Why does Excel select the range C14:C15?

The range C14:C15 automatically selected by Excel is not correct. Excel attempts to guess which cells you want to include in the function by looking for ranges that are adjacent to the selected cell and that contain numeric data.

Figure 2–23

3

- Click cell C4 and then drag through cell C12 to display the function with the new range in the formula bar and in the selected cell (Figure 2–24).

Figure 2–24

4

- Click the Enter box to determine the lowest value in the range C4:C12 and display the result in the formula bar and in the selected cell (Figure 2–25).

Q&A

How can I learn about other functions?

Excel has more than 400 additional functions that perform just about every type of calculation you can imagine. These functions are categorized in the Insert Function dialog box shown in Figure 2–19 on page EX 86. To view the categories, click the 'Or select a category' box arrow. To obtain a description of a selected function, select its name in the Insert Function dialog box. Excel displays the description of the function below the Select a function list in the dialog box.

MIN function determines lowest value in range C4:C12

result of MIN function appears in cell

	A	B	C	D	E	F	G	H	I	J
1	The Mobile Masses Store									
2	Biweekly Payroll Report									
3	Employee	Hire Date	Depender	Hours Worked	Hourly Pay Rate	Gross Pay	Federal Ta	State Tax	Net Pay	Tax %
4	Charvat, E	3/3/2009	1	65.25	20.5	1337.625	288.9271	53.505	995.1929	0.256
5	Chen, Bin	6/14/2010	2	80	25.85	2068	444.2592	82.72	1541.021	0.254826
6	Felski, No	10/11/2008	0	64.5	12.6	812.7	178.794	32.508	601.398	0.26
7	Kersey, Ja	3/4/2011	1	68.5	21.45	1469.325	317.9011	58.773	1092.651	0.256359
8	Merna, Th	1/15/2010	3	78.25	22.6	1768.45	373.0078	70.738	1324.704	0.250924
9	Pollitt, Sh	11/15/2008	2	49.25	18.25	898.8125	187.038	35.9525	675.8221	0.248095
10	Prasad, Ra	2/15/2008	0	33.5	9.35	313.225	68.9095	12.529	231.7865	0.26
11	Washingtc	5/11/2006	2	79.25	23.75	1882.188	403.3805	75.2875	1403.52	0.254315
12	Zica, Jame	4/14/2011	1	80	19.65	1572	340.4896	62.08	1168.63	0.256596
13	Totals			598.5		12122.33	2602.707	484.893	9034.725	0.254704
14	Average		1.333333							
15	Highest		3							
16	Lowest		0							
17										
18										

Figure 2–25

Other Ways

1. Click Insert Function box in the formula bar (if necessary, select Statistical category), click MIN

2. Click Sum button arrow (Formulas tab | Function Library group), click Min

3. Type =MIN in cell

To Copy a Range of Cells Across Columns to an Adjacent Range Using the Fill Handle

The next step is to copy the AVERAGE, MAX, and MIN functions in the range C14:C16 to the adjacent range D14:J16. The following steps use the fill handle to copy the functions.

1

- Select the source range from which to copy the functions, in this case C14:C16.

- Drag the fill handle in the lower-right corner of the selected range through cell J16 and continue to hold down the mouse button to begin a fill operation (Figure 2–26).

copy range C14:C16 selected

fill handle dragged to select destination area, range D14:J16

mouse pointer

	A	B	C	D	E	F	G	H	I	J
10	Prasad, Ra	2/15/2008				3.225	68.9095	12.5		
11	Washingtc	5/11/2006	2	79.25		32.188	403.3805	75.2875	1403.52	0.254315
12	Zica, Jame	4/14/2011	1	80		1572	340.4896	62.88	1168.63	0.256596
13	Totals			598.5		12122.33	2602.707	484.893	9034.725	0.254704
14	Average		1.333333							
15	Highest		3							
16	Lowest		0							
17										
18										
19										
20										
21										
22										
23										
24										

Biweekly Payroll Report

Figure 2–26

2

- Release the mouse button to copy the three functions to the selected range (Figure 2–27).

AVERAGE, MAX, and MIN functions in range C14:C16 copied to range D14:J16

9	Pollitt, Sh	11/15/2008								
10	Prasad, Ra	2/15/2008	0	33.5				.529	231.7865	0.26
11	Washingto	5/11/2006	2	79.25	23.75	1882.188	403.3805	75.2875	1403.52	0.254315
12	Zica, Jame	4/14/2011	1	80	19.65	1572	340.4896	62.88	1168.63	0.256596
13	Totals			598.5		12122.33	2602.707	484.893	9034.725	0.254704
14	Average		1.333333	66.5	19.33333	1346.925	289.1896	53.877	1003.858	0.255235
15	Highest		3	80	25.85	2068	444.2592	82.72	1541.021	0.26
16	Lowest		0	33.5	9.35	313.225	68.9095	12.529	231.7865	0.248095
17										
18										
19										
20										
21										
22										

Auto Fill Options button

Figure 2–27

Q&A

How can I be sure that the function arguments are proper for the cells in range D14:J16?

Remember that Excel adjusts the cell references in the copied functions so that each function refers to the range of numbers above it in the same column. Review the numbers in rows 14 through 16 in Figure 2–27. You should see that the functions in each column return the appropriate values, based on the numbers in rows 4 through 12 of that column.

3

- Select cell J14 and then press the DELETE key to delete the average of the tax % (Figure 2–28).

Q&A

Why is the formula in cell J14 deleted?

The average of the tax % in cell J14 is deleted because an average of percentages of this type is mathematically invalid.

Save button

The Mobile Masses Biweekly Payroll Report - Microsoft Excel

	A	B	C	D	E	F	G	H	I	J	K	L	M
1	The Mobile Masses Store												
2	Biweekly Payroll Report												
3	Employee	Hire Date	Dependen	Hours Worked	Hourly Pay Rate	Gross Pay	Federal Ta	State Tax	Net Pay	Tax %			
4	Charvat, E	3/3/2009	1	65.25	20.5	1337.625	288.9271	53.505	995.1929	0.256			
5	Chen, Bin	6/14/2010	2	80	25.85	2068	444.2592	82.72	1541.021	0.254826			
6	Felski, No	10/11/2008	0	64.5	12.6	812.7	178.794	32.508	601.398	0.26			
7	Kersey, Ja	3/4/2011	1	68.5	21.45	1469.325	317.9011	58.773	1092.651	0.256359			
8	Merna, Th	1/15/2010	3	78.25	22.6	1768.45	373.0078	70.738	1324.704	0.250924			
9	Pollitt, Sh	11/15/2008	2	49.25	18.25	898.8125	187.038	35.9525	675.8221	0.248095			
10	Prasad, Ra	2/15/2008	0	33.5	9.35	313.225	68.9095	12.529	231.7865	0.26			
11	Washingto	5/11/2006	2	79.25	23.75	1882.188	403.3805	75.2875	1403.52	0.254315			
12	Zica, Jame	4/14/2011	1	80	19.65	1572	340.4896	62.88	1168.63	0.256596			
13	Totals			598.5		12122.33	2602.707	484.893	9034.725	0.254704			
14	Average		1.333333	66.5	19.33333	1346.925	289.1896	53.877	1003.858				
15	Highest		3	80	25.85	2068	444.2592	82.72	1541.021	0.26			
16	Lowest		0	33.5	9.35	313.225	68.9095	12.529	231.7865	0.248095			
17													
18													
19													
20													
21													

average of percents in range J4:J12 mathematically invalid

Figure 2–28

Other Ways

1. Select source area, click Copy button (Home tab | Clipboard group), select destination area, click Paste button (Home tab | Clipboard group)

2. Right-click source area, click Copy on shortcut menu, right-click destination area, click Paste icon on shortcut menu

3. Select source area and then point to border of range; while holding down CTRL, drag source area to destination area

4. Select source area, press CTRL+C, select destination area, press CTRL+V

To Save a Workbook Using the Same File Name

Earlier in this project, an intermediate version of the workbook was saved using the file name, The Mobile Masses Biweekly Payroll Report. The following step saves the workbook a second time, using the same file name.

1 Click the Save button on the Quick Access Toolbar to overwrite the previously saved file.

Break Point: If you wish to take a break, this is a good place to do so. You can quit Excel now. To resume at a later time, start Excel, open the file called Mobile Masses Biweekly Payroll Report, and continue following the steps from this location forward.

Verifying Formulas Using Range Finder

One of the more common mistakes made with Excel is to include a wrong cell reference in a formula. An easy way to verify that a formula references the cells you want it to reference is to use the Excel Range Finder. Use **Range Finder** to check which cells are referenced in the formula assigned to the active cell. Range Finder allows you to make immediate changes to the cells referenced in a formula.

To use Range Finder to verify that a formula contains the intended cell references, double-click the cell with the formula you want to check. Excel responds by highlighting the cells referenced in the formula so that you can check that the cell references are correct.

Entering Functions
You can drag the Function Arguments dialog box (Figure 2–20 on page EX 86) out of the way in order to select a range. You also can click the Collapse Dialog button to the right of the Number 1 box to hide the Function Arguments dialog box. The dialog box then collapses and the Collapse Dialog button becomes an Expand Dialog box button. After selecting the range, click the Expand Dialog to expand the dialog box.

To Verify a Formula Using Range Finder

The following steps use Range Finder to check the formula in cell J4.

1
• Double-click cell J4 to activate Range Finder (Figure 2–29).

2
• Press the ESC key to quit Range Finder and then click anywhere in the worksheet, such as cell A18, to deselect the current cell.

Figure 2–29

Formatting the Worksheet

Although the worksheet contains the appropriate data, formulas, and functions, the text and numbers need to be formatted to improve their appearance and readability.

In Chapter 1, cell styles were used to format much of the worksheet. This section describes how to change the unformatted worksheet in Figure 2–30a to the formatted worksheet in Figure 2–30b using a theme and other commands on the Ribbon. The colors and fonts that are used in the worksheet shown in Figure 2–30b are those that are associated with the Trek theme.

(a) Unformatted Worksheet

(b) Formatted Worksheet

Figure 2–30

Plan
Ahead

Identify how to format various elements of the worksheet.
As you have learned, applying proper formatting to a worksheet improves its appeal and readability. The following list includes additional worksheet formatting considerations.

- **Consider using cell borders and fill colors for various portions of the worksheet.** Cell borders, or box borders, draw a border around a cell or range of cells to set the cell or range off from other portions of the worksheet. For example, worksheet titles often include cell borders. Similarly, the use of a fill color in a cell or range of cells sets off the cell or range from other portions of the worksheet and provides visual impact to draw the user's eye toward the cell or range.

- **Use good judgment when centering values in columns.** If a cell entry is short, such as the dependents in column C, centering the entries within their respective columns improves the appearance of the worksheet.

- **Consider the use of a different theme.** A **theme** is a predefined set of colors, fonts, chart styles, cell styles, and fill effects that can be applied to an entire workbook. Every new workbook that you create is assigned a default theme named Office. Excel, however, includes a variety of other themes that provide a range of visual effects for your workbooks.

- **Apply proper formatting for cells that include dates.** Excel provides a number of date formats so that date values can be formatted to meet your needs. How you decide to format a date depends on a number of factors. For example, dates that include years both before and after the year 2000 should be formatted with a four-digit year. Your organization or department may insist on the use of certain standard date formats. Industry standards also may indicate how you should format date values.

The following outlines the formatting suggested in the sketch of the worksheet in Figure 2–3 on page EX 70.

1. Workbook theme — Trek
2. Worksheet title and subtitle
   a. Alignment — center across columns A through J
   b. Cell style — Title
   c. Font size — title 18; subtitle 16
   d. Background color (range A1:J2) — Orange Accent 1, Lighter 60%
   e. Border — thick box border around range A1:J2
3. Column titles
   a. Cell style — Heading 3
   b. Alignment — center
4. Data
   a. Dates in column B — mm/dd/yy format
   b. Alignment — center data in range C4:C12
   c. Numbers in column D — Comma style and two decimal places; if a cell in range D4:D12 is greater than 70, then cell appears with background color of orange and a font color of white
   d. Numbers in top row (range E4:I4) — Accounting number format
   e. Numbers below top row (range E5:I12) — Comma style and decimal places
5. Total line
   a. Cell style — Total
   b. Numbers — Accounting number format

6. Average, highest, and lowest rows

   a. Font style of row titles in range A14:A16 — bold

   b. Numbers — Currency style with floating dollar sign in the range E14:I16

7. Percentages in column J

   a. Numbers — Percentage style with two decimal places

8. Column widths

   a. Columns A, B, and C — best fit

   b. Column H — 10.22 characters

   c. Column D, E, and J — 7.56 characters

9. Row heights

   a. Row 3 — 48.00 points

   b. Row 14 — 27.00 points

   c. Remaining rows — default

To Change the Workbook Theme

The Trek theme includes fonts and colors that provide the worksheet a professional and subtly colored appearance. The following steps change the workbook theme to the Trek theme.

1

- Display the Page Layout tab.

- Click the Themes button (Page Layout tab | Themes group) to display the Themes gallery.

- Scroll to the bottom of the gallery (Figure 2–31).

Experiment

- Point to several themes in the Themes gallery to see a live preview of the themes.

Q&A

Why should I change the theme of a workbook?

A company or department may standardize on a specific theme so that all of their documents have a similar appearance. Similarly, an individual may want to have a theme that sets his or her work apart from the work of others. Other Office programs, such as Word and PowerPoint, include the same themes included with Excel, meaning that all of your Microsoft Office documents can share a common theme.

Figure 2–31

❷

• Click Trek in the Themes gallery to change the workbook theme (Figure 2–32).

Figure 2–32

Why did the cells in the worksheet change?

The cells in the worksheet originally were formatted with the default font for the default Office theme. The default font for the Trek theme is different from that of the default font for the Office theme and, therefore, changed on the worksheet when you changed the theme. If you had modified the font for any of the cells, those cells would not receive the default font for the Trek theme.

To Format the Worksheet Titles

The following steps merge and center the worksheet titles, apply the Title cells style to the worksheet titles, and decrease the font of the worksheet subtitle.

❶ Display the Home tab.

❷ Select the range to be merged, A1:J1 in this case, and then click the Merge & Center button (Home tab | Alignment group) to merge and center the text in the selected range.

❸ Select the range A2:J2 and then click the Merge & Center button (Home tab | Alignment group) to merge and center the text in the selected range.

❹ Select the range to contain the Title cell style, in this case A1:A2, click the Cell Styles button (Home tab | Styles group) to display the cell styles gallery, and then click the Title cell style in the Cell Styles gallery to apply the Title cell style to the selected range.

❺ Select cell A2 and then click the Decrease Font Size button (Home tab | Font group) to decrease the font size of the selected cell to the next lowest font size (Figure 2–33 on the following page).

Q&A

What is the effect of clicking the Decrease Font Size button?

When you click the Decrease Font Size button, Excel assigns the next lowest font size in the Font Size gallery to the selected range. The Increase Font Size button works in a similar manner but causes Excel to assign the next highest font size in the Font Size gallery to the selected range.

BTW

Color Selection
Knowing how people perceive colors helps you emphasize parts of your worksheet. Warmer colors (red and orange) tend to reach toward the reader. Cooler colors (blue, green, and violet) tend to pull away from the reader. Bright colors jump out of a dark background and are easiest to see. White or yellow text on a dark blue, green, purple, or black background is ideal.

Figure 2–33

To Change the Background Color and Apply a Box Border to the Worksheet Title and Subtitle

The final formats assigned to the worksheet title and subtitle are the orange background color and thick box border (Figure 2–30b on page EX 92). The following steps complete the formatting of the worksheet titles.

1

• Select the range A1:A2 and then click the Fill Color button arrow (Home tab | Font group) to display the Fill Color gallery (Figure 2–34).

Experiment

• Point to a number of colors in the Fill Color gallery to display a live preview of the color in the range A1:A2.

Figure 2–34

2

• Click Orange, Accent 1, Lighter 60% (column 5, row 3) in the Fill Color gallery to change the background color of the range of cells (Figure 2–35).

Figure 2–35

3

• Click the Borders button arrow (Home tab | Font group) to display the Borders list (Figure 2–36).

Figure 2–36

4

• Click Thick Box Border in the Borders list to display a thick box border around the selected range.

• Click anywhere in the worksheet, such as cell A18, to deselect the current range (Figure 2–37).

Figure 2–37

Other Ways

1. Click Format Cells Dialog Box Launcher (Home tab | Font group), click appropriate tab (Format Cells dialog box), click desired format, click OK button

2. Right-click range, click Format Cells on shortcut menu, click appropriate tab (Format Cells dialog box), click desired format, click OK button

3. Press CTRL+1, click appropriate tab (Format Cells dialog box), click desired format, click OK button

Background Colors
The most popular background color is blue. Research shows that the color blue is used most often because this color connotes serenity, reflection, and proficiency.

To Apply a Cell Style to the Column Headings and Format the Total Rows

As shown in Figure 2–30b on page EX 92, the column titles (row 3) should have the Heading 3 cell style and the totals row (row 13) should have the Total cell style. The summary information headings in the range A14:A16 should be bold. The following steps assign these styles and formats to row 3 and row 13 and the range A14:A16.

1 Select the range to be formatted, cells A3:J3 in this case.

2 Apply the Heading 3 cell style to the range A3:J3.

3 Click the Center button (Home tab | Alignment group) to center the column headings.

4 Apply the Total cell style to the range A13:J13.

5 Bold the range A14:A16 (Figure 2–38).

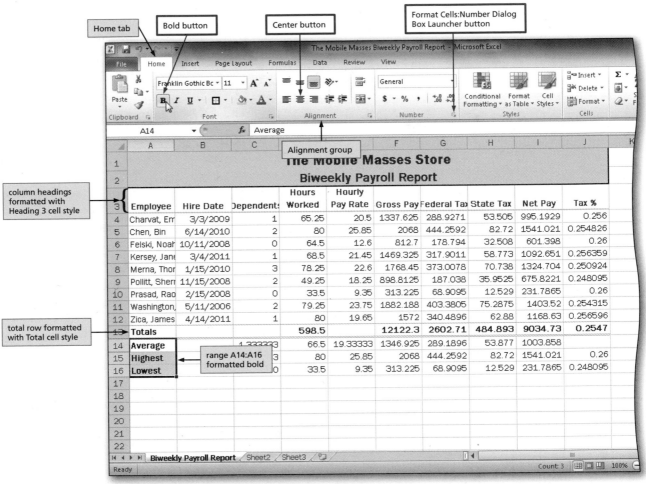

Figure 2–38

To Format Dates and Center Data in Cells

With the column titles and total rows formatted, the next step is to format the dates in column B and center the dependents in column C. The following steps format the dates in the range B4:B12 and center the data in the range C4:C12.

- Select the range to contain the new date format, cells B4:B12 in this case.

- Click the Format Cells: Number Dialog Box Launcher (Home tab | Number group) to display the Format Cells dialog box.

- If necessary, click the Number tab (Format Cells dialog box), click Date in the Category list, and then click 3/14/01 in the Type list to choose the format for the selected range (Figure 2–39).

Figure 2–39

2

- Click the OK button (Format Cells dialog box) to format the dates in the current column using the selected date format style.

3

- Select the range C4:C12 and then click the Center button (Home tab | Alignment group) to center the data in the selected range.

- Select cell E4 to deselect the selected range (Figure 2–40).

	A	B	C	D	E	F	G	H	I	J	K
1				**The Mobile Masses Store**							
2				**Biweekly Payroll Report**							
3	Employee	Hire Date	Dependents	Hours Worked	Hourly Pay Rate	Gross Pay	Federal Tax	State Tax	Net Pay	Tax %	
4	Charvat, Em	3/3/09	1	65.25	20.5	1337	cell E4 selected	53.505	995.1929	0.256	
5	Chen, Bin	6/14/10	2	80	25.85	2068	444.2592	82.72	1541.021	0.254826	
6	Felski, Noah	10/11/08	0	64.5	12.6	812.7	178.794	32.508	601.398	0.26	
7	Kersey, Jane	3/4/11	1	68.5	21.45	1469.325	317.9011	58.773	1092.651	0.256359	
8	Merna, Thor	1/15/10	3	78.25	22.6	1768.45	373.0078	70.738	1324.704	0.250924	
9	Pollitt, Sherr	11/15/08	2	49.25	18.25	898.8125	187.038	35.9525	675.8221	0.248095	
10	Prasad, Rao	2/15/08	0	33.5	9.35	313.225	68.9095	12.529	231.7865	0.26	
11	Washington,	5/11/06	2	79.25	23.75	1882.188	403.3805	75.2875	1403.52	0.254315	
12	Zica, James	4/14/11	1	80	19.65	1572	340.4896	62.88	1168.63	0.256596	
13	Totals			598.5		12122.3	2602.71	484.893	9034.73	0.2547	
14	Average		1.333333	66.5	19.33333	1346.925	289.1896	53.877	1003.858		
15	Highest		3	80	25.85	2068	444.2592	82.72	1541.021	0.26	
16	Lowest		0	33.5	9.35	313.225	68.9095	12.529	231.7865	0.248095	

Excel displays dates in range B4:B12 using date style format, mm/dd/yy

data centered in range C4:C12

Figure 2–40

Q&A

Can I format an entire column at once?

Yes. Rather than selecting the range B4:B12 in Step 1, you could have clicked the column B heading immediately above cell B1, and then clicked the Center button (Home tab | Alignment group). In this case, all cells in column B down to the last cell in the worksheet would have been formatted to use center alignment. This same procedure could have been used to format the dates in column C.

Other Ways

1. Right-click range, click Format Cells on shortcut menu, click appropriate tab (Format Cells dialog box), click desired format, click OK button

2. Press CTRL+1, click appropriate tab (Format Cells dialog box), click desired format, click OK button

Formatting Numbers Using the Ribbon

As shown in Figure 2–30b on page EX 92, the worksheet is formatted to resemble an accounting report. For example, in columns E through I, the numbers in the first row (row 4), the totals row (row 13), and the rows below the totals (rows 14 through 16) have dollar signs, while the remaining numbers (rows 5 through 12) in column E through column I do not.

Plan Ahead

Determine proper formatting for cells that include currency and other numeric amounts.

- To append a dollar sign to a number, you should use the Accounting number format. Excel displays numbers using the **Accounting number format** with a dollar sign to the left of the number, inserts a comma every three positions to the left of the decimal point, and displays numbers to the nearest cent (hundredths place). Clicking the Accounting Number Format button (Home tab | Number group) assigns the desired Accounting number format.

- When you use the Accounting Number Format button to assign the Accounting number format, Excel displays a **fixed dollar sign** to the far left in the cell, often with spaces between it and the first digit. To assign a **floating dollar sign** that appears immediately to the left of the first digit with no spaces, use the Currency style (Format Cells dialog box). Whether you use the Accounting number format or the Currency style format depends on a number of factors, including the preference of your organization, industry standards, and the aesthetics of the worksheet.

- The Comma style format is used to instruct Excel to display numbers with commas and no dollar signs. The **Comma style format**, which can be assigned to a range of cells by clicking the Comma Style button (Home tab | Number group), inserts a comma every three positions to the left of the decimal point and causes numbers to be displayed to the nearest hundredths.

To Apply an Accounting Number Format and Comma Style Format Using the Ribbon

The following steps assign formats using the Accounting Number Format button and the Comma Style button (Home tab | Number group). The Accounting Number format is applied to the currency amounts in rows 4 and 13. The Comma style is applied to the range E4:I12 and to column D (Hours Worked).

1

- Select the range to contain the Accounting Number Format, cells E4:I4 in this case.

- While holding down the CTRL key, select the range F13:I13 to select the nonadjacent range.

- Click the Accounting Number Format button (Home tab | Number group) to apply the Accounting number format with fixed dollar signs to the selected nonadjacent ranges (Figure 2–41).

Q&A

What is the effect of applying the Accounting number format?

The Accounting Number Format button assigns a fixed dollar sign to the numbers in the ranges E4:I4 and F13:I13. In each cell in these ranges, Excel displays the dollar sign to the far left with spaces between it and the first digit in the cell.

Figure 2–41

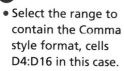

2

- Select the range to contain the Comma style format, cells E5:I12 in this case.

- Click the Comma Style button (Home tab | Number group) to assign the Comma style format to the selected range (Figure 2–42).

Figure 2–42

3

- Select the range to contain the Comma style format, cells D4:D16 in this case.

- Click the Comma Style button (Home tab | Number group) to assign the Comma style format to the selected range (Figure 2–43).

Figure 2–43

To Apply a Currency Style Format with a Floating Dollar Sign Using the Format Cells Dialog Box

The following steps use the Format Cells dialog box to apply the Currency style format with a floating dollar sign to the numbers in the range E14:I16.

1

- Select the range E14:I16 and then click the Format Cells: Number Dialog Box Launcher (Home tab | Number group) to display the Format Cells dialog box.

- If necessary, click the Number tab (Format Cells dialog box) to display the Number tab (Format Cells dialog box) (Figure 2–44).

Figure 2–44

2

- Click Currency in the Category list to select the necessary number format category, and then click the third style ($1,234.10) in the Negative numbers list (Format Cells dialog box) to select the desired currency format for negative numbers (Figure 2–45).

Q&A

How do I select the proper format?

You can choose from 12 categories of formats. Once you select a category, you can select the number of decimal places, whether or not a dollar sign should be displayed, and how negative numbers should appear. Selecting the appropriate negative numbers format is important, because doing so adds a space to the right of the number in order to align the numbers in the worksheet on the decimal points. Some of the available negative number formats do not align the numbers in the worksheet on the decimal points.

Figure 2–45

❸

- Click the OK button (Format Cells dialog box) to assign the Currency style format with a floating dollar sign to the selected range (Figure 2–46).

Q&A What is the difference between using the Accounting Number style and Currency style?

When using the Accounting Number Style button, recall that a floating dollar sign always appears immediately to the left of the first digit, and the fixed dollar sign always appears on the left side of the cell. Cell E4, for example, has a fixed dollar sign, while cell E14 has a floating dollar sign. The Currency style was assigned to cell E14 using the Format Cells dialog box and the result is a floating dollar sign.

	0	33.50			68.91			0.26
11/06	2	79.25	23.75	1,882.19	403.38	75.29	1,403.52	0.254315
14/11	1	80.00	19.65	1,572.00	340.49	62.88	1,168.63	0.256596
		8.50		$ 12,122.33	$ 2,602.71	$ 484.89	$ 9,034.73	0.2547
		66.50	$19.33	$1,346.93	$289.19	$53.88	$1,003.86	
		80.00	$25.85	$2,068.00	$444.26	$82.72	$1,541.02	0.26
		83.50	$9.35	$313.23	$68.91	$12.53	$231.79	0.248095

Excel displays range E14:I16 using Currency style format with floating dollar signs

Figure 2–46

Other Ways

1. Press CTRL+1, click Number tab (Format Cells dialog box), click Currency — in Category list, select format, click OK button
2. Press CTRL+SHIFT+DOLLAR SIGN ($)

To Apply a Percent Style Format and Use the Increase Decimal Button

The next step is to format the tax % in column J. Currently, Excel displays the numbers in column J as a decimal fraction (for example, 0.256 in cell J4). The following steps format the range J4:J16 to the Percent style format with two decimal places.

❶

- Select the range to format, cell J4:J16 in this case.

- Click the Percent Style button (Home tab | Number group) to display the numbers in the selected range as a rounded whole percent.

Q&A What is the result of clicking the Percent Style button?

The Percent Style button instructs Excel to display a value as a percentage, determined by multiplying the cell entry by 100, rounding the result to the nearest percent, and adding a percent sign. For example, when cell J4 is formatted using the Percent Style buttons, Excel displays the actual value 0.256 as 26%.

❷

- Click the Increase Decimal button (Home tab | Number group) two times to display the numbers in the selected range with two decimal places (Figure 2–47).

Percent Style button | Increase Decimal button

Decrease Decimal button

Number group

The Mobile Masses Store
Biweekly Payroll Report

dents	Hours Worked	Hourly Pay Rate	Gross Pay	Federal Tax	State Tax	Net Pay	Tax %
	65.25	$ 20.50	$ 1,337.63	$ 288.93	$ 53.51	$ 995.19	25.60%
	80.00	25.85	2,068.00	444.26	82.72	1,541.02	25.48%
	64.50	12.60	812.70	178.79	32.51	601.40	26.00%
	68.50	21.45	1,469.33	317.90	58.77	1,092.65	25.64%
	78.25	22.60	1,768.45	373		,324.70	25.09%
	49.25	18.25	898.81	187		675.82	24.81%
	33.50	9.35	313.23	68		231.79	26.00%
	79.25	23.75	1,882.19	403		,403.52	25.43%
	80.00	19.65	1,572.00	340.49	62.88	1,168.63	25.66%
	598.50		$ 12,122.33	$ 2,602.71	$ 484.89	$ 9,034.73	25.47%
333	66.50	$19.33	$1,346.93	$289.19	$53.88	$1,003.86	
3	80.00	$25.85	$2,068.00	$444.26	$82.72	$1,541.02	26.00%
0	33.50	$9.35	$313.23	$68.91	$12.53	$231.79	24.81%

Excel displays range J4:J16 using Percent style format with two decimal places

Figure 2–47

Other Ways

1. Right-click range, click Format Cells on shortcut menu, click Number tab (Format Cells dialog box), click Percentage — in Category list, select format, click OK button
2. Press CTRL+1, click Number tab (Format Cells dialog box), click Percentage — in Category list, select format, click OK button
3. Press CTRL+SHIFT+ percent sign (%)

Conditional Formatting

The next step is to emphasize the values greater than 70 in column D by formatting them to appear with an orange background and white font color (Figure 2–48).

Establish rules for conditional formatting.

- Excel lets you apply formatting that appears only when the value in a cell meets conditions that you specify. This type of formatting is called **conditional formatting**. You can apply conditional formatting to a cell, a range of cells, the entire worksheet, or the entire workbook. Usually, you apply conditional formatting to a range of cells that contains values you want to highlight, if conditions warrant.

- A **condition**, which is made up of two values and a relational operator, is true or false for each cell in the range. If the condition is true, then Excel applies the formatting. If the condition is false, then Excel suppresses the formatting. What makes conditional formatting so powerful is that the cell's appearance can change as you enter new values in the worksheet.

- As with worksheet formatting, follow the less-is-more rule when considering conditional formatting. Use conditional formatting to make cells and ranges stand out and raise attention. Too much conditional formatting can result in confusion for the reader of the worksheet.

BTW

Conditional Formatting
You can assign any format to a cell, a range of cells, a worksheet, or an entire workbook conditionally. If the value of the cell changes and no longer meets the specified condition, Excel suppresses the conditional formatting.

To Apply Conditional Formatting

The following steps assign conditional formatting to the range D4:D12, so that any cell value greater than 70 will cause Excel to display the number in the cell with an orange background and a white font color.

1

- Select the range D4:D12.

- Click the Conditional Formatting button (Home tab | Styles group) to display the Conditional Formatting list (Figure 2–48).

Figure 2–48

2

- Click New Rule in the Conditional Formatting list to display the New Formatting Rule dialog box.

- Click 'Format only cells that contain' in the Select a Rule Type area (New Formatting Rule dialog box) to change the 'Edit the Rule Description' area.

- In the 'Edit the Rule Description' area, click the box arrow in the relational operator box (second text box) to display a list of relational operators, and then select greater than to select the desired operator.

Figure 2–49

- Select the rightmost box, and then type 70 in the box in the 'Edit the Rule Description' area to enter the second value of the rule description (Figure 2–49).

Q&A

What do the changes in the 'Edit the Rule Description' indicate?

The 'Edit the Rule Description' area allows you to view and edit the rules for the conditional format. In this case, reading the area indicates that Excel should conditionally format only cells with cell values greater than 70.

3

- Click the Format button (New Formatting Rule dialog box) to display the Format Cells dialog box.

- If necessary, click the Font tab. Click the Color box arrow (Format Cells dialog box) to display the Color gallery and then click White, Background 1 (column 1, row 1) in the Color gallery to select the font color.

- Click the Fill tab (Format Cells dialog box) to display the Fill sheet and then click the orange color in column 5, row 5 to select the background color (Figure 2–50).

Figure 2–50

4

- Click the OK button (Format Cells dialog box) to close the Format Cells dialog box and display the New Formatting Rule dialog box with the desired font and background colors displayed in the Preview box (Figure 2–51).

New Formatting Rule dialog box

Preview box displays format assigned to cell in selected range if value in cell is greater than 70

OK button

Figure 2–51

5

- Click the OK button to assign the conditional format to the selected range.

- Click anywhere in the worksheet, such as cell A18, to deselect the current range (Figure 2–52).

Excel displays numbers greater than 70 in range D4:D12 with an orange background and white font color

Figure 2–52

Conditional Formatting Operators

As shown in Figure 2–49 on page EX 105, the second text box in the New Formatting Rule dialog box allows you to select a relational operator, such as less than, to use in the condition. The eight different relational operators from which you can choose for conditional formatting in the New Formatting Rule dialog box are summarized in Table 2–5.

Table 2–5 Summary of Conditional Formatting Relational Operators	
Relational Operator	**Description**
between	Cell value is between two numbers.
not between	Cell value is not between two numbers.
equal to	Cell value is equal to a number.
not equal to	Cell value is not equal to a number.
greater than	Cell value is greater than a number.
less than	Cell value is less than a number.
greater than or equal to	Cell value is greater than or equal to a number.
less than or equal to	Cell value is less than or equal to a number.

Changing the Widths of Columns and Heights of Rows

When Excel starts and displays a blank worksheet on the screen, all of the columns have a default width of 8.43 characters, or 64 pixels. These values may change depending on the theme applied to the workbook. For example, in this chapter, the Trek theme was applied to the workbook, resulting in columns having a default width of 8.11 characters. A character is defined as a letter, number, symbol, or punctuation mark in 11-point Calibri font, the default font used by Excel. An average of 8.43 characters in 11-point Calibri font will fit in a cell.

Another measure of the height and width of cells is pixels, which is short for picture element. A **pixel** is a dot on the screen that contains a color. The size of the dot is based on your screen's resolution. At the resolution of 1024 × 768 used in this book, 1024 pixels appear across the screen and 768 pixels appear down the screen for a total of 786,432 pixels. It is these 786,432 pixels that form the font and other items you see on the screen.

The default row height in a blank worksheet is 15 points (or 20 pixels). Recall from Chapter 1 that a point is equal to 1/72 of an inch. Thus, 15 points is equal to about 1/5 of an inch. You can change the width of the columns or height of the rows at any time to make the worksheet easier to read or to ensure that Excel displays an entry properly in a cell.

BTW

Hidden Rows and Columns
For some people, trying to unhide a range of columns using the mouse can be frustrating. An alternative is to use the keyboard: select the columns to the right and left of the hidden columns and then press CTRL+SHIFT+) (RIGHT PARENTHESIS). To use the keyboard to hide a range of columns, press CTRL+0 (ZERO). You also can use the keyboard to unhide a range of rows by selecting the rows immediately above and below the hidden rows and then pressing CTRL+SHIFT+((LEFT PARENTHESIS). To use the keyboard to hide a range of rows, press CTRL+9.

To Change the Widths of Columns

When changing the column width, you can set the width manually or you can instruct Excel to size the column to best fit. **Best fit** means that the width of the column will be increased or decreased so that the widest entry will fit in the column. Sometimes, you may prefer more or less white space in a column than best fit provides. To change the white space, Excel allows you to change column widths manually.

When the format you assign to a cell causes the entry to exceed the width of a column, Excel automatically changes the column width to best fit. If you do not assign a format to a cell or cells in a column, the column width will remain 8.43 characters. To set a column width to best fit, double-click the right boundary of the column heading above row 1.

The steps on the following pages change the column widths: column A, B, and C to best fit; column H to 10.22 characters; and columns D, E, and J to 7.56 characters.

1

- Drag through column headings A, B, and C above row 1 to select the columns.

- Point to the boundary on the right side of column heading C to cause the mouse pointer to become a split double arrow (Figure 2–53).

Q&A

What if I want to make a large change to the column width?

If you want to increase or decrease column width significantly, you can right-click a column heading and then use the Column Width command on the shortcut menu to change the column's width. To use this command, however, you must select one or more entire columns.

Figure 2–53

2

- Double-click the right boundary of column heading C to change the width of the selected columns to best fit.

- Point to the boundary on the right side of the column H heading above row 1.

- When the mouse pointer changes to a split double arrow, drag until the ScreenTip indicates Width: 10.22 (99 pixels). Do not release the mouse button (Figure 2–54).

Q&A

What happens if I change the column width to zero (0)?

If you decrease the column width to 0,

Figure 2–54

the column is hidden. **Hiding cells** is a technique you can use to hide data that might not be relevant to a particular report or sensitive data that you do not want others to see. To instruct Excel to display a hidden column, position the mouse pointer to the right of the column heading boundary where the hidden column is located and then drag to the right.

3

- Release the mouse button to change the column width.

- Click the column D heading above row 1 to select the column.

- While holding down the CTRL key, click the column E heading and then the column J heading above row 1 so that nonadjacent columns are selected (Figure 2–55).

Figure 2–55

4

- If necessary, scroll the worksheet to the right so that the right border of column J is visible. Point to the boundary on the right side of the column J heading above row 1.

- Drag until the ScreenTip indicates Width: 7.56 (75 pixels). Do not release the mouse button (Figure 2–56).

Figure 2–56

5

- Release the mouse button to change the column widths.

- If necessary, scroll the worksheet to the left so that the left border of column A is visible.

- Click anywhere in the worksheet, such as cell A18, to deselect the columns (Figure 2–57).

Other Ways

1. Right-click column heading or drag through multiple column headings and right-click, click Column Width on shortcut menu, enter desired column width, click OK button

Figure 2–57

To Change the Heights of Rows

When you increase the font size of a cell entry, such as the title in cell A1, Excel automatically increases the row height to best fit so that it can display the characters properly. Recall that Excel did this earlier when multiple lines were entered in a cell in row 3, and when the cell style of the worksheet title and subtitle was changed.

You also can increase or decrease the height of a row manually to improve the appearance of the worksheet. The following steps improve the appearance of the worksheet by increasing the height of row 3 to 48.00 points and increasing the height of row 14 to 27.00 points.

1

- Point to the boundary below row heading 3.

- Drag down until the ScreenTip indicates Height: 48.00 (64 pixels). Do not release the mouse button (Figure 2–58).

Figure 2–58

2

- Release the mouse button to change the row height.

- Point to the boundary below row heading 14.

- Drag down until the ScreenTip indicates Height: 27.00 (36 pixels). Do not release the mouse button (Figure 2–59).

Figure 2–59

3

- Release the mouse button to change the row height.

- Click anywhere in the worksheet, such as cell A18, to deselect the current cell (Figure 2–60).

Q&A

Can I hide a row?

Yes. As with column widths, when you decrease the row height to 0, the row is hidden. To instruct Excel to display a hidden row, position the mouse pointer just below the row heading boundary where the row is hidden and then drag down. To set a row height to best fit, double-click the bottom boundary of the row heading.

Figure 2–60

Other Ways
1. Right-click row heading or drag through multiple row headings and right-click, click Row Height   on shortcut menu, enter desired row height, click OK button

Break Point: If you wish to take a break, this is a good place to do so. Be sure to save the The Mobile Masses Biweekly Payroll Report file again and then you can quit Excel. To resume at a later time, start Excel, open the file called The Mobile Masses Biweekly Payroll Report and continue following the steps from this location forward.

BTW

Spell Checking
While Excel's spell checker is a valuable tool, it is not infallible. You should proofread your workbook carefully by pointing to each word and saying it aloud as you point to it. Be mindful of misused words such as its and it's, through and though, and to and too. Nothing undermines a good impression more than a professional looking report with misspelled words.

Checking Spelling

Excel includes a **spell checker** you can use to check a worksheet for spelling errors. The spell checker looks for spelling errors by comparing words on the worksheet against words contained in its standard dictionary. If you often use specialized terms that are not in the standard dictionary, you may want to add them to a custom dictionary using the Spelling dialog box.

When the spell checker finds a word that is not in either dictionary, it displays the word in the Spelling dialog box. You then can correct it if it is misspelled.

To Check Spelling on the Worksheet

To illustrate how Excel responds to a misspelled word, the following steps misspell purposely the word, Employee, in cell A3 as the word, Empolyee, as shown in Figure 2–61.

1

- Click cell A3 and then type **Empolyee** to misspell the word Employee.

- Select cell A1 so that the spell checker begins checking at the selected cell.

- Click Review on the Ribbon to display the Review tab.

- Click the Spelling button (Review tab | Proofing group) to run the spell checker and display the misspelled word in the Spelling dialog box (Figure 2–61).

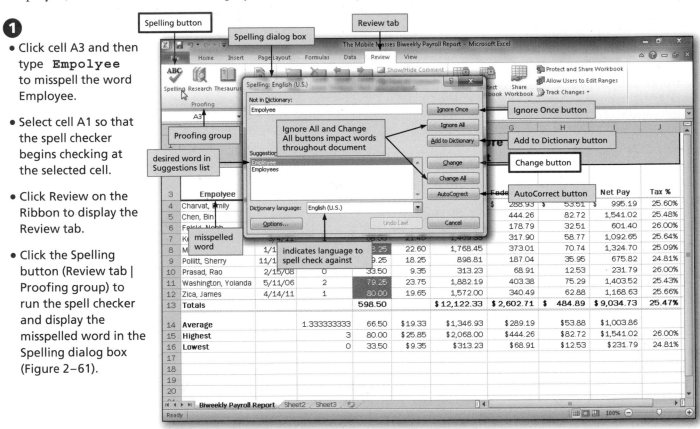

Figure 2–61

Q&A

What happens when the spell checker finds a misspelled word?

When the spell checker identifies that a cell contains a word not in its standard or custom dictionary, it selects that cell as the active cell and displays the Spelling dialog box. The Spelling dialog box lists the word not found in the dictionary and a list of suggested corrections (Figure 2–61).

2

- Click the Change button (Spelling dialog box) to change the misspelled word to the correct word (Figure 2–62).

- Click the Close button (Spelling dialog box) to close the Spelling dialog box.

- If the Microsoft Excel dialog box is displayed, click the OK button.

3

- Click anywhere in the worksheet, such as cell A18, to deselect the current cell.

- Display the Home tab.

- Click the Save button on the Quick Access Toolbar to save the workbook.

Figure 2–62

Q&A

What other actions can I take in the Spelling dialog box?

If one of the words in the Suggestions list is correct, click it and then click the Change button. If none of the suggestions is correct, type the correct word in the Not in Dictionary text box and then click the Change button. To change the word throughout the worksheet, click the Change All button instead of the Change button. To skip correcting the word, click the Ignore Once button. To have Excel ignore the word for the remainder of the worksheet, click the Ignore All button

Other Ways
1. Press F7

Additional Spell Checker Considerations

Consider these additional guidelines when using the spell checker:

- To check the spelling of the text in a single cell, double-click the cell to make the formula bar active and then click the Spelling button (Review tab | Proofing group).

- If you select a single cell so that the formula bar is not active and then start the spell checker, Excel checks the remainder of the worksheet, including notes and embedded charts.

- If you select a cell other than cell A1 before you start the spell checker, Excel will display a dialog box when the spell checker reaches the end of the worksheet, asking if you want to continue checking at the beginning.

- If you select a range of cells before starting the spell checker, Excel checks the spelling of the words only in the selected range.

- To check the spelling of all the sheets in a workbook, right-click any sheet tab, click Select All Sheets on the sheet tab shortcut menu, and then start the spell checker.

- To add words to the dictionary such as your last name, click the Add to Dictionary button in the Spelling dialog box (Figure 2–61) when Excel identifies the word as not in the dictionary.

- Click the AutoCorrect button (Spelling dialog box) to add the misspelled word and the correct version of the word to the AutoCorrect list. For example, suppose that you misspell the word, do, as the word, dox. When the spell checker displays the Spelling dialog box with the correct word, do, in the Change to box, click the AutoCorrect button. Then, anytime in the future that you type the word dox, Excel automatically will change it to the word, do.

BTW

Error Checking
Always take the time to check the formulas of a worksheet before submitting it to your supervisor. You can check formulas by clicking the Error Checking button (Formulas tab | Formula Auditing group). You also should test the formulas by employing data that tests the limits of formulas. Experienced spreadsheet specialists spend as much time testing a workbook as they do creating it, and they do so before placing the workbook into production.

Preparing to Print the Worksheet

Excel allows for a great deal of customization in how a worksheet appears when printed. For example, the margins on the page can be adjusted. A header or footer can be added to each printed page as well. Excel also has the capability to work on the worksheet in Page Layout view. **Page Layout view** allows you to create or modify a worksheet while viewing how it will look in printed format. The default view that you have worked in up until this point in the book is called **Normal view**.

Plan Ahead

> **Specify how the printed worksheet should appear.**
>
> Before printing a worksheet, you should consider how the worksheet will appear when printed. In order to fit as much information on the printed page as possible, the margins of the worksheet should be set to a reasonably small width and height. While the current version of a worksheet may print on one page, you may add more data in the future that causes the worksheet to extend to multiple pages. It is, therefore, a good idea to add a page header to the worksheet that prints in the top margin of each page. A **header** is common content that prints on every page of a worksheet. Landscape orientation is a good choice for large worksheets because the printed worksheet's width is greater than its length.

To Change the Worksheet's Margins, Header, and Orientation in Page Layout View

The following steps change to Page Layout view, narrow the margins of the worksheet, change the header of the worksheet, and set the orientation of the worksheet to landscape. Often, you may want to reduce margins so that the printed worksheet better fits the page. **Margins** are those portions of a printed page outside the main body of the printed document and always are blank when printed. Recall that in Chapter 1, the worksheet was printed in landscape orientation. The current worksheet also is too wide for a single page and requires landscape orientation to fit on one page in a readable manner.

- Click the Page Layout button on the status bar to view the worksheet in Page Layout view (Figure 2–63).

Q&A

What are some key features of Page Layout view?

Page Layout view shows the worksheet divided into pages. A gray background separates each page. The white areas surrounding each page indicate the print margins. The top of each page includes a Header area, and the bottom of each page includes a Footer area. Page Layout view also includes a ruler at the top of the page that assists you in placing objects on the page, such as charts and pictures.

Figure 2–63

2

- Display the Page Layout tab.

- Click the Margins button (Page Layout tab | Page Setup group) to display the Margins gallery (Figure 2–64).

Figure 2–64

3

- Click Narrow in the Margins gallery to change the worksheet margins to the Narrow margin style.

- Drag the scroll bar on the right side of the worksheet to the top so that row 1 of the worksheet is displayed.

- Click above the worksheet title in cell A1 in the center area of the Header area.

- Type **Samuel Snyder** and then press the ENTER key. Type **Chief Financial Officer** to complete the worksheet header (Figure 2–65).

Figure 2–65

Q&A

What else can I place in a header?

You can add text, page number information, date and time information, the file path of the workbook, the file name of the workbook, the sheet name of the workbook, and pictures to a header.

4

- Select cell B16 to deselect the header. Click the Orientation button (Page Layout tab | Page Setup group) to display the Orientation gallery (Figure 2–66).

Q&A

Why do I need to deselect the header?

Excel disables almost all of the buttons on the Ribbon as you edit a header or footer. In addition to the commands on the Design tab (Figure 2–65 on the previous page), only a few commands remain available on the Home tab on the Ribbon. To continue working in Excel, therefore, you should select a cell in the worksheet so that all of the commands on the Ribbon are available for your use.

Figure 2–66

5

- Click Landscape in the Orientation gallery to change the worksheet's orientation to landscape (Figure 2–67).

Q&A

Do I need to change the orientation every time I want to print the worksheet?

No. Once you change the orientation and save the workbook, Excel will save the orientation setting for that workbook until you change it. When you open a new workbook, Excel sets the orientation to portrait.

Figure 2–67

Other Ways

1. Click Page Setup Dialog Box Launcher (Page Layout tab | Page Setup group), click Page tab

   (Page Setup dialog box), click Portrait or Landscape, click OK button

Printing the Worksheet

Excel provides other options for printing a worksheet. The following sections print the worksheet and print a section of the worksheet.

To Print a Worksheet

The following steps print the worksheet.

1 Click File on the Ribbon to open the Backstage view.

2 Click the Print tab in the Backstage view to display the Print gallery.

3 If necessary, click the Printer Status button in the Print gallery to display a list of available Printer options and then click the desired printer to change the currently selected printer.

4 Click the Print button in the Print gallery to print the worksheet in landscape orientation on the currently selected printer.

5 When the printer stops, retrieve the hard copy (Figure 2–68).

BTW

Conserving Ink and Toner
If you want to conserve ink or toner, you can instruct Excel to print draft quality documents by clicking File on the Ribbon to open the Backstage view, clicking Options in the Backstage view to display the Excel Options dialog box, clicking Advanced in the left pane (Excel Options dialog box), scrolling to the Print area in the right pane, placing a check mark in the 'Use draft quality' check box, and then clicking the OK button. Then, use the Backstage view to print the document as usual.

BTW

Printing Document Properties
To print document properties, click File on the Ribbon to open the Backstage view, click the Print tab in the Backstage view to display the Print gallery, click the first button in the Settings area to display a list of options specifying what you can print, click Document Properties in the list to specify you want to print the document properties instead of the actual document, and then click the Print button in the Print gallery to print the document properties on the currently selected printer.

landscape orientation

Samuel Snyder
Chief Financial Officer

The Mobile Masses Store
Biweekly Payroll Report

Employee	Hire Date	Dependents	Hours Worked	Hourly Pay Rate	Gross Pay	Federal Tax	State Tax	Net Pay	Tax %
Charvat, Emily	3/3/09	1	65.25	$ 20.50	$ 1,337.63	$ 288.93	$ 53.51	$ 995.19	25.60%
Chen, Bin	6/14/10	2	80.00	25.85	2,068.00	444.26	82.72	1,541.02	25.48%
Felski, Noah	10/11/08	0	64.50	12.60	812.70	178.79	32.51	601.40	26.00%
Kersey, Jane	3/4/11	1	68.50	21.45	1,469.33	317.90	58.77	1,092.65	25.64%
Merna, Thomas	1/15/10	3	78.25	22.60	1,768.45	373.01	70.74	1,324.70	25.09%
Pollitt, Sherry	11/15/08	2	49.25	18.25	898.81	187.04	35.95	675.82	24.81%
Prasad, Rao	2/15/08	0	33.50	9.35	313.23	68.91	12.53	231.79	26.00%
Washington, Yolanda	5/11/06	2	79.25	23.75	1,882.19	403.38	75.29	1,403.52	25.43%
Zica, James	4/14/11	1	80.00	19.65	1,572.00	340.49	62.88	1,168.63	25.66%
Totals			598.50		$ 12,122.33	$ 2,602.71	$ 484.89	$ 9,034.73	25.47%
Average		1.333333333	66.50	$19.33	$1,346.93	$289.19	$53.88	$1,003.86	
Highest		3	80.00	$25.85	$2,008.00	$444.26	$82.72	$1,541.02	26.00%
Lowest		0	33.50	$9.35	$313.23	$68.91	$12.53	$231.79	24.81%

Figure 2–68

To Print a Section of the Worksheet

You might not always want to print the entire worksheet. You can print portions of the worksheet by selecting the range of cells to print and then clicking the Selection option button in the Print what area in the Print dialog box. The following steps print the range A3:F16.

1

- Select the range to print, cells A3:F16 in this case.

- Click File on the Ribbon to open the Backstage view.

- Click the Print tab to display the Print gallery.

- Click Print Active Sheets in the Settings area (Print tab | Print gallery) to display a list of options that determine what Excel should print (Figure 2–69).

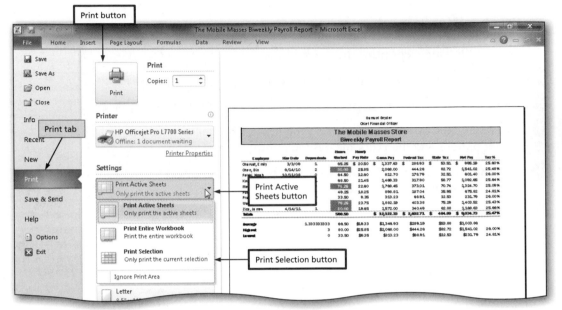

Figure 2–69

2

- Click Print Selection to instruct Excel to print only the selected range.

- Click the Print button in the Print gallery to print the selected range of the worksheet on the currently selected printer (Figure 2–70).

- Click the Normal button on the status bar to return to Normal view.

- Click cell A18 to deselect the range A3:F16.

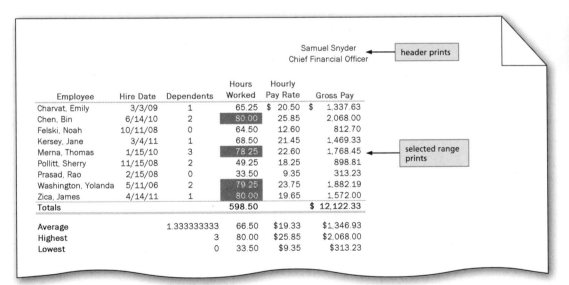

Figure 2–70

Q&A | What are my options for telling Excel what to print?

Excel includes three options to allow you to determine what should be printed (Figure 2–69). As shown in the previous steps, the Print Selection button instructs Excel to print the selected range. The Print Active Sheets button instructs Excel to print the active worksheet (the worksheet currently on the screen) or the selected worksheets. Finally, the Print Entire Workbook button instructs Excel to print all of the worksheets in the workbook.

Other Ways

1. Select range, click Print Area button (Page Layout tab | Page Setup group), click Set Print Area, click Quick Print button on Quick Access Toolbar, click Print Area, click Clear Print Area

2. Select range, click Print Area button (Page Layout tab | Page Setup group), click Set Print Area, click File tab to open Backstage view, click Print tab, click Print button

Displaying and Printing the Formulas Version of the Worksheet

BTW

Values versus Formulas
When completing class assignments, do not enter numbers in cells that require formulas. Most instructors will check both the values version and formulas version of your worksheets. The formulas version verifies that you entered formulas, rather than numbers, in formula-based cells.

Thus far, you have been working with the **values version** of the worksheet, which shows the results of the formulas you have entered, rather than the actual formulas. Excel also can display and print the **formulas version** of the worksheet, which shows the actual formulas you have entered, rather than the resulting values.

The formulas version is useful for debugging a worksheet. **Debugging** is the process of finding and correcting errors in the worksheet. Viewing and printing the formulas version instead of the values version makes it easier to see any mistakes in the formulas.

When you change from the values version to the formulas version, Excel increases the width of the columns so that the formulas and text do not overflow into adjacent cells on the right. The formulas version of the worksheet, thus, usually is significantly wider than the values version. To fit the wide printout on one page, you can use landscape orientation, which has already been selected for the workbook, and the Fit to option in the Page sheet in the Page Setup dialog box.

To Display the Formulas in the Worksheet and Fit the Printout on One Page

The following steps change the view of the worksheet from the values version to the formulas version of the worksheet and then print the formulas version on one page.

1

- Press CTRL+ACCENT MARK (`) to display the worksheet with formulas.

- Click the right horizontal scroll arrow until column J appears (Figure 2–71).

2

- Click the Page Setup Dialog Box Launcher (Page Layout tab | Page Setup group) to display the Page Setup dialog box.

Figure 2–71

3

- If necessary, click Landscape in the Orientation area to select it.

- If necessary, click Fit to in the Scaling area to select it.

4

- Click the Print button (Page Setup dialog box) to print the formulas in the worksheet on one page in landscape orientation (Figure 2–72). If necessary, in the Backstage view, select the Print Active Sheets option in the Settings area of the Print gallery.

- When Excel displays the Backstage view, click the Print button to print the worksheet.

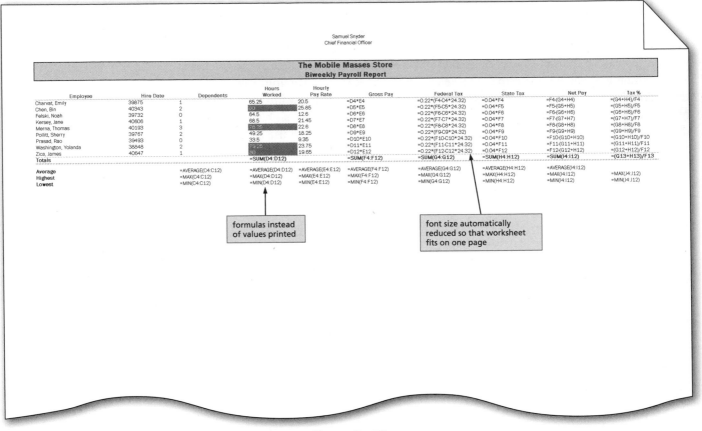

Figure 2–72

5

- After viewing and printing the formulas version, press CTRL+ACCENT MARK (`) to instruct Excel to display the values version.

- Click the left horizontal scroll arrow until column A appears.

To Change the Print Scaling Option Back to 100%

Depending on your printer, you may have to change the Print Scaling option back to 100% after using the Fit to option. Doing so will cause the worksheet to print at the default print scaling of 100%. The following steps reset the Print Scaling option so that future worksheets print at 100%, instead of being resized to print on one page.

1 If necessary, display the Page Layout tab and then click the Page Setup Dialog Box Launcher (Page Layout tab | Page Setup group) to display the Page Setup dialog box.

2 Click Adjust to in the Scaling area to select the Adjust to setting.

3 If necessary, type 100 in the Adjust to box to adjust the print scaling to a new percentage.

4 Click the OK button (Page Setup dialog box) to set the print scaling to normal.

5 Display the Home tab.

Q&A What is the purpose of the Adjust to box in the Page Setup dialog box?

The Adjust to box allows you to specify the percentage of reduction or enlargement in the printout of a worksheet. The default percentage is 100%. When you click the Fit to option, this percentage automatically changes to the percentage required to fit the printout on one page.

BTW

Quick Reference
For a table that lists how to complete the tasks covered in this book using the mouse, Ribbon, shortcut menu, and keyboard, see the Quick Reference Summary at the back of this book, or visit the Excel 2010 Quick Reference Web page (scsite.com/ex2010/qr).

To Save the Workbook and Quit Excel

With the workbook complete, the following steps save the workbook and quit Excel.

1 Click the Save button on the Quick Access Toolbar.

2 Click the Close button on the upper-right corner of the title bar.

Chapter Summary

In this chapter you have learned how to enter formulas, calculate an average, find the highest and lowest numbers in a range, verify formulas using Range Finder, added borders, align text, format numbers, change column widths and row heights, and add conditional formatting to a range of numbers. In addition, you learned to spell check a worksheet, print a section of a worksheet, and display and print the formulas version of the worksheet using the Fit to option. The items listed below include all the new Excel skills you have learned in this chapter.

1. Enter a Formula Using the Keyboard (EX 75)
2. Enter Formulas Using Point Mode (EX 77)
3. Copy Formulas Using the Fill Handle (EX 80)
4. Determine the Average of a Range of Numbers Using the Keyboard and Mouse (EX 84)
5. Determine the Highest Number in a Range of Numbers Using the Insert Function Box (EX 86)
6. Determine the Lowest Number in a Range of Numbers Using the Sum Menu (EX 87)
7. Copy a Range of Cells Across Columns to an Adjacent Range Using the Fill Handle (EX 89)
8. Verify a Formula Using Range Finder (EX 91)
9. Change the Workbook Theme (EX 94)
10. Change the Background Color and Apply a Box Border to the Worksheet Title and Subtitle (EX 96)
11. Format Dates and Center Data in Cells (EX 98)
12. Apply an Accounting Number Format and Comma Style Format Using the Ribbon (EX 100)
13. Apply a Currency Style Format with a Floating Dollar Sign Using the Format Cells Dialog Box (EX 102)
14. Apply a Percent Style Format and Use the Increase Decimal Button (EX 103)
15. Apply Conditional Formatting (EX 104)
16. Change the Widths of Columns (EX 107)
17. Change the Heights of Rows (EX 110)
18. Check Spelling on the Worksheet (EX 112)
19. Change the Worksheet's Margins, Header, and Orientation in Page Layout View (EX 114)
20. Print a Section of the Worksheet (EX 118)
21. Display the Formulas in the Worksheet and Fit the Printout on One Page (EX 119)

Learn It Online

Test your knowledge of chapter content and key terms.

Instructions: To complete the Learn It Online exercises, start your browser, click the Address bar, and then enter `scsite.com/ex2010/learn` as the Web address. When the Excel 2010 Learn It Online page is displayed, click the link for the exercise you want to complete and then read the instructions.

Chapter Reinforcement TF, MC, and SA
A series of true/false, multiple choice, and short answer questions that test your knowledge of the chapter content.

Flash Cards
An interactive learning environment where you identify chapter key terms associated with displayed definitions.

Practice Test
A series of multiple choice questions that test your knowledge of chapter content and key terms.

Who Wants To Be a Computer Genius?
An interactive game that challenges your knowledge of chapter content in the style of a television quiz show.

Wheel of Terms
An interactive game that challenges your knowledge of chapter key terms in the style of the television show *Wheel of Fortune*.

Crossword Puzzle Challenge
A crossword puzzle that challenges your knowledge of key terms presented in the chapter.

Apply Your Knowledge

Reinforce the skills and apply the concepts you learned in this chapter.

Profit Analysis Worksheet
Instructions: The purpose of this exercise is to open a partially completed workbook, enter formulas and functions, copy the formulas and functions, and then format the worksheet titles and numbers. As shown in Figure 2–73, the completed worksheet analyzes the costs associated with a police department's fleet of vehicles.

	A	B	C	D	E	F	G
1			Village of Scott Police Department				
2			Monthly Vehicle Cost-per-Mile Summary				
3	Vehicle ID	Miles Driven	Cost per Mile	Maintenance Cost	Mileage Cost	Total Cost	Total Cost per Mile
4	670543	2,007	$ 0.49	$ 242.80	$ 983.43	$ 1,226.23	$ 0.61
5	979253	3,192	0.48	446.37	1,532.16	1,978.53	0.62
6	948173	3,802	0.65	472.47	2,471.30	2,943.77	0.77
7	837625	2,080	0.62	432.25	1,289.60	1,721.85	0.83
8	824664	2,475	0.56	369.88	1,386.00	1,755.88	0.71
9	655385	3,294	0.50	352.05	1,647.00	1,999.05	0.61
10	836417	3,640	0.70	417.80	2,548.00	2,965.80	0.81
11	993617	3,395	0.70	390.39	2,376.50	2,766.89	0.81
12	779468	4,075	0.55	442.17	2,241.25	2,683.42	0.66
13	Totals	27,960		$ 3,566.18	$ 16,475.24	$ 20,041.42	$ 0.72
14	Highest	4,075	$0.70	$472.47	$2,548.00	$2,965.80	$0.83
15	Lowest	2,007	$0.48	$242.80	$983.43	$1,226.23	$0.61
16	Average	3,107	$0.58	$396.24	$1,830.58	$2,226.82	$0.72
17							
18							
19							
20							

Figure 2–73

1. Start Excel. Open the workbook Apply 2-1 Village of Scott Police Department. See the inside back cover of this book for instructions for downloading the Data Files for Students or see your instructor for information on accessing the files required in this book.

2. Use the following formulas in cells E4, F4, and G4:

   Mileage Cost (cell E4) = Miles Driven * Cost per Mile or = B4 * C4

   Total Cost (cell F4) = Maintenance Cost + Mileage Cost or = D4 + E4

   Total Cost per Mile (cell G4) = Total Cost / Miles Driven or = F4 / B4

   Use the fill handle to copy the three formulas in the range E4:G4 to the range E5:G12.

3. Determine totals for the miles driven, maintenance cost, mileage cost, and total cost in row 13. Copy the formula in cell G12 to G13 to assign the formula in cell G12 to G13 in the total line. If necessary, reapply the Total cell style to cell G13.

4. In the range B14:B16, determine the highest value, lowest value, and average value, respectively, for the values in the range B4:B12. Use the fill handle to copy the three functions to the range C14:G16.

5. Format the worksheet as follows:

   a. change the workbook theme to Foundry by using the Themes button (Page Layout tab | Themes group)

   b. cell A1 — change to Title cell style

   c. cell A2 — change to a font size of 16

   d. cells A1:A2 — Rose background color and a thick box border

   e. cells C4:G4 and D13:G13 — Accounting number format with two decimal places and fixed dollar signs by using the Accounting Number Format button (Home tab | Number group)

   f. cells C5:G12 — Comma style format with two decimal places by using the Comma Style button (Home tab | Number group)

   g. cells B4:B16 — Comma style format with no decimal places

   h. cells C14:G16 — Currency style format with floating dollar signs by using the Format Cells: Number Dialog Box Launcher (Home tab | Number group)

   i. cells G4:G12 — apply conditional formatting so that cells with a value greater than 0.80 appear with a rose background color

6. Switch to Page Layout View and delete any current text in the Header area. Enter your name, course, laboratory assignment number, and any other information, as specified by your instructor, in the Header area. Preview and print the worksheet in landscape orientation. Change the document properties, as specified by your instructor. Save the workbook using the file name, Apply 2-1 Village of Scott Police Department Complete.

7. Use Range Finder to verify the formula in cell G13.

Continued >

Apply Your Knowledge *continued*

8. Print the range A3:D16. Press CTRL+ACCENT MARK (`) to change the display from the values version of the worksheet to the formulas version. Print the formulas version in landscape orientation on one page (Figure 2–74) by using the Fit to option in the Page sheet in the Page Setup dialog box. Press CTRL+ACCENT MARK (`) to change the display of the worksheet back to the values version. Close the workbook without saving it.

9. Submit the workbook and results as specified by your instructor.

Jeff Quasney
Apply 2-1 Village of Scott Police Department

Village of Scott Police Department
Monthly Vehicle Cost-per-Mile Summary

Vehicle ID	Miles Driven	Cost per Mile	Maintenance Cost	Mileage Cost	Total Cost	Total Cost per Mile
670543	2007	0.49	242.8	=B4*C4	=D4+E4	=F4/B4
979253	3192	0.48	446.37	=B5*C5	=D5+E5	=F5/B5
948173	3802	0.65	472.47	=B6*C6	=D6+E6	=F6/B6
837625	2080	0.62	432.25	=B7*C7	=D7+E7	=F7/B7
824664	2475	0.56	369.88	=B8*C8	=D8+E8	=F8/B8
685385	3294	0.5	352.05	=B9*C9	=D9+E9	=F9/B9
836417	3640	0.7	417.8	=B10*C10	=D10+E10	=F10/B10
993617	3395	0.7	390.39	=B11*C11	=D11+E11	=F11/B11
779468	4075	0.55	442.17	=B12*C12	=D12+E12	=F12/B12
Totals	=SUM(B4:B12)		=SUM(D4:D12)	=SUM(E4:E12)	=SUM(F4:F12)	=F13/B13
Highest	=MAX(B4:B12)	=MAX(C4:C12)	=MAX(D4:D12)	=MAX(E4:E12)	=MAX(F4:F12)	=MAX(G4:G12)
Lowest	=MIN(B4:B12)	=MIN(C4:C12)	=MIN(D4:D12)	=MIN(E4:E12)	=MIN(F4:F12)	=MIN(G4:G12)
Average	=AVERAGE(B4:B12)	=AVERAGE(C4:C12)	=AVERAGE(D4:D12)	=AVERAGE(E4:E12)	=AVERAGE(F4:F12)	=AVERAGE(G4:G12)

Figure 2–74

Extend Your Knowledge

Extend the skills you learned in this chapter and experiment with new skills. You may need to use Help to complete the assignment.

Applying Conditional Formatting to Cells

Instructions: Start Excel. Open the workbook Extend 2-1 State Wildlife Department Employee Ratings. See the inside back cover of this book for instructions for downloading the Data Files for Students, or see your instructor for information on accessing the files required in this book. Perform the following tasks to apply three types of conditional formatting to cells in a worksheet:

1. Select the range C4:C18. Click the Conditional Formatting button (Home tab | Styles group) and then click New Rule in the Conditional Formatting list. Select 'Format only top or bottom ranked values' in the Select a Rule Type area (Conditional Formatting Rules Manager dialog box), as shown in Figure 2–75. Enter any value between 10 and 25 in the text box in the Edit the Rule Description (New Formatting Rule dialog box) area, and click the '% of the selected range' check box to select it. Click the Format button, and choose a blue background to assign this conditional format. Click the OK button in each dialog box and view the worksheet.

2. With range C4:C18 selected, apply a conditional format to the range that uses a green background color to highlight cells with scores that are below average.

3. With range D4:D18 selected, apply a conditional format to the range that uses an orange background to highlight cells that contain Exemplary or Exceeds Requirements.

4. With range B4:B18 selected, apply a conditional format to the range that uses a red background color to highlight cells with duplicate student names.

5. Change the document properties as specified by your instructor. Save the workbook using the file name, Extend 2-1 State Wildlife Department Employee Ratings Complete. Submit the revised workbook as specified by your instructor.

Figure 2–75

Make It Right

Analyze a workbook and correct all errors and/or improve the design.

Correcting Formatting, Functions, and Formulas in a Worksheet

Instructions: Start Excel. Open the workbook Make It Right 2-1 Dion Designwear Profit Analysis. See the inside back cover of this book for instructions for downloading the Data Files for Students, or see your instructor for information on accessing the files required for this book.

In this exercise you will learn how to correct formatting, functions, and formula problems in a worksheet (Figure 2–76).

Product	Desciption	Cost	Profit	Units Sold	Total Sales	Total Profit	% Profit
			Dion Designwear				
			Profit Anaylsis				
4835	Coat	$247.63	$144.83	95,159	$37,346,101.14	$13,781,877.97	36.903%
7563	Custom	210.08	142.18	75,762	26,687,922.12	10,771,841.16	40.362%
8191	Dress	186.53	99.48	69,297	19,819,634.97	6,893,665.56	34.782%
8409	Hat	146.82	59.97	39,164	8,098,723.56	2,348,665.08	29.000%
5677	Jacket	140.68	85.63	38,261	8,658,846.91	3,276,289.43	37.837%
8985	Shirt	68.38	8.15	42,420	3,246,402.60	345,723.00	10.649%
5871	Slacks	144.54	30.44	68,536	11,992,429.28	2,086,235.84	17.396%
7796	Sleepwear	93.74	11.80	77,413	8,170,168.02	913,473.40	11.181%
7777	Suit	305.91	126.00	19,999	8,637,768.09	2,519,874.00	29.173%
8178	Sweater	112.21	9.24	61,257	7,439,662.65	566,014.68	7.608%
Totals				**587,268**	**$140,097,659.34**	**$43,503,660.12**	**31.052%**
Lowest		$68.38	$8.15	19,999	$3,246,402.60	$345,723.00	7.608%
Highest		$305.91	$144.83	95,159	$37,346,101.14	$13,781,877.97	40.362%
Average		$156.54	$71.77	54,679	$14,009,765.93	$3,302,420.24	25.489%

Figure 2–76

Continued >

STUDENT ASSIGNMENTS

Make It Right *continued*

Perform the following tasks:

1. Add a thick box border around the title and subtitle so that they appear more separated from the rest of the worksheet.

2. Adjust the width of column D to 8.11 pixels so that the word in the column header does not wrap. Adjust the column widths of columns F and G to best fit.

3. Spell check the worksheet and correct any spelling mistakes that are found, but ignore any spelling mistakes found with the worksheet title and the product descriptions.

4. Center the values in the Product column.

5. The averages in several columns do not include the product in row 4. Adjust the functions in these cells so that all products are included in the calculation.

6. The total sales calculations should be:

   Total Sales = Units Sold * (Cost + Profit)

   Adjust the formulas in the range F4:F13 so that the correct formula is used.

7. The value for the lowest value in column E was entered as a number rather than as a function. Replace the value with the appropriate function.

8. The currency values in rows 4 and 14 should be formatted with the Accounting Number Format button (Home tab | Number group). They are currently formatted with the Currency format (floating dollar sign). The Accounting number format displays a fixed dollar sign.

9. Delete the function in the cell containing the average of % Profit because it is mathematically invalid.

10. Change the document properties as specified by your instructor. Save the workbook using the file name, Make It Right 2–1 Dion Designwear Profit Analysis Corrected. Submit the revised workbook as specified by your instructor.

In the Lab

Design and/or create a workbook using the guidelines, concepts, and skills presented in this chapter. Labs 1, 2, and 3 are listed in order of increasing difficulty.

Lab 1: Accounts Receivable Balance Worksheet

Problem: You are a part-time assistant in the accounting department at Aficionado Guitar Parts, a Chicago-based supplier of custom guitar parts. You have been asked to use Excel to generate a report that summarizes the monthly accounts receivable balance (Figure 2–77). A chart of the balances also is desired. The customer data in Table 2–6 is available for test purposes.

Table 2–6 Aficionado Guitar Parts Accounts Receivable Data				
Customer	**Beginning Balance**	**Credits**	**Payments**	**Purchases**
Cervantes, Katriel	803.01	56.92	277.02	207.94
Cummings, Trenton	285.05	87.41	182.11	218.22
Danielsson, Oliver	411.45	79.33	180.09	364.02
Kalinowski, Jadwiga	438.37	60.90	331.10	190.39
Lanctot, Royce	378.81	48.55	126.15	211.38
Raglow, Dora	710.99	55.62	231.37	274.71
Tuan, Lin	318.86	85.01	129.67	332.89

Instructions Part 1:   Create a worksheet similar to the one shown in Figure 2–77. Include the five columns of customer data in Table 2–6 in the report, plus two additional columns to compute a service charge and a new balance for each customer. Assume no negative unpaid monthly balances.

	A	B	C	D	E	F	G
1	**Aficionado Guitar Parts**						
2	**Monthy Accounts Receivable Balance Report**						
3	Customer	Beginning Balance	Credits	Payments	Purchases	Service Charge	New Balance
4	Cervantes, Katriel	$803.01	$56.92	$277.02	$207.94	$15.24	$692.25
5	Cummings, Trenton	285.05	87.41	182.11	218.22	0.50	234.25
6	Danielsson, Oliver	411.45	79.33	180.09	364.02	4.94	520.99
7	Kalinowski, Jadwiga	438.37	60.90	331.10	190.39	1.51	238.27
8	Lanctot, Royce	378.81	48.55	126.15	211.38	6.63	422.12
9	Raglow, Dora	710.99	55.62	231.37	274.71	13.78	712.49
10	Tuan, Lin	318.86	85.01	129.67	332.89	3.39	440.46
11	Totals	$3,346.54	$473.74	$1,457.51	$1,799.55	$46.00	$3,260.84
12	Highest	$803.01	$87.41	$331.10	$364.02	$15.24	$712.49
13	Lowest	$285.05	$48.55	$126.15	$190.39	$0.50	$234.25
14	Average	$478.08	$67.68	$208.22	$257.08	$6.57	$465.83
15							
16							

Figure 2–77

Perform the following tasks:

1. Enter and format the worksheet title **Aficionado Guitar Parts** and worksheet subtitle **Monthly Accounts Receivable Balance Report** in cells A1 and A2. Change the theme of the worksheet to the Trek theme. Apply the Title cell style to cells A1 and A2. Change the font size in cell A1 to 28 points. Merge and center the worksheet title and subtitle across columns A through G. Change the background color of cells A1 and A2 to the Red standard color. Change the font color of cells A1 and A2 to the White theme color. Draw a thick box border around the range A1:A2.

2. Change the width of column A to 20.00 points. Change the widths of columns B through G to 12.00 points. Change the heights of row 3 to 36.00 points and row 12 to 30.00 points.

3. Enter the column titles in row 3 and row titles in the range A11:A14, as shown in Figure 2–77. Center the column titles in the range A3:G3. Apply the Heading 3 cell style to the range A3:G3. Apply the Total cell style to the range A11:G11. Bold the titles in the range A12:A14. Change the font size in the range A3:G14 to 12 points.

4. Enter the data in Table 2–6 in the range A4:E10.

5. Use the following formulas to determine the service charge in column F and the new balance in column G for the first customer. Copy the two formulas down through the remaining customers.

   a. Service Charge (cell F4) = 3.25% * (Beginning Balance – Payments – Credits)

   b. New Balance (G4) = Beginning Balance + Purchases – Credits – Payments + Service Charge

6. Determine the totals in row 11.

7. Determine the maximum, minimum, and average values in cells B12:B14 for the range B4:B10, and then copy the range B12:B14 to C12:G14.

Continued >

In the Lab *continued*

8. Format the numbers as follows: (a) assign the Currency style with a floating dollar sign to the cells containing numeric data in the ranges B4:G4 and B11:G14, and (b) assign a number style with two decimal places and a thousand's separator (currency with no dollar sign) to the range B5:G10.

9. Use conditional formatting to change the formatting to white font on a red background in any cell in the range F4:F10 that contains a value greater than 10.

10. Change the worksheet name from Sheet1 to Accounts Receivable and the sheet tab color to the Red standard color. Change the document properties, as specified by your instructor. Change the worksheet header with your name, course number, and other information as specified by your instructor.

11. Spell check the worksheet. Preview and then print the worksheet in landscape orientation. Save the workbook using the file name, Lab 2-1 Part 1 Aficionado Guitar Parts Accounts Receivable Balance Report.

12. Print the range A3:D14. Print the formulas version on another page. Close the workbook without saving the changes. Submit the assignment as specified by your instructor.

Instructions Part 2: In this part of the exercise, you will create a 3-D Bar chart on a new worksheet in the workbook (Figure 2–78). If necessary, use Excel Help to obtain information on inserting a chart on a separate sheet in the workbook.

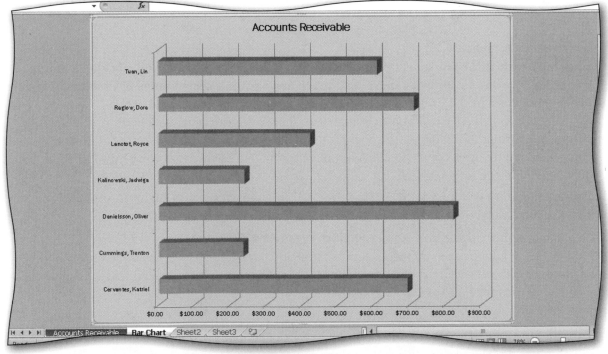

Figure 2–78

1. Open the workbook Lab 2-1 Part 1 Aficionado Guitar Parts Accounts Receivable Balance Report workbook created in Part 1. Save the workbook using the file name, Lab 2-1 Part 2 Aficionado Guitar Parts Accounts Receivable Balance Report.

2. Use the CTRL key and mouse to select the nonadjacent chart ranges A4:A10 and G4:G10. That is, select the range A4:A10 and while holding down the CTRL key, select the range G4:G10.

3. Click the Bar button (Insert tab | Charts group) and then select Clustered Bar in 3-D in the 3-D Bar area. When the chart is displayed on the worksheet, click the Move Chart button (Chart Tools Design tab | Location group). When the Move Chart dialog box appears, click New sheet and then type Bar Chart for the sheet name. Click the OK button (Move Chart dialog box). Change the sheet tab color to the Green standard color.

4. When the chart is displayed on the new worksheet, click the Series 1 series label and then press the DELETE key to delete it. Click the chart area, which is a blank area near the edge of the chart, click the Shape Fill button (Chart Tools Format tab | Shape Styles group), and then select Orange, Accent 1, Lighter 60% in the gallery (column 5, row 3). Click one of the bars in the chart. Click the Shape Fill button (Chart Tools Format tab | Shape Styles group) and then select the Green standard color. Click the Chart Title button (Chart Tools Layout tab | Labels group) and then select Above Chart in the Chart Title gallery. If necessary, use the scroll bar on the right side of the worksheet to scroll to the top of the chart. Click the edge of the chart title to select it and then type `Accounts Receivable` as the chart title.

5. Drag the Accounts Receivable tab at the bottom of the worksheet to the left of the Bar Chart tab to reorder the sheets in the workbook. Preview and print the chart.

6. Click the Accounts Receivable sheet tab. Change the following beginning balances: customer Oliver Danielsson to $702.13 and customer Lin Tuan to $482.74. The company also decided to change the service charge from 3.25% to 2.75% for all customers. After copying the adjusted formula in cell F4 to the range F5:F10, click the Auto Fill Options button and then click Fill without Formatting to maintain the original formatting in the range F5:F10. The total new balance in cell G11 should equal $3,720.82.

7. Select both sheets by holding down the SHIFT key and then clicking the Bar Chart tab. Preview and print the selected sheets. Save the workbook. Submit the assignment as specified by your instructor.

In the Lab

Lab 2: Sales Summary Worksheet

Problem: You have been asked to build a worksheet for a start-up company, Electry Auto, that analyzes the financing needs for the company's first six months in business. The company plans to begin operations in January with an initial investment of $500,000.00. The expected revenue and costs for the company's first six months are shown in Table 2–7. The desired worksheet is shown in Figure 2–79 on the following page. The initial investment is shown at the starting balance for January (cell B4). The amount of financing required by the company is shown as the lowest ending balance (cell F12).

Table 2–7 Electry Auto Start-Up Financing Needs Data

Month	Revenue	Costs
January	105000	220000
February	82000	260000
March	200000	255000
April	250000	320000
May	325000	420000
June	510000	540000

Continued >

In the Lab *continued*

Instructions Part 1: Perform the following tasks to build the worksheet shown in Figure 2–79.

	A	B	C	D	E	F
1			**Electry Auto**			
2			Start-Up Financing Needs			
3	**Month**	**Starting Balance**	**Revenue**	**Costs**	**Net Income**	**Ending Balance**
4	January	$ 500,000.00	$ 105,000.00	$ 220,000.00	$ (115,000.00)	$ 385,000.00
5	February	385,000.00	82,000.00	260,000.00	(178,000.00)	207,000.00
6	March	207,000.00	200,000.00	255,000.00	(55,000.00)	152,000.00
7	April	152,000.00	250,000.00	320,000.00	(70,000.00)	82,000.00
8	May	82,000.00	325,000.00	420,000.00	(95,000.00)	(13,000.00)
9	June	(13,000.00)	510,000.00	540,000.00	(30,000.00)	(43,000.00)
10	*Average*	$218,833.33	$245,333.33	$335,833.33	($90,500.00)	$128,333.33
11	*Highest*	$500,000.00	$510,000.00	$540,000.00	($30,000.00)	$385,000.00
12	*Lowest*	($13,000.00)	$82,000.00	$220,000.00	($178,000.00)	($43,000.00)
13						
14						
15						
16						
17						
18						

Figure 2–79

1. Start Excel. Apply the Concourse theme to a new workbook.

2. Increase the width of column A to 10.00 and the width of columns B through F to 14.00.

3. Enter the worksheet title `Electry Auto` in cell A1 and the worksheet subtitle `Start-Up Financing Needs` in cell A2. Enter the column titles in row 3, as shown in Figure 2–79. In row 3, use ALT+ENTER to start a new line in a cell.

4. Enter the start-up financing needs data described in Table 2–7 in columns A, C, and D in rows 4 through 9. Enter the initial starting balance (cell B4) of 500000.00. Enter the row titles in the range A10:A12, as shown in Figure 2–79.

5. For the months of February through March, the starting balance is equal to the previous month's ending balance. Obtain the starting balance for February by setting the starting balance of February to the ending balance of January. Use a cell reference rather than typing in the data. Copy the formula for February to the remaining months.

6. Obtain the net income amounts in column E by subtracting the costs in column D from the revenues in column C. Enter the formula in cell E4 and copy it to the range E5:E9. Obtain the ending balance amounts in column F by adding the starting balance in column B to the net income in column F. Enter the formula in cell F4 and copy it to the range F5:F9.

7. In the range B10:B12, use the AVERAGE, MAX, and MIN functions to determine the average value, highest value, and lowest value in the range B4:B9. Copy the range B10:B12 to the range C10:F12.

8. One at a time, merge and center the worksheet title and subtitle across columns A through F. Select cells A1 and A2 and change the background color to light blue (column 7 in the Standard Colors area in the Fill Color gallery). Apply the Title cell style to cells A1 and A2. Change the worksheet title in cell A1 to 28-point white (column 1, row 1 on the Font Color gallery). Change the worksheet subtitle to the same color. Assign a thick box border to the range A1:A2.

9. Center the titles in row 3, columns A through F. Apply the Heading 3 cell style to the range A3:F3. Use the Italic button (Home tab | Font group) to italicize the column titles in row 3 and the row titles in the range A10:A12.

10. Assign a thick box border to the range A10:F12. Change the background and font color for cell F12 to the same colors applied to the worksheet title in Step 8.

11. Change the row heights of row 3 to 36.00 points and row 10 to 30.00 points.

12. Assign the Accounting number format to the range B4:F4. Assign the Comma style format to the range B5:F9. Assign a Currency format with a floating dollar sign to the range B10:F12.

13. Rename the sheet tab as Start-Up Financing Needs. Apply the Light Blue color to the sheet tab. Change the document properties, as specified by your instructor. Change the worksheet header with your name, course number, and other information as specified by your instructor. Save the workbook using the file name Lab 2-1 Part 1 Electry Auto Start-Up Financing Needs. Print the entire worksheet in landscape orientation. Next, print only the range A3:B9.

14. Display the formulas version by pressing CTRL+ACCENT MARK (`). Print the formulas version using the Fit to option button in the Scaling area on the Page tab in the Page Setup dialog box. After printing the worksheet, reset the Scaling option by selecting the Adjust to option button on the Page tab in the Page Setup dialog box and changing the percent value to 100%. Change the display from the formulas version to the values version by pressing CTRL+ACCENT MARK (`). Do not save the workbook.

15. Submit the revised workbook as requested by your instructor.

Instructions Part 2:   In this part of the exercise, you will change the revenue amounts until the lowest ending balance is greater than zero, indicating that the company does not require financing in its first six months of operation. Open the workbook created in Part 1 and save the workbook as Lab 2-1 Part 2 Electry Auto Start-Up Financing Needs. Manually increment each of the six values in the revenue column by $1,000.00 until the lowest ending balance in cell F12 is greater than zero. The value of cell F12 should equal $5,000.00 All six values in column C must be incremented the same number of times. Update the worksheet header and save the workbook. Print the worksheet. Submit the assignment as specified by your instructor.

Instructions Part 3:   In this part of the exercise, you will change the monthly costs until the lowest ending balance is greater than zero, indicating that the company does not require financing in its first six months of operation. Open the workbook created in Part 1 and then save the workbook as Lab 2-1 Part 3 Electry Auto Start-Up Financing Needs. Manually decrement each of the six values in the costs column by $1,000.00 until the lowest ending balance in cell F12 is greater than zero. Decrement all six values in column C the same number of times. Your worksheet is correct when the lowest ending balance in cell F12 is $5,000.00. Update the worksheet header and save the workbook. Print the worksheet. Submit the assignment as specified by your instructor.

In the Lab

Lab 3: Stock Club Investment Analysis

Problem: Several years ago, you and a large group of friends started a stock club. Each year every member invests more money per month. You have decided to create a portfolio worksheet (Figure 2–80) that summarizes the club's current stock holdings so that you can share the information with your group of friends. The club's portfolio is summarized in Table 2–8. Table 2–8 also shows the general layout of the worksheet to be created.

A18

	A	B	C	D	E	F	G	H	I	J
1					Sock-It-Away Stock Club					
2					Summary of Investments					
3	Company	Stock Symbol	Purchase Date	Shares	Initial Price per Share	Initial Cost	Current Price per Share	Current Value	Gain/Loss	Percent Gain/Loss
4	Apple	AAPL	3/3/2007	250	$ 86.17	$ 21,542.50	$ 75.32	$ 18,830.00	$ (2,712.50)	-12.59%
5	Caterpillar	CAT	6/14/2008	200	81.74	16,348.00	69.02	13,804.00	(2,544.00)	-15.56%
6	Disney	DIS	10/11/2006	300	31.06	9,318.00	37.38	11,214.00	1,896.00	20.35%
7	General Electric	GE	3/4/2009	500	7.24	3,620.00	9.39	4,695.00	1,075.00	29.70%
8	MetLife	MET	1/15/2008	200	60.92	12,184.00	77.09	15,418.00	3,234.00	26.54%
9	Microsoft	MSFT	11/15/2006	500	29.20	14,600.00	36.30	18,150.00	3,550.00	24.32%
10	PepsiCo	PEP	2/15/2006	350	57.86	20,251.00	70.65	24,727.50	4,476.50	22.11%
11	Target	TGT	5/11/2004	450	44.11	19,849.50	44.02	19,809.00	(40.50)	-0.20%
12	Wal-Mart	WMT	4/14/2009	250	50.81	12,702.50	57.20	14,300.00	1,597.50	12.58%
13	Totals					$ 130,415.50		$ 140,947.50	$ 10,532.00	8.08%
14	Average			333.3333	$49.90	$14,490.61	$52.93	$15,660.83	$1,170.22	
15	Highest			500	$86.17	$21,542.50	$77.09	$24,727.50	$4,476.50	29.70%
16	Lowest			200	$7.24	$3,620.00	$9.39	$4,695.00	($2,712.50)	-15.56%
17										
18										
19										

Figure 2–80

Table 2–8 Sock-It-Away Stock Club

Company	Stock Symbol	Purchase Date	Shares	Initial Price per Share	Initial Cost	Current Price per Share	Current Value	Gain/ Loss	Percent Gain/ Loss
Apple	AAPL	3/3/2007	250	86.17	Formula A	75.32	Formula B	Formula C	Formula D
Caterpillar	CAT	6/14/2008	200	81.74		69.02			
Disney	DIS	10/11/2006	300	31.06		37.38			
General Electric	GE	3/4/2009	500	7.24		9.39			
MetLife	MET	1/15/2008	200	60.92		77.09			
Microsoft	MSFT	11/15/2006	500	29.20		36.30			
PepsiCo	PEP	2/15/2006	350	57.86		70.65			
Target	TGT	5/11/2004	450	44.11		44.02			
Wal-Mart	WMT	4/14/2009	250	50.81		57.20			
Totals			Formula E						
Average			Formula F						
Highest			Formula G						
Lowest			Formula H						

Instructions: Perform the following tasks:

1. Start Excel. Enter the worksheet titles Sock-It-Away Stock Club in cell A1 and Summary of Investments in cell A2.

2. Enter the column titles and data in Table 2–8 beginning in row 3.

3. Change the column widths and row heights as follows: column A — 11.78; column C — 10.00; columns E and G — 7.44; columns F, H, and I — 13.00; column J — 8.22; row 3 — 56.25 points; row 14 — 27.00 points.

4. Enter the following formulas in row 4 and then copy them down through row 12:

   a. Enter Formula A in cell F4: Initial Cost = Shares × Initial Price per Share

   b. Enter Formula B in cell H4: Current Value = Shares × Current Price Per Share

   c. Enter Formula C in cell I4: Gain/Loss = Current Value – Initial Cost

   d. Enter Formula D in cell J4: Percent Gain/Loss = Gain/Loss / Initial Cost

5. Compute the totals for initial cost, current value, gain/loss, and percent gain loss. For the percent gain/loss in cell J13, copy cell J12 to J13 using the fill handle.

6. In cells D14, D15, and D16, enter Formulas E, F, and G using the AVERAGE, MAX, and MIN functions. Copy the three functions across through the range J14: J16. Delete the invalid formula in cell J14.

7. Format the worksheet as follows:

   a. Apply the Trek theme to the worksheet.

   b. Format the worksheet title with Title cell style. Merge and center across columns A through J.

   c. Format the worksheet subtitle with Franklin Gothic Book font, 16 point font size, Black, Text 1 theme font color. Merge and Center across columns A through J.

   d. Format the worksheet title and subtitle background with Orange, Accent 1, Lighter 60% theme color and a thick box border.

   e. Format row 3 with the Heading 3 cell style and row 13 with the Total cell style.

   f. Format the data in rows 4 through 12: center data in column B; format dates in column C to the mm/dd/yy date format; range E4:I4 — Accounting number format style with fixed dollar sign; range E5:I12 — Comma style; range J4:J13 — Percent style with two decimal places; cells F13, H13, and I13 — Accounting Number format with fixed dollar sign.

   g. Format E14:I16 — Currency format with floating decimal places; J15:J16 — Percent style with two decimal places.

   h. Format J4:J12 — apply conditional formatting so that if a cell in range is less than 0, then cell appears with a pink background color.

8. Spell check the worksheet. Change the name of the sheet tab to Summary of Investments and apply the Orange, Accent 1, Darker 25% theme color to the sheet tab. Update the document properties, and save the workbook using the file name, Lab 2-3 Sock-It-Away Stock Club Summary of Investments. Print the worksheet in landscape orientation. Print the formulas version on one page. Close the workbook without saving changes. Submit the assignment as specified by your instructor.

Cases and Places

Apply your creative thinking and problem-solving skills to design and implement a solution.

1: Analyzing Emergency Student Loans

Academic

The Student Assistance office at your school provides emergency loans at simple interest. The data obtained from six types of loans and the desired report format are shown in Table 2–9. The required formulas are shown in Table 2–10. Use the concepts and techniques presented in this chapter to create and format the worksheet. Include total, average, maximum, and minimum values for Principal, Interest, and Amount Due.

Table 2–9 Emergency Student Loan Data and Worksheet Layout			
Loan Type	Principal	Rate	Time in Years
Academic Supplies	$40,000	7.5%	.4
Medical Emergency	$25,500	12%	.33
Personal Emergency	$12,750	8.25%	.5
Room and Board	$27,000	6.5%	1
Travel Expenses	$4,550	12%	.5
Tuition Reimbursement	$107,000	6%	1

Table 2–10 Emergency Student Loan Formulas
Interest = Principal × Rate × Time
Amount Due = Principal + Interest
Average = AVERAGE function
Minimum = MIN function
Maximum = MAX function

2: Analyzing Energy Consumption

Personal

Your parents believe that your late night studying sessions and household appliance usage contribute to excessive electricity bills. You have decided to try to prove them wrong by analyzing your daily and monthly electricity consumption. You research the energy consumption of your personal items and appliance usage to obtain consumption costs per hour for each item. Table 2–11 contains the data and format for the report you want to create.

Use the concepts and techniques presented in this project to create and format the worksheet. Include an embedded 3-D Pie chart that shows the cost per month. Use Microsoft Excel Help to create a professional looking 3-D Pie chart with title and data labels.

Table 2–11 Appliance Electricity Usage Costs

Appliance	Cost per Hour	Hours Used Daily	Total Cost Per Day	Total Cost per Month (30 Days)
Clothes dryer	$0.325	1		
Computer	$0.02	6		
DVD player	$0.035	1		
Light bulbs	$0.043	8		
Refrigerator	$0.035	24		
Stereo	$0.02	5		
Television	$0.04	4		
Washing machine	$0.03	2		

3: Analyzing Profit Potential

Professional

You work for HumiCorp, an online retailer of home humidifiers. Your manager wants to know the profit potential of their inventory based on the items in inventory listed in Table 2–12. Table 2–12 contains the format of the desired report. The required formulas are shown in Table 2–13. Use the concepts and techniques developed in this chapter to create and format the worksheet. The company just received 67 additional desk-sized humidifiers and shipped out 48 room-sized humidifiers. Update the appropriate cells to reflect the change in inventory.

Table 2–12 HumiCorp Inventory Profit Potential Data and Worksheet Layout

Item	Units on Hand	Unit Cost	Total Cost	Unit Price	Total Value	Potential Profit
Desk	187	27.58	Formula A	Formula B	Formula C	Formula D
Filtered home-sized	42	324.14				
Filtered room-sized	118	86.55				
Home-sized	103	253.91				
Room-sized	97	53.69				
Total	—	—	—	—	—	—
Average	Formula E					
Lowest	Formula F					
Highest	Formula G					

Table 2–13 HumiCorp Inventory Profit Potential Formulas

Formula A = Units on Hand × Unit Cost
Formula B = Unit Cost × (1 / (1 − .66))
Formula C = Units on Hand × Unit Price
Formula D = Total Value − Total Cost
Formula E = AVERAGE function
Formula F = MIN function
Formula G = MAX function

3 | What-If Analysis, Charting, and Working with Large Worksheets

Objectives

You will have mastered the material in this chapter when you can:

- Rotate text in a cell
- Create a series of month names
- Copy, paste, insert, and delete cells
- Format numbers using format symbols
- Freeze and unfreeze rows and columns
- Show and format the system date
- Use absolute and mixed cell references in a formula
- Use the IF function to perform a logical test

- Create Sparkline charts
- Use the Format Painter button to format cells
- Create a 3-D Pie chart on a separate chart sheet
- Rearrange worksheet tabs
- Change the worksheet view
- Answer what-if questions
- Goal seek to answer what-if questions

3 | What-If Analysis, Charting, and Working with Large Worksheets

Introduction

Worksheets normally are much larger than those created in the previous chapters, often extending beyond the size of the Excel window. Because you cannot see the entire worksheet on the screen at one time, working with a large worksheet sometimes can be frustrating. This chapter introduces several Excel commands that allow you to control what is displayed on the screen so that you can view critical parts of a large worksheet at one time. One command allows you to freeze rows and columns so that Excel always displays them on the screen. Another command splits the worksheet into separate windowpanes so that you can view different parts of a worksheet on the screen at one time.

When you set up a worksheet, you should use cell references in formulas whenever possible, rather than constant values. The use of a cell reference allows you to change a value in multiple formulas by changing the value in a single cell. The cell references in a formula are called assumptions. Assumptions are values in cells that you can change to determine new values for formulas. This chapter emphasizes the use of assumptions and shows how to use Excel to answer what-if questions, such as what happens to the six-month operating income if you decrease the marketing expenses assumption by 3 percent? Being able to analyze quickly the effect of changing values in a worksheet is an important skill in making business decisions.

This chapter also introduces you to techniques that will enhance your ability to create worksheets and draw charts. From your work in Chapter 1, you are aware of how easily you can create charts. This chapter covers additional charting techniques that allow you to convey a message in a dramatic pictorial fashion, such as Sparkline charts and an exploded 3-D pie chart. This chapter also covers other methods for entering values in cells, such as allowing Excel to enter values for you based on a pattern of values that you create, and formatting these values. In addition, you will learn how to use absolute cell references and how to use the IF function to assign a value to a cell based on a logical test.

Project — Financial Projection Worksheet with What-If Analysis and Chart

The project in the chapter follows proper design guidelines and uses Excel to create the worksheet and pie chart shown in Figures 3–1a and 3–1b. Modern Music Shops operates several stores that sell and service musical instruments. Each June and December, the director of finance and accounting submits a plan to the management team to show projected monthly sales revenues, costs of goods sold, gross margin, expenses, and operating income for the next six months. The director requires an easy-to-read worksheet that shows financial projections for the next six months. The worksheet should allow for quick analysis if projections for certain numbers change, such as the percentage of expenses allocated to marketing. In addition, a 3-D pie chart is required that shows the projected operating income contribution for each of the six months.

Figure 3–1 (a) Worksheet

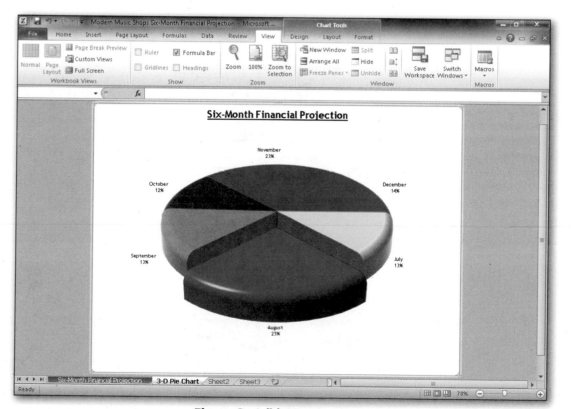

Figure 3–1 (b) 3-D Pie Chart

The requirements document for the Modern Music Shops Six-Month Financial Projection worksheet is shown in Figure 3–2. It includes the needs, source of data, summary of calculations, chart requirements, and other facts about its development.

REQUEST FOR NEW WORKBOOK

Date Submitted:	April 9, 2012
Submitted By:	Marcus Olek
Worksheet Title:	Modern Music Shops' Six-Month Financial Projection
Needs:	The needs are: (1) a worksheet (Figure 3-3a on page EX 142) that shows Modern Music Shops' projected monthly sales, cost of goods sold, gross margin, expenses, and operating income for a six-month period; and (2) a 3-D Pie chart (Figure 3-3b on page EX 142) that shows the projected contribution of each month's operating income to the six-month period operating income.
Source of Data:	The data supplied by the Finance department includes projections of the monthly sales and expenses (Table 3-1 on page EX 143) that are based on prior years. All the remaining numbers in the worksheet are determined from these 13 numbers using formulas.
Calculations:	The following calculations must be made for each month: 1. Cost of Goods Sold = Revenue – Revenue × Margin 2. Gross Margin = Revenue – Cost of Goods Sold 3. Bonus Expense = $200,000.00 if the Revenue exceeds the Revenue for Bonus; otherwise Bonus Expense = 0 4. Commission Expense = Commission Assumption × Revenue 5. Marketing Expense = Marketing Assumption × Revenue 6. Research and Development = Research and Development Assumption × Revenue 7. Support, General, and Administrative Expense = Support, General, and Administrative Assumption × Revenue 8. Total Expenses = Sum of Expenses 9. Operating Income = Gross Margin – Total Expenses
Chart Requirements:	Show Sparkline charts for Revenue and each of the items noted in the calculations area above. A 3-D Pie chart is required on a separate sheet (Figure 3-3b) to show the contribution of each month's operating income to the six-month period operating income. The chart should also emphasize the month with the greatest operating income.

Approvals

Approval Status:	X	Approved
		Rejected
Approved By:		Farah Qadir, CFO
Date:		April 16, 2012
Assigned To:		J. Quasney, Spreadsheet Specialist

Figure 3–2

Overview

As you read this chapter, you will learn how to create the worksheet shown in Figure 3–1 by performing these general tasks:

- Create a series of month names
- Use absolute cell references in a formula
- Use the IF function to perform a logical test
- Create Sparkline charts in a range of cells
- Use the Format Painter button to format cells
- Create a 3-D pie chart on a separate chart sheet
- Answer what-if questions
- Manipulate large worksheets

BTW

Excel's Usefulness
Just a short time ago, a what-if question of any complexity could be answered only by using a large, expensive computer programmed by highly paid computer professionals, and generating a result could take days. Excel gives the noncomputer professional the ability to get complex business-related questions answered instantaneously and economically.

Plan Ahead

General Project Decisions

While creating an Excel worksheet, you need to make several decisions that will determine the appearance and characteristics of the finished worksheet. As you create the worksheet required to meet the requirements shown in Figure 3–2, you should follow these general guidelines:

1. **Plan the layout of the worksheet.** Worksheets that include financial data associated with time frames typically include dates, such as months, quarters, or years, as column headers. What-if assumptions should not clutter the worksheet, but placing them in an easily located portion of the worksheet allows for quicker creation of new projections.

2. **Determine the necessary formulas and functions needed.** Often, financial calculations rely on strict definitions and commonly accepted formulas for performing the calculations. Look for such situations and always use the accepted formulas. When using a what-if section on a worksheet, make certain to create formulas that use the what-if criteria. When a requirement necessitates a calculation only under a certain condition, a function can check for the condition and make the calculation when necessary.

3. **Specify how to best utilize Sparkline charts.** Sparkline charts allow worksheet users quickly to visualize information in a small chart within a cell. The use of multiple Sparkline charts in the worksheet will provide the user with a visual comparison of the various data items for each month. The user, therefore, can see trends for each line item over time and also compare relationships among various line items.

4. **Identify how to format various elements of the worksheet.** Format separate parts of a worksheet, such as what-if assumptions, in a manner that indicates that they are separate from the main area of the worksheet. Other financial items, such as sales revenue and expenses, are distinct categories of financial data and should be separated visually. Totals and subtotals should stand out to draw the reader's attention.

5. **Specify how charts should convey necessary information.** As you have learned, different chart types convey different messages and are appropriate in different situations. For example, a 3-D pie chart is a good way to compare visually a small set of numbers. Often one or two slices of a pie chart displays as exploded, meaning that the slice appears pulled away from the cart, in order to emphasize the slice to the user. Format chart data points so that the worksheet user's eye is drawn to important information.

6. **Perform what-if analysis and goal seeking using the best techniques.** What-if analysis allows you quickly to answer questions regarding various predictions. A what-if area of a worksheet allows users of the worksheet efficiently to ask questions. Goal seeking allows you automatically to modify values in a what-if area of a worksheet based on a goal that you have for another cell in the worksheet.

When necessary, more specific details concerning the above guidelines are presented at appropriate points in the chapter. The chapter also will identify the actions you perform and decisions made regarding these guidelines during the creation of the worksheet shown in Figure 3–1 on page EX 139.

Using a sketch of the worksheet can help you visualize its design. The sketch of the worksheet consists of titles, column and row headings, location of data values, calculations, and a rough idea of the desired formatting (Figure 3–3a). The sketch of the 3-D pie chart shows the expected contribution of each month's operating income to the six-month operating income (Figure 3–3b). The assumptions will be entered at the top of the worksheet (Figure 3–3a). The projected monthly sales revenue will be entered in row 13 of the worksheet. The projected monthly sales revenue and the assumptions shown in Table 3–1 will be used to calculate the remaining numbers in the worksheet.

Figure 3–3 (a) Worksheet Sketch

Figure 3–3 (b) 3-D Pie Chart Sketch

With a solid understanding of the requirements document, an understanding of the necessary decisions, and a sketch of the worksheet, the next step is to use Excel to create the worksheet.

Table 3–1 Modern Music Shops Six-Month Financial Projections Data and What-If Assumptions	
Projected Monthly Total Sales Revenues	
July	$3,113,612.16
August	7,962,235.53
September	5,112,268.58
October	2,924,627.87
November	7,630,534.65
December	3,424,270.23
What-If Assumptions	
Bonus	$200,000.00
Commission	5.75%
Margin	57.50%
Marketing	15.00%
Research and Development	7.50%
Sales Revenue for Bonus	$3,500,000.00
Support, General, and Administrative	18.75%

To Start Excel

If you are using a computer to step through the project in this chapter and you want your screens to match the figures in this book, you should change your screen's resolution to 1024 × 768. For information about how to change a computer's resolution, refer to the Introduction to Office 2010 and Windows 7 chapter at the beginning of this book.

The following steps, which assume Windows 7 is running, start Excel based on a typical installation. You may need to ask your instructor how to start Excel for your computer. For a detailed example of the procedure summarized below, refer to the Office 2010 and Windows 7 chapter at the beginning of this book.

1 Click the Start button on the Windows 7 taskbar to display the Start menu.

2 Type **Microsoft Excel** as the search text in the 'Search programs and files' text box, and watch the search results appear on the Start menu.

3 Click Microsoft Excel 2010 in the search results on the Start menu to start Excel and display a new blank workbook in the Excel window.

4 If the Excel window is not maximized, click the Maximize button next to the Close button on its title bar to maximize the window.

For an introduction to Windows 7 and instruction about how to perform basic Windows 7 tasks, read the Office 2010 and Windows 7 chapter at the beginning of this book, where you can learn how to resize windows, change screen resolution, create folders, move and rename files, use Windows Help, and much more.

BTW

For an introduction to Office 2010 and instruction about how to perform basic tasks in Office 2010 programs, read the Office 2010 and Windows 7 chapter at the beginning of this book, where you can learn how to start a program, use the Ribbon, save a file, open a file, quit a program, use Help, and much more.

To Enter the Worksheet Titles, Change Document Properties, Apply a Theme, and Save the Workbook

The worksheet contains two titles, initially in cells A8 and A9. In the previous chapters, titles were centered across the worksheet. With large worksheets that extend beyond the size of a window, it is best to enter titles left-aligned as shown in the sketch of the worksheet in Figure 3–3a because the worksheet prints with the title on the first page if the worksheet requires multiple pages, and the user more easily finds the worksheet title when necessary. The following steps enter the worksheet titles, change the workbook theme to Opulent, change document properties, and then save the workbook.

1 Select cell A8 and then type `Modern Music Shops` as the worksheet title.

2 Select cell A9 and then type `Six-Month Financial Projection` as the worksheet subtitle and then press the ENTER key to enter the worksheet subtitle.

3 Change the document properties as specified by your instructor.

4 Apply the Opulent theme to the workbook.

5 With a USB flash drive connected to one of the computer's USB ports, click the Save button on the Quick Access Toolbar to display the Save As dialog box.

6 Type `Modern Music Shops Six-Month Financial Projection` in the File name text box to change the file name. Do not press the ENTER key after typing the file name because you do not want to close the dialog box at this time.

7 Navigate to the desired save location (in this case, the Excel folder in the CIS 101 folder [or your class folder] on the USB flash drive).

8 Click the Save button (Save As dialog box) to save the document in the selected folder on the selected drive with the entered file name.

BTW

The Ribbon and Screen Resolution
Excel may change how the groups and buttons within the groups appear on the Ribbon, depending on the computer's screen resolution. Thus, your Ribbon may look different from the ones in this book if you are using a screen resolution other than 1024 x 768.

Rotating Text and Using the Fill Handle to Create a Series

The data on the worksheet, including month names and the What-If Assumptions section, now can be added to the worksheet.

BTW

BTWs
For a complete list of the BTWs found in the margins of this book, visit the Excel 2010 BTW Web page (scsite.com/ex2010/btw).

Plan Ahead

> **Plan the layout of the worksheet.**
> Excel allows you to rotate text in a cell. Rotated text often provides a strong visual appeal. Rotated text also allows you to fit more text into a smaller column width. Chapters 1 and 2 used the fill handle to copy a cell or a range of cells to adjacent cells. The fill handle also allows creation of a series of numbers, dates, or month names automatically. Using the fill handle in this way eliminates the need to type in such data, saving time and eliminating typographical errors.

To Rotate Text and Use the Fill Handle to Create a Series of Month Names

The design of the worksheet calls specifically for only six months of data. Because there always will be only six months of data in the worksheet, the months should be placed across the top of the worksheet as column headings rather than as row headings. The data for the worksheet includes more data items regarding each month than there are months, and, possibly, more expense categories could be added in the future. A proper layout, therefore, includes placing each month as column headings.

When you first enter text, its angle is zero degrees (0°), and it reads from left to right in a cell. Excel allows you to rotate text in a cell counterclockwise by entering a number between 1° and 90°.

The following steps enter the month name, July, in cell B10; format cell B10 (including rotating the text); and then use the fill handle to enter the remaining month names in the range C10:G10.

1

- If necessary, select the Home tab and then select cell B10 because this cell will include the first month name in the series of month names.

- Type **July** as the cell entry and then click the Enter box.

- Click the Format Cells: Alignment Dialog Box Launcher (Home tab | Alignment group) to display the Format Cells dialog box (Figure 3–4).

Figure 3–4

2

- Click the 45° point in the Orientation area (Format Cells dialog box) to move the Text hand in the Orientation area to the 45° point and to display a new orientation in the Degrees box (Figure 3–5).

Figure 3–5

3

- Click the OK button to rotate the text in the active cell and automatically increase the height of the current row to best fit the rotated text.

- Point to the fill handle on the lower-right corner of cell B10 to display the crosshair mouse pointer in preparation of filling the month series (Figure 3–6).

Figure 3–6

4

- Drag the fill handle to the right to select the range to fill, C10:G10 in this case. Do not release the mouse button (Figure 3–7).

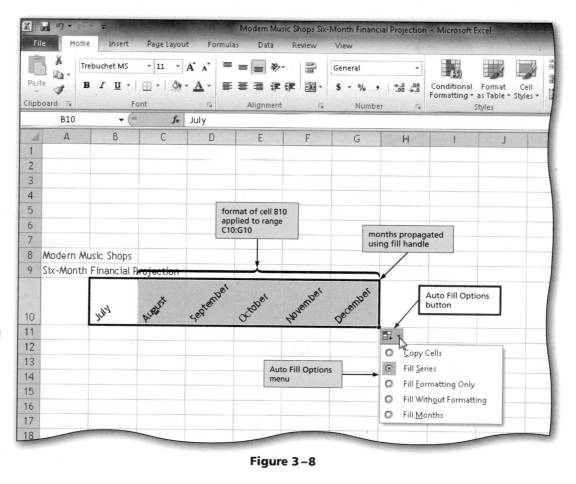

Figure 3–7

5

- Release the mouse button to create a month name series in the selected range and copy the format of the selected cell to the selected range.

- Click the Auto Fill Options button below the lower-right corner of the fill area to display the Auto Fill Options menu (Figure 3–8).

Q&A

What if I do not want to copy the format of cell B10 during the auto fill operation?

In addition to creating a series of values, dragging the fill handle instructs Excel to copy the format of cell B10 to the range C10:G10. With some fill operations, you may not want to copy the formats of the source cell or range to the destination cell or range. If this is the case, click the Auto Fill Options button after the range fills and then select the option you desire on the Auto Fill Options menu (Figure 3–8).

Figure 3–8

6
- Click the Auto Fill Options button to hide the Auto Fill Options menu.

- Select cell H10, type `Total,` and then press the RIGHT ARROW key to enter a column heading.

- Type Chart in cell I10 and then press the RIGHT ARROW key to enter a column heading.

Q&A

Why is the word Total automatically formatted with a 45° rotation?

Excel tries to save you time by automatically recognizing the adjacent cell format in cell G10 and applying it to cell H10. Such behavior also occurs when typing the column heading in cell I10.

Other Ways

1. Enter start month in cell, apply formatting, right-drag fill handle in direction to fill, click Fill Months on shortcut menu

2. Enter start month in cell, apply formatting, select range, click Fill button (Home tab | Editing group), click Series, click AutoFill

---

Using the Auto Fill Options Menu

As shown in Figure 3–8 on the previous page, Fill Series is the default option that Excel uses to fill an area, which means it fills the destination area with a series, using the same formatting as the source area. If you choose another option on the Auto Fill Options menu, then Excel immediately changes the contents of the destination range. Following the use of the fill handle, the Auto Fill Options button remains active until you begin the next Excel operation. Table 3–2 summarizes the options on the Auto Fill Options menu.

Table 3–2 Options Available on the Auto Fill Options Menu	
Auto Fill Option	**Description**
Copy Cells	Fill destination area with contents using format of source area. Do not create a series.
Fill Series	Fill destination area with series using format of source area. This option is the default.
Fill Formatting Only	Fill destination area using format of source area. No content is copied unless fill is series.
Fill Without Formatting	Fill destination area with contents, without the formatting of source area.
Fill Months	Fill destination area with series of months using format of source area. Same as Fill Series and shows as an option only if source area contains a month.

You can use the fill handle to create a series longer than the one shown in Figure 3–8. If you drag the fill handle past cell G10 in Step 4, Excel continues to increment the months and logically will repeat July, August, and so on, if you extend the range far enough to the right.

You can create several different types of series using the fill handle. Table 3–3 illustrates several examples. Notice in examples 4 through 7, 9, and 11 that, if you use the fill handle to create a series of numbers or nonsequential months, you must enter the first item in the series in one cell and the second item in the series in an adjacent cell. Excel still creates the series, however, if the first two items are in a range and the cells between the items are empty. Next, select both cells and drag the fill handle through the destination area.

Table 3–3 Examples of Series Using the Fill Handle

Example	Contents of Cell(s) Copied Using the Fill Handle	Next Three Values of Extended Series
1	4:00	5:00, 6:00, 7:00
2	Qtr2	Qtr3, Qtr4, Qtr1
3	Quarter 1	Quarter 2, Quarter 3, Quarter 4
4	22-Jul, 22-Sep	22-Nov, 22-Jan, 22-Mar
5	2012, 2013	2014, 2015, 2016
6	1, 2	3, 4, 5
7	625, 600	575, 550, 525
8	Mon	Tue, Wed, Thu
9	Sunday, Tuesday	Thursday, Saturday, Monday
10	4th Section	5th Section, 6th Section, 7th Section
11	−205, −208	−211, −214, −217

BTW

Custom Fill Sequences
You can create your own custom lists for use with the fill handle. For example, if you often type in the same list of products or names into Excel, you can create a custom fill sequence. You then can type the first product or name and then use the fill handle automatically to fill in the remaining products or names. To create a custom fill sequence, open the Excel Options dialog box by clicking the Options button in the Backstage view. Click the Advanced tab (Excel Options dialog box) and then click the Edit Custom Lists button (Excel Options dialog box).

To Increase Column Widths

In Chapter 2, you increased column widths after the values were entered into the worksheet. Sometimes, you may want to increase the column widths before you enter the values and, if necessary, adjust them later. The following steps increase the column widths.

1

- Move the mouse pointer to the boundary between column heading A and column heading B so that the mouse pointer changes to a split double arrow in preparation of adjusting the column widths.

- Drag the mouse pointer to the right until the ScreenTip displays the desired column width, Width: 36.00 (293 pixels) in this case. Do not release the mouse button (Figure 3–9).

Figure 3–9

2

- Release the mouse button to change the width of the column.

- Click column heading B to select the column and then drag through column heading G to select the range in which to change the widths.

- Move the mouse pointer to the boundary between column headings B and C in preparation of resizing column B, and then drag the mouse to the right until the ScreenTip displays the desired width, Width: 14.88 (124 pixels) in this case. Do not release the mouse button (Figure 3–10).

Figure 3–10

3

- Release the mouse button to change the width of the selected columns.

- If necessary, scroll the worksheet so that column H is visible and then use the technique described in Step 1 to increase the width of column H to 16.00.

To Enter Row Titles

Excel allows you to indent text in cells. Often, indentation sets off titles, such as row titles, from other titles to create a hierarchy, such as you may find in a table of contents in a book. The following steps enter the row titles in column A and indent several of the row titles.

1

- If necessary, scroll the worksheet so that column A and row 23 are visible and then enter the row titles in the range A11:A23 but without the indents (Figure 3–11).

- Select cell A12 and then click the Increase Indent button (Home tab | Alignment group) to increase the indentation of the text in the selected cell.

- Select the range A16:A20 and then click the Increase Indent button (Home tab | Alignment group) to increase the indentation of the text in the selected range (Figure 3–11).

Figure 3–11

2

- Select cell A1 to finish entering the row titles and deselect the current cell.

Q&A

What happens when I click the Increase Indent button?

The Increase Indent button (Home tab | Alignment group) indents the contents of a cell to the right by three spaces each time you click it. The Decrease Indent button decreases the indent by three spaces each time you click it.

Other Ways

1. To indent, right-click range, click Format Cells on shortcut menu, click Alignment tab (Format Cells dialog box), click Left (Indent) in Horizontal list, type number of spaces to indent in Indent text box, click OK button (Format Cells dialog box)

Copying a Range of Cells to a Nonadjacent Destination Area

The What-If Assumptions section should be placed in an area of the worksheet that is accessible easily yet does not impair the view of the main section of the worksheet. As shown in Figure 3–3a on page EX 142, the What-If Assumptions should be placed above the calculations in the worksheet. Additionally, the row titles in the Expenses area are the same as the row titles in the What-If Assumptions table, with the exception of the two additional entries in cells A4 (Margin) and A7 (Sales Revenue for Bonus). Hence, the What-If Assumptions table row titles can be created by copying the range A16:A20 to the range A2:A6 and then inserting two rows for the additional entries in cells A4 and A7. The source area (range A16:A20) is not adjacent to the destination area (range A2:A6). The first two chapters used the fill handle to copy a source area to an adjacent destination area. To copy a source area to a nonadjacent destination area, however, you cannot use the fill handle.

A more versatile method of copying a source area is to use the Copy button and Paste button (Home tab | Clipboard group). You can use these two buttons to copy a source area to an adjacent or nonadjacent destination area.

BTW

Fitting Entries in a Cell
An alternative to increasing column widths or row heights is to shrink the characters in a cell to fit the current width of the column. To shrink to fit, click Format Cells: Alignment Dialog Box Button Launcher (Home tab | Alignment group), and click Shrink to fit in the Text control area. After shrinking entries to fit in cells, consider using the Zoom slider on the status bar to make the entries more readable.

To Copy a Range of Cells to a Nonadjacent Destination Area

The Copy button copies the contents and format of the source area to the **Office Clipboard**, a reserved place in the computer's memory that allows you to collect text and graphics from an Office document and then paste them into almost any other type of document. The Paste button copies the item from the Office Clipboard to the destination area.

The following steps enter the what-if area row heading and use the Copy and Paste buttons to copy the range A16:A20 to the nonadjacent range A2:A6.

1

- With cell A1 selected, type **What-If Assumptions** as the new row title.

- Select the range A16:A20 and then click the Copy button (Home tab | Clipboard group) to copy the values and formats of the selected range, A16:A20 in this case, to the Office Clipboard.

- Select cell A2, the top cell in the destination area (Figure 3–12).

Q&A

Why do I not need to select the entire destination area?

You are not required to select the entire destination area (range A2:A6) before clicking the Paste button (Home tab | Clipboard group). Excel needs to know only the upper-left cell of the destination area. In the case of a single column range, such as A2:A6, the top cell of the destination area (cell A2) also is the upper-left cell of the destination area.

Figure 3–12

2

- Click the Paste button (Home tab | Clipboard group) to copy the values and formats of the last item placed on the Office Clipboard, range A16:A20 in this case, to the destination area, A2:A6 in this case (Figure 3–13).

Q&A

What if data already existed in the destination area?

When you complete a copy, the values and formats in the destination area are replaced with the values and formats of the source area. Any data contained in the destination area prior to the copy and paste is lost. If you accidentally delete valuable data, immediately click the Undo button on the Quick Access Toolbar.

3

- Press the ESC key to remove the marquee from the source area and disable the Paste button (Home tab | Clipboard group).

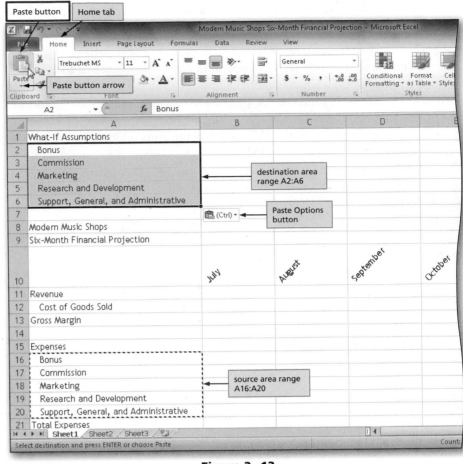

Figure 3–13

Other Ways

1. Right-click source area, click Copy on shortcut menu, right-click destination area, click Paste icon on shortcut menu

2. Select source area and point on border of range; while holding down CTRL key, drag source area to destination area

3. Select source area, press CTRL+C, select destination area, press CTRL+V

BTW

Q&As
For a complete list of the Q&As found in many of the step-by-step sequences in this book, visit the Excel 2010 Q&A Web page (scsite.com/ex2010/qa).

Using the Paste Options Menu

After you click the Paste button, Excel immediately displays the Paste Options button, as shown in Figure 3–13. If you click the Paste Options button arrow and select an option on the Paste Options gallery, Excel modifies the most recent paste operation based on your selection. Table 3–4 summarizes the options available on the Paste Options gallery. When the Paste Options button is visible, you can use shortcut keys to access the paste commands available in the Paste Options gallery. Additionally, you can use combinations of the options in the Paste Options gallery to customize your paste operation. That is, after clicking one of the icons in the Paste Options gallery, you can open the gallery again to further adjust your paste operation. The Paste button (Home tab | Clipboard group) includes an arrow that, when clicked, displays the same options as does the Paste Options button arrow.

Table 3–4 Options Available in the Paste Options Gallery			
Paste Option Icon	Paste Option	Shortcut Key	Description
	Paste	CTRL+P	Copy contents and format of source area. This option is the default.
	Formulas	CTRL+F	Copy formulas from the source area, but not the contents and format.
	Formulas & Number Formatting	CTRL+O	Copy formulas and format for numbers and formulas of source area, but not the contents.
	Keep Source Formatting	CTRL+K	Copy contents, format, and styles of source area.
	No Borders	CTRL+B	Copy contents and format of source area, but not any borders.
	Keep Source Column Widths	CTRL+W	Copy contents and format of source area. Change destination column widths to source column widths.
	Transpose	CTRL+T	Copy the contents and format of the source area, but transpose, or swap, the rows and columns.
	Values	CTRL+V	Copy contents of source area, but not the formatting for formulas.
	Values & Number Formatting	CTRL+A	Copy contents and format of source area for numbers or formulas, but use format of destination area for text.
	Values & Source Formatting	CTRL+E	Copy contents and formatting of source area, but not the formula.
	Formatting	CTRL+R	Copy format of source area, but not the contents.
	Paste Link	CTRL+N	Copy contents and format and link cells so that a change to the cells in source area updates the corresponding cells in destination area.
	Picture	CTRL+U	Copy an image of the source area as a picture.
	Linked Pictures	CTRL+I	Copy an image of the source area as a picture so that a change to the cells in source area updates the picture in destination area.

An alternative to clicking the Paste button is to press the ENTER key. The ENTER key completes the paste operation, removes the marquee from the source area, and disables the Paste button so that you cannot paste the copied source area to other destination areas. The ENTER key was not used in the previous set of steps so that the capabilities of the Paste Options button could be discussed. The Paste Options button does not appear on the screen when you use the ENTER key to complete the paste operation.

Using Drag and Drop to Move or Copy Cells

You also can use the mouse to move or copy cells. First, you select the source area and point to the border of the cell or range. You know you are pointing to the border of the cell or range when the mouse pointer changes to a block arrow. To move the selected cell or cells, drag the selection to the destination area. To copy a selection, hold down the CTRL key while dragging the selection to the destination area. You know Excel is in copy mode when a small plus sign appears next to the block arrow mouse pointer. Be sure to release the mouse button before you release the CTRL key. Using the mouse to move or copy cells is called **drag and drop**.

BTW

Cutting

When you cut a cell or range of cells using the Cut command on a shortcut menu or Cut button (Home tab | Clipboard group), Excel copies the cells to the Office Clipboard, but does not remove the cells from the source area until you paste the cells in the destination area by either clicking the Paste button (Home tab | Clipboard group) or pressing the ENTER key. When you complete the paste, Excel clears the cell's or range of cell's entries and their formats from the source area.

Using Cut and Paste to Move Cells

Another way to move cells is to select them, click the Cut button (Home tab | Clipboard group) (Figure 3–12 on page EX 151) to remove them from the worksheet and copy them to the Office Clipboard, select the destination area, and then click the Paste button (Home tab | Clipboard group) or press the ENTER key. You also can use the Cut command on the shortcut menu, instead of the Cut button.

Inserting and Deleting Cells in a Worksheet

At any time while the worksheet is on the screen, you can insert cells to enter new data or delete cells to remove unwanted data. You can insert or delete individual cells; a range of cells, rows, columns; or entire worksheets.

To Insert a Row

According to the sketch of the worksheet in Figure 3–3a on page EX 142, two rows must be inserted in the What-If Assumptions table, one between Commission and Marketing for the Margin assumption and another between Research and Development and Support, General, and Administrative for the Sales Revenue for Bonus assumption. The following steps insert the new rows into the worksheet.

1

- Right-click row heading 4, the row below where you want to insert a row, to display the shortcut menu and the Mini toolbar (Figure 3–14).

Figure 3–14

2

- Click Insert on the shortcut menu to insert a new row in the worksheet by shifting the selected row and all rows below it down one row.

- Select cell A4 in the new row and then enter **Margin** to enter a new row title (Figure 3–15).

Q&A

What is the resulting format of the new row?

The cells in the new row inherit the formats of the cells in the row above them. You can change this behavior by clicking the Insert Options button that appears immediately below the inserted row. Following the insertion of a row, the Insert Options button allows you to select from the following options: (1) 'Format Same As Above'; (2) 'Format Same As Below'; and (3) Clear Formatting. The 'Format Same as Above' option is the default. The Insert Options button remains active until you begin the next Excel operation. Excel does not display the Insert Options button if the initial row does not contain any formatted data.

Figure 3–15

3

- Right-click row heading 7 to display a shortcut menu and then click Insert on the shortcut menu to insert a new row in the worksheet.

- Select cell A7 in the new row and then enter **Sales Revenue for Bonus** to enter a new row title (Figure 3–16).

Q&A

What would happen if cells in the shifted rows were included in formulas?

If the rows that shift down include cell references in formulas located in the worksheet, Excel automatically would adjust the cell references in the formulas to their new locations. Thus, in Step 2, if a formula in the worksheet references a cell in row 7 before the insert, then Excel adjusts the cell reference in the formula to row 8 after the insert.

Figure 3–16

Other Ways

1. Insert (Home tab | Cells group), click Insert Sheet Rows

2. Press CTRL + SHIFT + PLUS SIGN, click Entire row, click OK button

BTW

Inserting Multiple Rows
If you want to insert multiple rows, you have two choices. You can insert a single row by using the Insert command on the shortcut menu and then repeatedly press F4 to continue inserting rows. Alternatively, you can select any number of existing rows to choose the number of rows that you want to insert. For instance, if you want to insert five rows, select five existing rows in the worksheet, right-click the rows, and then click Insert on the shortcut menu.

BTW

Dragging Ranges
You can move and insert a selected cell or range between existing cells by holding down the SHIFT key while you drag the selection to the gridline where you want to insert the selected cell or range. You also can copy and insert by holding down the CTRL+SHIFT keys while you drag the selection to the desired gridline.

BTW

Ranges and Undo
The incorrect use of copying, deleting, inserting, and moving ranges of cells have the potential to render a worksheet useless. Carefully review the results of these actions before continuing on to the next task. If you are not sure the result of the action is correct, click the Undo button on the Quick Access Toolbar.

Inserting Columns

You insert columns into a worksheet in the same way you insert rows. To insert columns, select one or more columns immediately to the right of where you want Excel to insert the new column or columns. Select the number of columns you want to insert. Next, click the Insert button arrow (Home tab | Cells group) and then click Insert Sheet Columns in the Insert list or right-click the selected column(s), then click Insert on the shortcut menu. The Insert command on the shortcut menu requires that you select an entire column (or columns) to insert a column (or columns). Following the insertion of a column, Excel displays the Insert Options button, which allows you to modify the insertion in a fashion similar to that discussed earlier when inserting rows.

Inserting Single Cells or a Range of Cells

The Insert command on the shortcut menu or the Insert Cells command on the Insert list of the Insert button (Home tab | Cells group) allows you to insert a single cell or a range of cells. You should be aware that if you shift a single cell or a range of cells, however, it no longer lines up with its associated cells. To ensure that the values in the worksheet do not get out of order, spreadsheet experts recommend that you insert only entire rows or entire columns. When you insert a single cell or a range of cells, Excel displays the Insert Options button so that you can change the format of the inserted cell, using options similar to those for inserting rows and columns.

Deleting Columns and Rows

The Delete button (Home tab | Cells group) or the Delete command on the shortcut menu removes cells (including the data and format) from the worksheet. Deleting cells is not the same as clearing cells. The Clear command, described in Chapter 1 on page EX 52, clears the data from the cells, but the cells remain in the worksheet. The Delete command removes the cells from the worksheet and shifts the remaining rows up (when you delete rows) or shifts the remaining columns to the left (when you delete columns). If formulas located in other cells reference cells in the deleted row or column, Excel does not adjust these cell references. Excel displays the error message **#REF!** in those cells to indicate a cell reference error. For example, if cell A7 contains the formula =A4+A5 and you delete row 5, Excel assigns the formula =A4+#REF! to cell A6 (originally cell A7) and displays the error message #REF! in cell A6. Excel also displays an Error Options button when you select the cell containing the error message #REF!, which allows you to select options to determine the nature of the problem.

To Enter Numbers with Format Symbols

The next step in creating the Six-Month Financial Projection worksheet is to enter the what-if assumptions values in the range B2:B8. The numbers in the table can be entered and then formatted as in Chapters 1 and 2, or each one can be entered with format symbols. When a number is entered with a **format symbol**, Excel immediately displays it with the assigned format. Valid format symbols include the dollar sign ($), comma (,), and percent sign (%).

If you enter a whole number, it appears without any decimal places. If you enter a number with one or more decimal places and a format symbol, Excel displays the number with two decimal places. Table 3–5 illustrates several examples of numbers entered with format symbols. The number in parentheses in column 4 indicates the number of decimal places.

Table 3–5 Numbers Entered with Format Symbols

Format Symbol	Typed in Formula Bar	Displays in Cell	Comparable Format
,	374, 149	374, 149	Comma(0)
	5,833.6	5,833.60	Comma(2)
$	$58917	$58,917	Currency(0)
	$842.51	$842.51	Currency(2)
	$63,574.9	$63,574.90	Currency(2)
%	85%	85%	Percent(0)
	12.80%	12.80%	Percent(2)
	68.4222%	68.2242%	Percent(4)

The following step enters the numbers in the What-If Assumptions table with format symbols.

1

- Enter `200,000.00` in cell B2, `5.75%` in cell B3, `57.50%` in cell B4, `15.00%` in cell B5, `7.50%` in cell B6, `3,500,000.00` in cell B7, and `18.75%` in cell B8 to display the entries using formats based on the format symbols entered with the numbers (Figure 3–17).

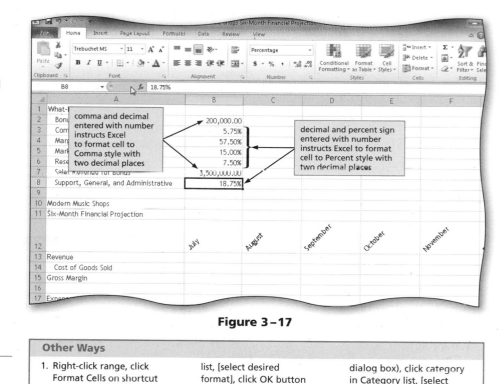

Figure 3–17

Other Ways

1. Right-click range, click Format Cells on shortcut menu, click Number tab (Format Cells dialog box), click category in Category list, [select desired format], click OK button (Format Cells dialog box)

2. Press CTRL + 1, click Number tab (Format Cells dialog box), click category in Category list, [select desired format], click OK button (Format Cells dialog box)

To Freeze Column and Row Titles

Freezing worksheet titles is a useful technique for viewing large worksheets that extend beyond the window. Normally, when you scroll down or to the right, the column titles in row 12 and the row titles in column A that define the numbers no longer appear on the screen. This makes it difficult to remember what the numbers in these rows and columns represent. To alleviate this problem, Excel allows you to **freeze the titles**, so that Excel displays the titles on the screen, no matter how far down or to the right you scroll.

The steps on the following page use the Freeze Panes button (View tab | Window group) to freeze the worksheet title and column titles in rows 10, 11, and 12, and the row titles in column A.

1

- Scroll the worksheet to ensure that Excel displays row 10 as the first row and column A on the screen.

- Select cell B13 to select the cell on which to freeze panes.

- Display the View tab and then click the Freeze Panes button (View tab | Window group) to display the Freeze Panes gallery (Figure 3–18).

Q&A

Why should I ensure that row 10 is the first row displayed?

Before freezing the titles, it is important that Excel display the first row that you want frozen as the first row displayed. For example, if cell B13 was selected while displaying row 1, then Excel would freeze the what-if assumptions and only show a few rows of data in the Six-Month Financial Project area of the worksheet. To ensure that you can view as much data as possible, always scroll to a row that maximizes the view of your important data before freezing panes.

Figure 3–18

2

- Click Freeze Panes in the Freeze Panes gallery to freeze rows and columns to the left and above the selected cell, column A and rows 10 through 12 in this case (Figure 3–19).

Q&A

What happens after I click the Freeze Panes command?

Excel displays a thin black line on the right side of column A, indicating the split between the frozen row titles in column A and the rest of the worksheet. It also displays a thin black line below row 12, indicating the split between the frozen column titles in rows 10 through 12 and the rest of the worksheet (Figure 3–19).

Figure 3–19

To Enter the Projected Monthly Sales

The following steps enter the projected revenue, listed earlier in Table 3–1 on page EX 143, in row 13 and compute the projected six-month revenue in cell H13.

1 If necessary, display the Home tab.

2 Enter `3113612.16` in cell B13, `7962235.53` in cell C13, `5112268.58` in cell D13, `2924627.87` in cell E13, `7630534.65` in cell F13, and `3424270.23` in cell G13.

3 Select cell H13 and then click the Sum button (Home tab | Editing group) twice to create a sum in the selected cell (Figure 3–20).

BTW

Freezing Titles
If you want to freeze only column headings, select the appropriate cell in column A before you click the Freeze Panes button (View tab | Window group). If you want to freeze only row titles, select the appropriate cell in row 1 before you click the Freeze Panes button (View tab | Window group). To freeze both column headings and row titles, select the cell that is the intersection of the column and row titles before you click the Freeze Panes button (View tab | Window group).

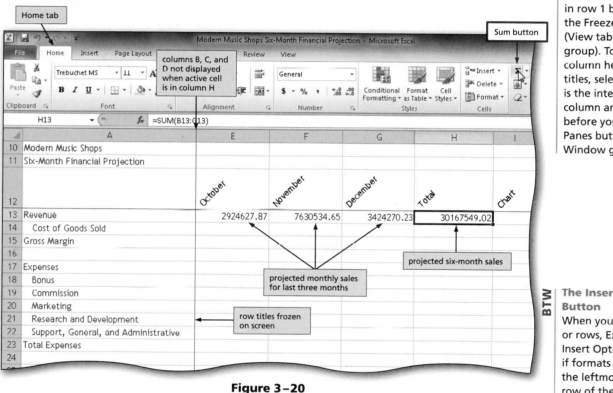

Figure 3–20

BTW

The Insert Options Button
When you insert columns or rows, Excel displays the Insert Options button only if formats are assigned to the leftmost column or top row of the selection.

To Enter and Format the System Date

The sketch of the worksheet in Figure 3–3a on page EX 142 includes a date stamp on the right side of the heading section. A **date stamp** shows the date a workbook, report, or other document was created or the period it represents. In business, a report often is meaningless without a date stamp. For example, if a printout of the worksheet in this chapter were distributed to the company's analysts, the date stamp would show when the six-month projections were made, as well as what period the report represents.

A simple way to create a date stamp is to use the NOW function to enter the system date tracked by your computer in a cell in the worksheet. The **NOW function** is one of 22 date and time functions available in Excel. When assigned to a cell, the NOW function returns a number that corresponds to the system date and time beginning with December 31, 1899. For example, January 1, 1900 equals 1, January 2, 1900 equals 2, and so on. Noon equals .5. Thus, noon on January 1, 1900 equals 1.5 and 6 P.M. on January 1, 1900 equals 1.75. If the computer's system date is set to the current date, which normally it is, then the date stamp is equivalent to the current date.

The steps on the following pages enter the NOW function and then change the format from mm/dd/yyyy hh:mm to mm/dd/yyyy.

①

- Select cell I11 and then click the Insert Function box in the formula bar to display the Insert Function dialog box.

- Click the 'Or select a category' box arrow (Insert Function dialog box) and then select Date & Time in the list to populate the 'Select a function' list with data and time functions.

- Scroll down in the 'Select a function list' and then click NOW to select the required function (Figure 3–21).

Figure 3–21

②

- Click the OK button (Insert Function dialog box) to close the Insert Function dialog box and display the Function Arguments dialog box.

- Click the OK button (Function Arguments dialog box) to display the system date and time in the selected cell, using the default date and time format mm/dd/yyyy hh:mm.

- Right-click cell I11 to display a shortcut menu and Mini toolbar (Figure 3–22).

Q&A

Why does the date appear with the mm/dd/yyyy hh:mm format?

Excel automatically formats the result of the NOW function as a date, using the date and time format, mm/dd/yyyy hh:mm, where the first mm is the month, dd is the day of the month, yyyy is the year, hh is the hour of the day, and mm is the minutes past the hour.

Figure 3–22

3

• Click Format Cells on the shortcut menu to display the Format Cells dialog box.

• If necessary, click the Number tab (Format Cells dialog box) to display the Number sheet.

• Click Date in the Category list (Format Cells dialog box) to display the types of date formats in the Type list. Scroll down in the Type list and then click 3/14/2001 to display a sample of the data in the active cell, I11 in this case, using the selected format in the Sample area (Figure 3–23).

Q&A Why do the dates in the Type box show March 14, 2001 instead of the current date?

The date March 14, 2001 is used as a sample date in the Format cells dialog box.

Figure 3–23

4

• Click the OK button (Format Cells dialog box) to display the system date in the format mm/dd/yyyy.

• Double-click the border between columns I and J to change the width of the column to best fit (Figure 3–24).

Q&A How does Excel format a date?

In Figure 3–24, the date is displayed right-aligned in the cell because

Figure 3–24

Excel treats a date as a number formatted to display as a date. If you assign the General format (Excel's default format for numbers) to a date in a cell, the date is displayed as a number with two decimal places. For example, if the system time and date is 9:00 AM on November 13, 2012 and the cell containing the NOW function is assigned the General format, then Excel displays the following number in the cell:

41226.375

Number of days since   Time of day is 9:00 AM
December 31, 1899   (Portion of day complete)

The whole number portion of the number (41226) represents the number of days since December 31, 1899. The decimal portion of the number (.375) represents 9:00 AM as the time of day, at which point 37.5% of the day is complete. To assign the General format to a cell, click General in the Category list in the Format Cells dialog box (Figure 3–23).

Other Ways

1. Click Date & Time (Formulas tab | Function Library group), click now

2. Press CTRL + SEMICOLON (not a volatile date)

3. Press CTRL + SHIFT + # to format date to day-month-year

Break Point: If you wish to stop working through the chapter at this point, you can quit Excel now and then resume the project at a later point in time by starting Excel, opening the file called Modern Music Shops Six-Month Financial Projection, and continuing to follow the steps from this location forward.

Absolute versus Relative Addressing

The next sections describe the formulas and functions needed to complete the calculations in the worksheet.

As you learned in Chapters 1 and 2, Excel modifies cell references when copying formulas. While copying formulas, however, sometimes you do not want Excel to change cell references. To keep a cell reference constant when copying a formula or function, Excel uses a technique called absolute cell referencing. To specify an absolute cell reference in a formula, enter a dollar sign ($) before any column letters or row numbers you want to keep constant in formulas you plan to copy. For example, $B$4 is an absolute cell reference, whereas B4 is a relative cell reference. Both reference the same cell. The difference becomes apparent when they are copied to a destination area. A formula using the **absolute cell reference** $B$4 instructs Excel to keep the cell reference B4 constant (absolute) in the formula as it copies it to the destination area. A formula using the **relative cell reference** B4 instructs Excel to adjust the cell reference as it copies it to the destination area. A cell reference with only one dollar sign before either the column or the row is called a **mixed cell reference**. When planning formulas, be aware of when you need to use absolute, relative, and mixed cell references. Table 3−6 gives some additional examples of each of these types of cell references.

Table 3−6 Examples of Absolute, Relative, and Mixed Cell References		
Cell Reference	**Type of Reference**	**Meaning**
$B$4	Absolute cell reference	Both column and row references remain the same when you copy this cell, because the cell references are absolute.
B$4	Mixed reference	This cell reference is mixed. The column reference changes when you copy this cell to another column because it is relative. The row reference does not change because it is absolute.
$B4	Mixed reference	This cell reference is mixed. The column reference does not change because it is absolute. The row reference changes when you copy this cell reference to another row because it is relative.
B4	Relative cell reference	Both column and row references are relative. When copied to another cell, both the column and row in the cell reference are adjusted to reflect the new location.

The next step is to enter the formulas that calculate the following values for July: cost of goods sold (cell B14), gross margin (cell B15), expenses (range B18:B22), total expenses (cell B23), and the operating income (cell B25). The formulas are based on the projected monthly revenue in cell B13 and the assumptions in the range B2:B8.

To Enter a Formula Containing Absolute Cell References

The formulas for each column (month) are the same, except for the reference to the projected monthly revenue in row 13, which varies according to the month (B13 for July, C13 for August, and so on). Thus, the formulas for July can be entered in column B and then copied to columns C through G. Table 3−7 shows the formulas for determining the July cost of goods sold, gross margin, expenses, total expenses, and operating income in column B.

Table 3–7 Formulas for Determining Cost of Goods Sold, Margin, Expenses, Total Expenses, and Operating Income for July

Cell	Row Title	Formula	Comment
B14	Cost of Goods Sold	=B13 * (1 – B4)	Revenue times (1 minus Margin %)
B15	Gross Margin	= B13 – B14	Revenue minus Cost of Goods Sold
B18	Bonus	=IF(B13 >= B7, B2, 0)	Bonus equals value in B2 or 0
B19	Commission	=B13 * B3	Revenue times Commission %
B20	Marketing	=B13 * B5	Revenue times Marketing %
B21	Research and Development	=B13 * B6	Revenue times Research and Development %
B22	Support, General, and Administrative	=B13 * B8	Revenue times Support, General, and Administrative %
B23	Total Expenses	=SUM(B18:B22)	Sum of July Expenses
B25	Operating Income	=B15 – B23	Gross Margin minus Total Expenses

As the formulas are entered as shown in Table 3–7 in column B for July and then copied to columns C through G (August through December) in the worksheet, Excel will adjust the cell references for each column automatically. Thus, after the copy, the August Commission expense in cell C19 would be =C13 * C3. While the cell reference C13 (February Revenue) is correct, the cell reference C3 references an empty cell. The formula for cell C7 should read =C13 * B3, rather than =C13 * C3, because B3 references the Commission % value in the What-If Assumptions table. In this instance, a way is needed to keep a cell reference in a formula the same, or constant, when it is copied.

The following steps enter the cost of goods formula = B13*(1 – $B$4) in cell B14 using Point mode. To enter an absolute cell reference, you can type the dollar sign ($) as part of the cell reference or enter it by pressing F4 with the insertion point in or to the right of the cell reference to change it to absolute.

1

- Press CTRL+HOME to select cell B13 and then click cell B14 to show cell B13 and to select the cell in which to enter the first formula.

- Type = (equal sign), select cell B13, type *(1–b4 to continue entering the formula, and then press F4 to change the most recently typed cell reference, in this case cell b4, from a relative cell reference to an absolute cell reference. Type) to complete the formula (Figure 3–25).

Q&A Is an absolute reference required in this formula?

No, because a mixed cell reference could have been used. The formula in cell B14 will be copied across columns, rather than down rows. So, the formula entered in cell B14 in Step 1 could have been entered as =B13*(1–$B4), rather than =B13*(1–$B$4). That is, the formula could have included the mixed cell reference $B4, rather than the absolute cell reference $B$4. When you copy a formula across columns, the row does not change anyway. The key is to ensure that column B remains constant as you copy the formula across columns. To change the absolute cell reference to a mixed cell reference, continue to press the F4 key until you achieve the desired cell reference.

Figure 3–25

2

- Click the Enter box in the formula bar to display the result, 1323285.168, instead of the formula in B14 (Figure 3–26).

Figure 3–26

3

- Click cell B15 to select the cell in which to enter the next formula, type = (equal sign), click cell B13, type − (minus sign), and then click cell B14 to add a reference to the cell to the formula.

- Click the Enter box in the formula bar to display the result in the selected cell, in this case gross margin for July, 1790326.992, in cell B15 (Figure 3–27).

Figure 3–27

Making Decisions — The IF Function

Logical Operators in IF Functions

IF functions can use logical operators, such as AND, OR, and NOT. For example, the three IF functions =IF(AND(A1>C1, B1<C2), "OK", "Not OK") and =IF(OR(K5>J5, C3<K6), "OK", "Not OK") and =IF(NOT(B10<C10), "OK", "Not OK") use logical operators. In the first example, both logical tests must be true for the value_if_true OK to be assigned to the cell. In the second example, one or the other logical tests must be true for the value_if_true OK to be assigned to the cell. In the third example, the logical test B10<C10 must be false for the value_if_true OK to be assigned to the cell.

According to the Request for New Workbook in Figure 3–2 on page EX 140, if the projected July revenue in cell B13 is greater than or equal to the sales revenue for bonus in cell B7 (3,500,000.00), then the July bonus value in cell B18 is equal to the bonus value in cell B2 (200,000.00); otherwise, cell B18 is equal to 0. One way to assign the July bonus value in cell B18 is to check to see if the revenue in cell B13 equals or exceeds the sales revenue for the bonus amount in cell B7 and, if so, then to enter 200,000.00 in cell B18. You can use this manual process for all six months by checking the values for the corresponding months.

Because the data in the worksheet changes each time a report is prepared or the figures are adjusted, however, it is preferable to have Excel assign the monthly bonus to the entries in the appropriate cells automatically. To do so, cell B18 must include a formula or function that displays 200,000.00 or 0.00 (zero), depending on whether the projected July revenue in cell B13 is greater than, equal to, or less than the sales revenue for bonus value in cell B7.

The **IF function** is useful when you want to assign a value to a cell based on a logical test. For example, using the IF function, cell B18 can be assigned the following IF function:

$$=IF(B13>=\$B\$7, \$B\$2, 0)$$

logical_test   value_if_true   value_if_false

The IF function instructs Excel that, if the projected July revenue in cell B13 is greater than or equal to the sales revenue for bonus value in cell B7, then Excel should display the value 200000 in cell B2, in cell B18. If the projected July revenue in cell B13 is less than the sales revenue for bonus value in cell B7, then Excel displays a 0 (zero) in cell B18.

The general form of the IF function is:

=IF(logical_test, value_if_true, value_if_false)

The argument, logical_test, is made up of two expressions and a comparison operator. Each expression can be a cell reference, a number, text, a function, or a formula. Valid comparison operators, their meaning, and examples of their use in IF functions are shown in Table 3–8. The argument, value_if_true, is the value you want Excel to display in the cell when the logical test is true. The argument, value_if_false, is the value you want Excel to display in the cell when the logical test is false.

Table 3–8 Comparison Operators		
Comparison Operator	**Meaning**	**Example**
=	Equal to	=IF(B12 = 200, F3 * H4, E10 + F3)
<	Less than	=IF(G56 * Q56 < D12, $M$10, B9 ^ 5)
>	Greater than	=IF(MIN(A12:A52) > 75, 0, 1)
>=	Greater than or equal to	=IF($T$9 >= B7, P3 - H12, 1000)
<=	Less than or equal to	=IF(C9 * G2 <= 99, $T35, 350 * C9)
<>	Not equal to	=IF(G15 <> 1, "No","Yes")

To Enter an IF Function

The following steps assign the IF function =IF(B13>=$B$7,$B$2,0) to cell B18. This IF function determines whether or not the worksheet assigns a bonus for July.

1

- Click cell B18 to select the cell for the next formula.

- Click the Insert Function box in the formula bar to display the Insert Function dialog box.

- Click the 'Or select a category' box arrow (Insert Function dialog box) and then select Logical in the list to populate the 'Select a function' list with logic functions.

- Click IF in the 'Select a function list' to select the required function (Figure 3–28).

Figure 3–28

2

- Click the OK button (Insert Function dialog box) to display the Function Arguments dialog box.

- Type **b13>=b7** in the Logical test box to enter a logical test for the IF function.

- Type **b2** in the Value_if_true box to enter the result of the IF function if the logical test is true.

- Type **0** in the Value_if_false box to enter the result of the IF function if the logical test is false (Figure 3–29).

Figure 3–29

3

- Click the OK button (Function Arguments dialog box) to insert the IF function in the selected cell (Figure 3–30).

Figure 3–30

Q&A

Why is the value 0 displayed in cell B18?

The value that Excel displays in cell B18 depends on the values assigned to cells B13, B2, and B7. For example, if the value for July revenue in cell B13 is increased above 3,500,000.00, then the IF function in cell B18 will cause Excel to display 200,000.00. If you change the sales revenue for bonus in cell B7 from 3,500,000.00 to another number and the value in cell B13 is greater than or equal to the value in cell B7, it will change the results in cell B18 as well.

Other Ways

1. Click Logical button (Formulas tab | Function Library group), click IF

To Enter the Remaining July Formulas

The July commission expense in cell B19 is equal to the revenue in cell B13 times the commission assumption in cell B3 (5.75%). The July marketing expense in cell B20 is equal to the projected July revenue in cell B13 times the marketing assumption in cell B5 (15.00%). Similar formulas determine the remaining July expenses in cells B21 and B22.

The total expenses value in cell B23 is equal to the sum of the expenses in the range B18:B22. The operating income in cell B25 is equal to the gross margin in cell B15 minus the total expenses in cell B23. The formulas are short, and therefore, they are typed in the following steps, rather than entered using Point mode.

1 Select cell B19. Type =b13 * b3 and then press the DOWN ARROW key to enter the formula in the selected cell. Type =b13 * b5 and then press the DOWN ARROW key to enter the formula in the selected cell. Type =b13 * b6 and then press the DOWN ARROW key to enter the formula in the selected cell. Type =b13 * b8 and then press the DOWN ARROW key to enter the formula in the selected cell.

2 With cell B23 selected, click the Sum button (Home tab | Editing group) twice to insert a SUM function in the selected cell. Select cell B25 to prepare to enter the next formula. Type =b15−b23 and then press the ENTER key to enter the formula in the selected cell.

3 Press CTRL+ACCENT MARK (`) to display the formulas version of the worksheet (Figure 3–31).

4 When you are finished viewing the formulas version, press CTRL+ACCENT MARK (`) to display the values version of the worksheet.

Q&A Why should I view the formulas version of the worksheet?

Viewing the formulas version (Figure 3–31) of the worksheet allows you to check the formulas assigned to the range B14:B25. Recall that formulas were entered in lowercase. You can see that Excel converts all the formulas from lowercase to uppercase.

BTW

Replacing a Formula with a Constant
By doing the following, you can replace a formula with its result so that the cell value remains constant: (1) click the cell with the formula; (2) press F2 or click in the formula bar; (3) press F9 to display the value in the formula bar; and (4) press the ENTER key.

	July		August
	3113612.16		7962235.53
	=B13*(1-$B$4)		
	=B13-B14		
	=IF(B13>=$B$7,$B$2,0)	in formulas version, Excel displays formulas for July	
	=B13*$B$3		
	=B13*$B$5		
	=B13*$B$6		
nistrative	=B13*$B$8		
	=SUM(B18:B22)		
	=B15-B23		

100%

Figure 3–31

To Copy Formulas with Absolute Cell References Using the Fill Handle

The following steps use the fill handle to copy the July formulas in column B to the other five months in columns C through G.

1

- Select the range B14:B25 and then point to the fill handle in the lower-right corner of the selected cell, B25 in this case, to display the crosshair mouse pointer (Figure 3–32).

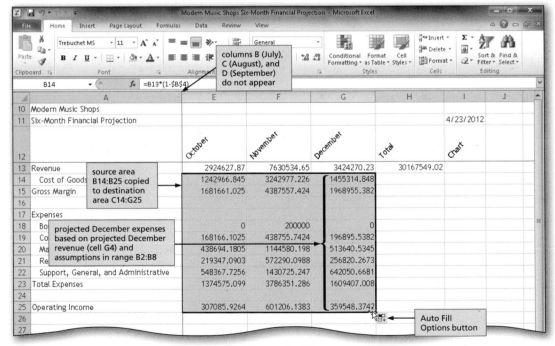

Figure 3–32

2

- Drag the fill handle to the right to copy the formulas from the source area, B14:B25 in this case, to the destination area, C14:G25 in this case, and display the calculated amounts and Auto Fill Options button (Figure 3–33).

Q&A

What happens to the formulas after performing the copy operation?

Because the formulas in the range B14:B25 use absolute cell references, the formulas still refer to the current values in the Assumptions table when the formulas are copied to the range C14:G25.

Figure 3–33

Q&A

What happened to columns B, C, and D?

As shown in Figure 3–33, as the fill handle is dragged to the right, columns B, C, and D no longer appear on the screen because column A now acts just as the row numbers do in that columns scrolled off of the visible portion of the worksheet disappear behind column A. Column A, however, remains on the screen, because the row titles were frozen earlier in this chapter.

To Determine Row Totals in Nonadjacent Cells

The following steps determine the row totals in column H. To determine the row totals using the Sum button, select only the cells in column H containing numbers in adjacent cells to the left. If, for example, you select the range H14:H25, Excel will display 0s as the sum of empty rows in cells H16, H17, and H24.

1 Select the range H14:H15. While holding down the CTRL key, select the range H18:H23 and cell H25, as shown in Figure 3–34.

2 Click the Sum button (Home tab | Editing group) to display the row totals in the selected ranges (Figure 3–34).

BTW

Error Messages
When Excel cannot calculate a formula, it displays an error message in a cell. These error messages always begin with a number sign (#). The more commonly occurring error messages are as follows: #DIV/0! (tries to divide by zero); #NAME? (uses a name Excel does not recognize); #N/A (refers to a value not available); #NULL! (specifies an invalid intersection of two areas); #NUM! (uses a number incorrectly); #REF (refers to a cell that is not valid); #VALUE! (uses an incorrect argument or operand); and ##### (refers to cells not wide enough to display entire entry).

	Home tab					Sum button	

	A	E	F	G	H	
10	Modern Music Shops					
11	Six-Month Financial Projection				4/23/2012	
12		October	November	December	Total	Chart
13	Revenue	2924627.87	7630534.65	3424270.23	30167549.02	
14	Cost of Goods Sold	1242966.845	3242977.226	1455314.848	12821208.33	
15	Gross Margin	1681661.025	4387557.424	1968955.382	17346340.69	
16						
17	Expenses					
18	Bonus	0	200000	0	600000	
19	Commission	168166.1025	438755.7424	196895.5382	1734634.069	
20	Marketing	438694.1805	1144580.198	513640.5345	4525132.353	
21	Research and Development	219347.0903	572290.0988	256820.2673	2262566.177	
22	Support, General, and Administrative	548367.7256	1430725.247	642050.6681	5656415.441	
23	Total Expenses	1374575.099	3786351.286	1609407.008	14778748.04	
24						
25	Operating Income	307085.9264	601206.1383	359548.3742	2567592.647	
26						
27						

H25 ▼ *fx* =SUM(B25:G25)

Editing group

projected six-month cost of goods sold, gross margin, expenses by category, and operating income

Figure 3–34

To Unfreeze the Worksheet Titles and Save the Workbook

All the text, data, and formulas have been entered into the worksheet. The following steps unfreeze the titles to allow you to work with the worksheet without frozen rows and columns, and save the workbook using its current file name, Modern Music Shops Six-Month Financial Projection.

1 Press CTRL+HOME to select cell B13 and view the upper-left corner of the screen.

2 Display the View tab and then click the Freeze Panes button (View tab | Window group) to display the Freeze Panes gallery.

3 Click Unfreeze Panes in the Freeze Panes gallery to unfreeze the frozen columns and rows.

4 Display the Home tab and then click the Save button on the Quick Access Toolbar to save the workbook.

Q&A Why does pressing CTRL+HOME select cell B13?

When the titles are frozen and you press CTRL+HOME, Excel selects the upper-left cell of the unfrozen section of the worksheet. For example, in Step 1 of the previous steps, Excel selected cell B13. When the titles are unfrozen, pressing CTRL+HOME selects cell A1.

Nested Forms of the IF Function

A **nested IF function** is one in which the action to be taken for the true or false case includes yet another IF function. The second IF function is considered to be nested, or layered, within the first. Study the nested IF function below, which determines the eligibility of a student to go on a field trip. The school permits the student to attend the field trip if the student's age is at least 14 and the student has provided a signed permission form. Assume the following in this example: (1) the nested IF function is assigned to cell L9, which instructs Excel to display one of three messages in the cell; (2) cell L7 contains a student's age; and (3) cell L8 contains a Y or N, based on whether the person provided a signed permission form.

Using IFERROR
Similar to the IF function, the IFERROR function checks a formula for correctness. For example, =IFERROR(formula, "Error Message") examines the formula argument. If an error appears (such as #N/A), Excel displays the Error Message text in the cell instead of the Excel #N/A error.

=IF(L7>=14, IF(L8="Y","Allowed","Can Travel, but No Permission"),"Too Young to Travel")

The nested IF function instructs Excel to display one, and only one, of the following three messages in cell L9: (1) Allowed; or (2) Can Travel, but No Permission; or (3) Too Young to Travel.

You can nest IF functions as deep as you want, but after you get beyond a nest of three IF functions, the logic becomes difficult to follow and alternative solutions, such as the use of multiple cells and simple IF functions, should be considered.

Adding and Formatting Sparkline Charts

Sometimes you may want to condense a range of data into a small chart in order to show a trend or variation in the range. Excel's standard charts may be too large or extensive for your needs. An Excel **Sparkline chart** provides a simple way to show trends and variations in a range of data within a single cell. Excel includes three types of Sparkline charts: Line, Column, and Win/Loss. Because they exist in only one cell, you should use Sparkline charts to convey succinct, eye-catching summaries of the data they represent.

To Add a Sparkline Chart to the Worksheet

Each of the rows of monthly data, including those containing formulas, provides useful information easily summarized by a Line Sparkline chart. A Line Sparkline chart is a good choice because it shows trends over the six-month period for each row of data.

The following steps add a Line Sparkline chart to cell I13 and then use the fill handle to create Line Sparkline charts in the range I14:I25 that represent the monthly data in rows 13 through 25.

1

- Scroll the worksheet so that both columns B and I are displayed on the screen.

- Select cell I13 to prepare to insert a Sparkline chart in the cell.

- Display the Insert tab and then click Line (Insert tab | Sparklines group) to display the Create Sparklines dialog box (Figure 3–35).

Figure 3–35

2

- Drag through the range B13:G13 to select the range. Do not release the mouse (Figure 3–36).

Q&A

What happened to the Create Sparklines dialog box?

When a dialog box includes a Collapse Dialog Box button (Figure 3–35), selecting cells or a range collapses the dialog box so that only the current text box is displayed. Once the selection is made, the dialog box expands back to its original size. You also can click the Collapse Dialog Box button to make your selection and then click the Expand Dialog Box button (Figure 3–36) to expand the dialog box.

Figure 3–36

3

- Release the mouse button to insert the selected range, B13:G13 in this case, in the Data Range text box.

- Click the OK button (Create Sparklines dialog box) to insert a Line Sparkline chart in the selected cell and display the Sparkline Tools contextual tab (Figure 3–37).

Figure 3–37

To Format and Copy the Sparkline Chart

Just as with standard charts, Excel provides formatting options for Sparkline charts. Sparkline chart formatting is restricted greatly as compared to standard charts. As shown in Figure 3–37, the Show group (Sparkline Tools Design tab) allows you to highlight various points in the chart. Markers provide a point on the chart for each cell represented in the chart. The Style group (Sparkline Tools Design tab) allows you to specify the style and color for the parts of a Sparkline chart.

The steps on the following page format the Sparkline chart in cell I13 using the Style 13 Sparkline chart style.

1

- Click the More button (Sparkline Tools Design tab | Style group) to display the Style gallery (Figure 3–38).

Figure 3–38

2

- Click Sparkline Style Accent 1, (no dark or light) in the Styles gallery to apply the style to the Sparkline chart in the selected cell, I13 in this case.

- Point to the fill handle in cell I13 and then drag through cell I25 to copy the Line Sparkline chart.

- Select cell I27 (Figure 3–39).

Q&A

Why do Sparkline charts not appear in cells I16, I17, and I24?

Excel does not draw Sparkline charts if the range for the Sparkline chart contains no data. In this case the ranges B16:G16, B17:G17, and B24:G24 do not contain data, so Excel draws no Sparkline chart. If you add data to cells in those ranges, then Excel automatically would draw Line Sparkline charts for the rows to which you added data because the Sparkline charts were defined for cells I16, I17, and I24 by the drag operation.

Figure 3–39

Formatting the Worksheet

The worksheet created thus far shows the financial projections for the six-month period, from July to December. Its appearance is uninteresting, however, even though some minimal formatting (formatting assumptions numbers, changing the column widths, formatting the date, and formatting the Sparkline chart) was performed earlier. This section will complete the formatting of the worksheet to make the numbers easier to read and to emphasize the titles, assumptions, categories, and totals as shown in Figure 3–40.

Identify how to format various elements of the worksheet.
A worksheet, such as the one presented in this chapter, should be formatted in the following manner: (1) format the numbers; (2) format the worksheet title, column titles, row titles, and total rows; and (3) format an assumptions table. Numbers in heading rows and total rows should be formatted with a currency symbol. Other dollar amounts should be formatted with a Comma style. An assumptions table should be diminished in its formatting so that it does not distract from the main calculations and data in the worksheet. Assigning the data in an assumptions table a smaller font size would set it apart from other data formatted with a larger font size.

Plan Ahead

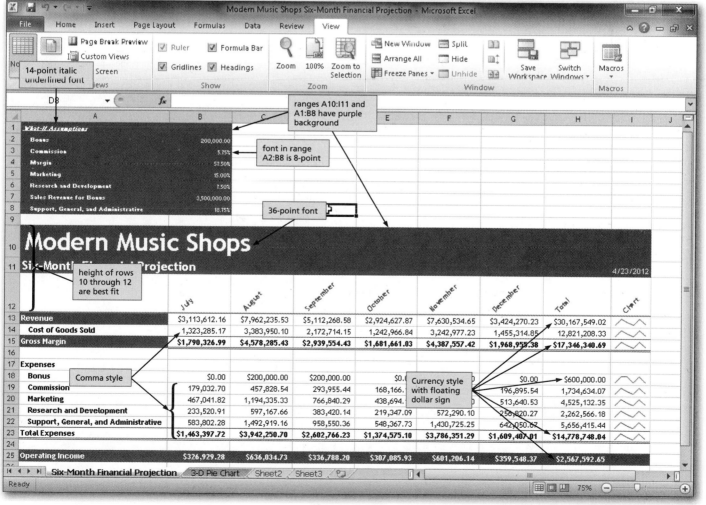

Figure 3–40

To Assign Formats to Nonadjacent Ranges

The numbers in the range B13:H25 are to be formatted as follows:

1. Assign the Currency style with a floating dollar sign to rows 13, 15, 18, 23, and 25.

2. Assign a Comma style to rows 14 and 19 through 22.

The following steps assign formats to the numbers in rows 13 through 25.

1

- Select the range B13:H13 as the first range to format.

- While holding down the CTRL key, select the nonadjacent ranges B15:H15, B18:H18, B23:H23, and B25:H25, and then release the CTRL key to select nonadjacent ranges.

- Click the Format Cells: Number Dialog Box Launcher (Home tab | Number group) to display the Format Cells dialog box.

- Click Currency in the Category list (Format Cells dialog box), if necessary select 2 in the Decimal places box, if necessary click $ in the Symbol list to ensure a dollar sign shows in the cells to be formatted, and click the black font color ($1,234.10) in the Negative numbers list to prepare the desired Currency style for the selected ranges (Figure 3–41).

Figure 3–41

Q&A

Why was the particular style chosen for the negative numbers?

In accounting, negative numbers often are shown with parentheses surrounding the value rather than with a negative sign preceding the value. Thus, the format (1,234.10) in the Negative numbers list was clicked. The data being used in this chapter contains no negative numbers. You must select a format for negative numbers, however, and you must be consistent if you are choosing different formats in a column; otherwise, the decimal points may not line up.

Q&A

Why is the Format Cells dialog box used to create the format for the ranges in this step?

The requirements for this worksheet call for a floating dollar sign. To assign a Currency style with a floating dollar sign, use the Format Cells dialog box rather than the Accounting Style button (Home tab | Number group), which assigns a fixed dollar sign.

2

- Click the OK button (Format Cells dialog box) to close the Format Cells dialog box and apply the desired format to the selected ranges.

- Select the range B14:H14 as the next range to format.

- While holding down the CTRL key, select the range B19:H22, and then release the CTRL key to select nonadjacent ranges.

- Click the Format Cells: Number Dialog Box Launcher (Home tab | Number group) to display the Format Cells dialog box.

Figure 3–42

- Click Currency in the Category list (Format Cells dialog box), if necessary select 2 in the Decimal places box, click None in the Symbol list so a dollar sign does not show in the cells to be formatted, and click the black font color (1,234.10) in the Negative numbers list (Figure 3–42).

3

- Click the OK button (Format Cells dialog box) to close the Format Cells dialog box and apply the desired format to the selected ranges.

- Select cell B27 to select an empty cell and display the formatted numbers as shown in Figure 3–43.

Figure 3–43

Q&A

Why is the Format Cells dialog box used to create the style for the ranges in Steps 2 and 3?

The Format Cells dialog box is used to assign the Comma style, because the Comma Style button (Home tab | Number group) assigns a format that displays a dash (–) when a cell has a value of 0. The specifications for this worksheet call for displaying a value of 0 as 0.00 (see cell B18 in Figure 3–40) rather than as a dash. To create a Comma style using the Format Cells dialog box, you can assign a Currency style with no dollar sign.

Other Ways

1. Right-click range, click Format Cells on shortcut menu, click Number tab (Format Cells dialog box), click category in Category list, select format, click OK button (Format Cells dialog box)

2. Press CTRL+1, click Number tab (Format Cells dialog box), click category in Category list, select format, click OK button (Format Cells dialog box)

To Format the Worksheet Titles

The following steps emphasize the worksheet titles in cells A10 and A11 by changing the font, size, and color. The steps also format all of the row headers in column A with a bold font style.

1

- Press CTRL+HOME to select cell A1 and then click the column A heading to select the column.

- Click the Bold button (Home tab | Font group) to bold all of the data in the selected column.

- Select cell A10, click the Font Size box arrow (Home tab | Font group), and then click 36 in the Font Size list to increase the font size of the selected cell.

- Select cell A11, click the Font Size box arrow, and then click 18 in the Font Size list to increase the font size of the selected cell (Figure 3–44).

2

- Select the range A10:I11 and then click the Fill Color button arrow (Home tab | Font group) to display the Fill Color gallery.

- Click Purple, Accent 2, Darker 25% (column 6, row 5) in the Fill Color gallery to add a background color to the selected range.

- Click the Font Color button arrow (Home tab | Font group) and then select White, Background 1 (column 1, row 1) in the Font Color gallery to change the font color of the selected range (Figure 3–45).

Figure 3–44

Figure 3–45

Other Ways

1. Right-click range, click Format Cells on shortcut menu, click Fill tab (Format Cells dialog box) to color background (or click Font tab to color font), click OK button

2. Press CTRL + 1, click Fill tab (Format Cells dialog box) to color background (or click Font tab to color font), click OK button

To Assign Cell Styles to Nonadjacent Rows and Colors to a Cell

The next step to improving the appearance of the worksheet is to format the heading in row 12 and the totals in rows 15, 23, and 25. The following steps format the heading in row 13 with the Heading 3 cell style and the totals in rows 15, 23, and 25 with the Total cell style. Cell A13 also is formatted with a background color and font color.

1 Select the range A12:I12 and apply the Heading 3 cell style.

2 Select the range A15:I15 and while holding down the CTRL key, select the ranges A23:I23 and A25:I25.

3 Apply the Total cell style to the selected nonadjacent ranges.

4 Select cell A13, click the Fill Color button arrow (Home tab | Font group), and then click the Purple, Accent 2, Darker 25% color (column 6, row 5) in the Fill Color gallery.

5 Click the Font Color button arrow (Home tab | Font group) and then click the White, Background 1 color (column 1, row 1) in the Font Color gallery (Figure 3–46).

Figure 3–46

To Copy a Cell's Format Using the Format Painter Button

Using the Format Painter, you can format a cell quickly by copying a cell's format to another cell or a range of cells. The following steps format cells A15 and the range A25:I25 using the Format Painter.

1

- If necessary, click cell A13 to select a source cell for the format to paint.

- Double-click the Format Painter button (Home tab | Clipboard group) and then move the mouse pointer onto the worksheet to cause the mouse pointer to change to a block plus sign with a paintbrush (Figure 3–47).

Figure 3–47

2

- Click cell A15 to assign the format of the source cell, A13 in this case, to the destination cell, A15 in this case (Figure 3–48).

Figure 3–48

3

- With the mouse pointer still a block plus sign with a paintbrush, drag through the range A25:I25 to assign the format of the source cell, A13 in this case, to the destination range, A25:I25 in this case.

- Press the ESC key to stop the format painter.

- Apply the Currency style to the range B25:H25 to cause the cells in the range to appear with a floating dollar sign and two decimal places and then scroll the worksheet so that column A is displayed (Figure 3–49).

B25   =B15-B23

	A	B	C	D	E	F
10	**Modern Music Shops**					
11	**Six-Month Financial Projection**					
12		July	August	September	October	November
13	Revenue	$3,113,612.16	$7,962,235.53	$5,112,268.58	$2,924,627.87	$7,630,5
14	Cost of Goods Sold	1,323,285.17	3,383,950.10	2,172,714.15	1,242,966.84	3,242,9
15	Gross Margin	$1,790,326.99	$4,578,285.43	$2,939,554.43	$1,681,661.03	$4,387,5
16						
17	Expenses					
18	Bonus	.00	$200,000.00	$200,000.00	$0.00	$200,
19	Commission	179,032.70	457,828.54	293,955.44	168,166.10	438,
20	Marketing	467,041.82	1,194,335.33	766,840.29	438,694.18	1,144,
21	Research and Development	233,520.91	597,167.66	383,420.14	219,347.09	572,
22	Support, General, and Administrative	583,802.28	1,492,919.16	958,550.36	548,367.73	1,430,7
23	Total Expenses	$1,463,397.72	$3,942,250.70	$2,602,766.23	$1,374,575.10	$3,786,35
24						
25	Operating Income	$326,929.28	$636,034.73	$336,788.20	$307,085.93	$601,20
26						
27						

format copied to range A25:H25 and Currency style applied to range B25:I25

Figure 3–49

Q&A

Why does the Currency style need to be reapplied to the range B25:H25?

Sometimes, the use of the format painter results in unintended outcomes. In this case, the changing of the background fill color and font color for the range B25:H25 resulted in the loss of the Currency style because the format being copied did not included the Currency style. Reapplying the Currency style to the range results in the proper number style, fill color, and font color.

Other Ways

1. Click Copy button (Home tab | Clipboard group), select cell, click Paste button arrow (Home tab | Clipboard group), click Formatting icon on Paste gallery

2. Right-click cell, click Copy, right-click cell, click Formatting icon on shortcut menu

To Format the What-If Assumptions Table and Save the Workbook

The last step to improving the appearance of the worksheet is to format the What-If Assumptions table in the range A1:B8. The specifications in Figure 3–40 on page EX 173 require an 8-point italic underlined font for the title in cell A1 and 8-point font in the range A2:B8. The following steps format the What-If Assumptions table.

1 Press CTRL+HOME to select cell A1.

2 Click the Font Size button arrow (Home tab | Font group) and then click 8 in the Font Size list to decrease the font size of the selected cell.

3 Click the Italic button (Home tab | Font Group) and then click the Underline button (Home tab | Font group) to italicize and underline the text in the selected cell.

4 Select the range A2:B8, click the Font Size button arrow (Home tab | Font group) and then click 8 in the Font Size list to apply a smaller font size to the selected range.

5 Select the range A1:B8 and then click the Fill Color button (Home tab | Font group) to apply the most recently used background color to the selected range.

BTW

Painting a Format to Nonadjacent Ranges
Double-click the Format Painter button (Home tab | Clipboard group) and then drag through the nonadjacent ranges to paint the formats to the ranges. Click the Format Painter button (Home tab | Clipboard group) to deactivate it.

BTW

Selecting Nonadjacent Ranges
One of the more difficult tasks to learn is selecting nonadjacent ranges. To complete this task, do not hold down the CTRL key when you select the first range because Excel will consider the current active cell to be the first selection, and you may not want the current active cell in the selection. Once the first range is selected, hold down the CTRL key and drag through the nonadjacent ranges. If a desired range is not visible in the window, use the scroll arrows to view the range. You need not hold down the CTRL key while you scroll.

6 Click the Font Color button (Home tab | Font group) to apply the most recently used font color to the selected range.

7 Click cell D8 to deselect the range A2:B8 and display the What-If Assumptions table, as shown in Figure 3–50.

8 Save the workbook.

Q&A

What happens when I click the Italic and Underline buttons?

Recall that when you assign the italic font style to a cell, Excel slants the characters slightly to the right, as shown in cell A1 in Figure 3–50. The **underline** format underlines only the characters in the cell, rather than the entire cell, as is the case when you assign a cell a bottom border.

Figure 3–50

Break Point: If you wish to stop working through the chapter at this point, you can quit Excel now and then resume the project at a later point in time by starting Excel, opening the file called Modern Music Shops Six-Month Financial Projection, and continuing to follow the steps from this location forward.

BTW

Charts
When you change a value on which a chart is dependent, Excel immediately redraws the chart based on the new value. With bar charts, you can drag the bar in the chart in one direction or another to change the corresponding value in the worksheet.

Adding a 3-D Pie Chart to the Workbook

The next step in the chapter is to draw the 3-D Pie chart on a separate sheet in the workbook, as shown in Figure 3–51. Use a **pie chart** to show the relationship or proportion of parts to a whole. Each slice (or wedge) of the pie shows what percent that slice contributes to the total (100%).

The 3-D Pie chart in Figure 3–51 shows the contribution of each month's projected operating income to the six-month projected operating income. The 3-D Pie chart makes it easy to evaluate the contribution of one month in comparison to the other months.

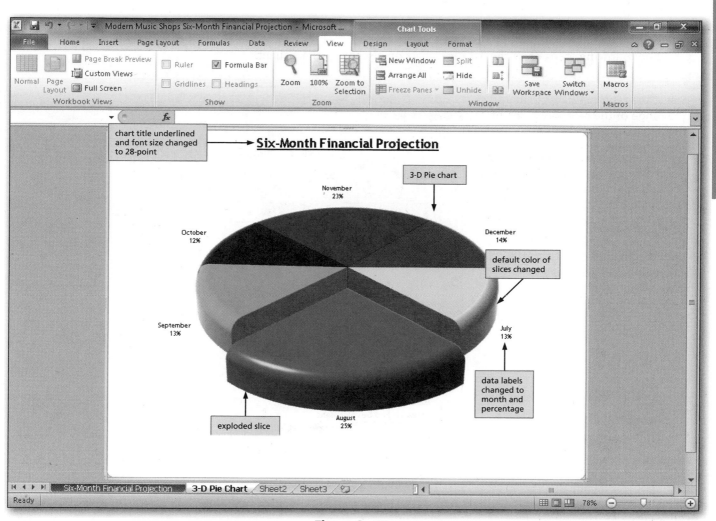

Figure 3–51

Unlike the 3-D Column chart created in Chapter 1, the 3-D Pie chart shown in Figure 3–51 is not embedded in the worksheet. Instead, the Pie chart resides on a separate sheet, called a **chart sheet**, which contains only the chart.

In this worksheet, the ranges to chart are the nonadjacent ranges B12:G12 (month names) and B25:G25 (monthly operating incomes). The month names in the range B12:G12 will identify the slices of the Pie chart; these entries are called **category names**. The range B25:G25 contains the data that determines the size of the slices in the pie; these entries are called the **data series**. Because six months are being charted, the 3-D Pie chart contains six slices.

The sketch of the 3-D Pie chart in Figure 3–3b on page EX 142 also calls for emphasizing the month of August by offsetting its slice from the main portion. A Pie chart with one or more slices offset is called an **exploded Pie chart**.

As shown in Figure 3–51, the default 3-D Pie chart also has been enhanced by rotating it, changing the colors of the slices, adding a bevel, and modifying the chart title and labels that identify the slices.

BTW

Chart Items
When you rest the mouse pointer over a chart item, such as a legend, bar, or axis, Excel displays a chart tip containing the name of the item.

To Draw a 3-D Pie Chart on a Separate Chart Sheet

The following steps draw the 3-D Pie chart on a separate chart sheet.

1

- Select the range B12:G12 to identify the range of the category name of the 3-D Pie Chart.

- If necessary, scroll the worksheet so that row 25 is displayed, and while holding down the CTRL key, select the range B25:G25.

- Display the Insert tab.

- Click the Pie button (Insert tab | Charts group) to display the Pie gallery (Figure 3–52).

Figure 3–52

2

- Click Pie in 3-D chart in the Pie gallery to select the desired chart type.

- When Excel draws the chart, click the Move Chart button (Chart Tools Design tab | Location group) to display the Move Chart dialog box (Figure 3–53).

Figure 3–53

3

- Click New sheet (Move Chart dialog box) and then type `3-D Pie Chart` in the 'New sheet name' text box to enter a sheet tab name for the chart sheet.

- Click the OK button (Move Chart dialog box) to move the chart to a new chart sheet with a new sheet name, 3-D Pie Chart in this case (Figure 3–54).

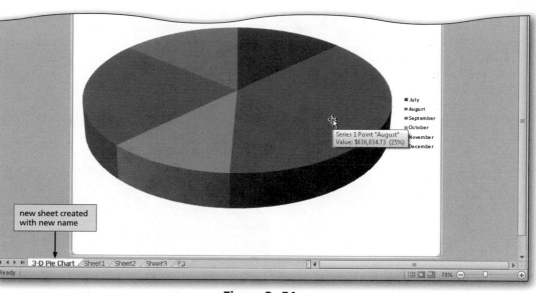

new sheet created with new name

Figure 3–54

Other Ways

1. Select range to chart, press F11

To Insert a Chart Title and Data Labels

The next step is to insert a chart title and labels that identify the slices. Before you can format a chart item, such as the chart title or data labels, you must select it. The following steps insert a chart title, remove the legend, and add data labels.

1

- Click anywhere in the chart area outside the chart to select the chart.

- Display the Chart Tools Layout tab and then click the Chart Title button (Chart Tools Layout tab | Labels group) to display the Chart Title gallery.

- Click the Centered Overlay Title command in the Chart Title gallery to add a chart title centered on top of the chart.

- Select the text in the chart title and then type `Six-Month Financial Projection` to add a new chart title (Figure 3–55).

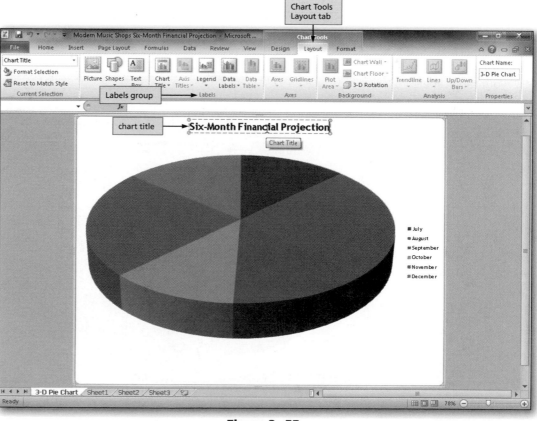

Figure 3–55

2

• Select the text in the new title and then display the Home tab.

• Click the Underline button (Home tab | Font group) to assign an underline font style to the chart title (Figure 3–56).

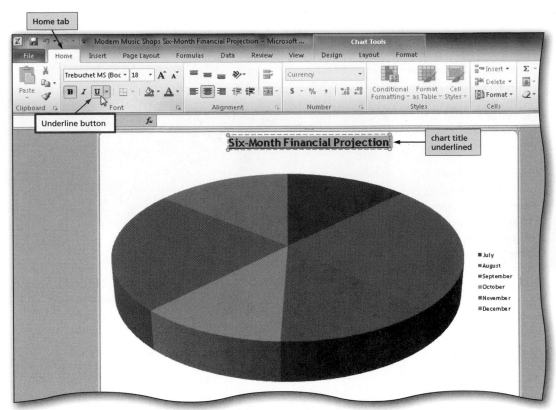

Figure 3–56

3

• Display the Chart Tools Layout tab and then click the Legend button (Chart Tools Layout tab | Labels group) to display the Legend gallery (Figure 3–57).

Figure 3–57

4

- Click the None Legend option in the Legend gallery to turn off the legend on the chart.

- Click the Data Labels button (Layout tab | Labels group) and then click Outside End in the Data Labels gallery to display data labels outside the chart at the end of each slice (Figure 3–58).

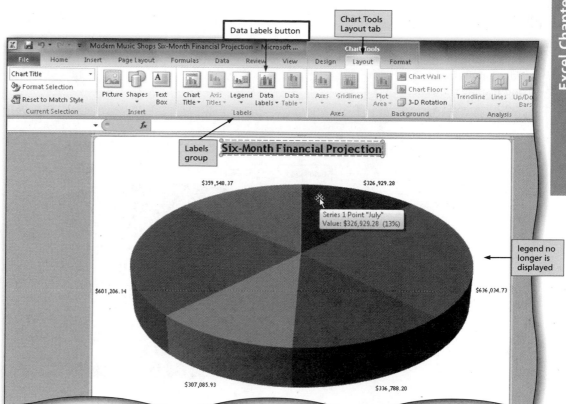

Figure 3–58

5

- If necessary, right-click any data label to select all of the data labels on the chart and to display a shortcut menu.

- Click the Format Data Labels command on the shortcut menu to display the Format Data Labels dialog box.

- If necessary, click the Series Name, Value, and Show Leader Lines check boxes to deselect them (Format Data Labels dialog box) and then click the Category Name and Percentage check boxes to cause the data labels to be displayed with category names and percent values, rather than currency values (Figure 3–59).

Figure 3–59

6

• Click the Close button to close the Format Data Labels dialog box and display the chart (Figure 3–60).

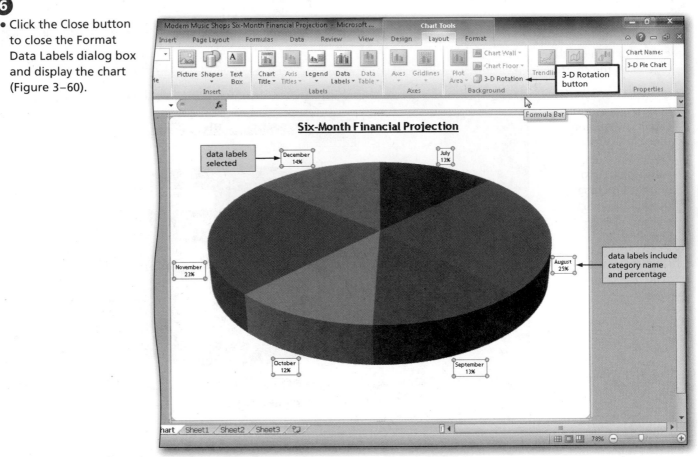

Figure 3–60

To Rotate the 3-D Pie Chart

With a three-dimensional chart, you can change the view to better show the section of the chart you are trying to emphasize. Excel allows you to control the rotation angle, elevation, perspective, height, and angle of the axes.

When Excel initially draws a Pie chart, it always positions the chart so that one of the dividing lines between two slices is a straight line pointing to 12 o'clock (or 0°). As shown in Figure 3–60, the line that divides the December and July slices currently is set to 0°. This line defines the rotation angle of the 3-D Pie chart.

To obtain a better view of the offset August slice, the largest slice, the 3-D Pie chart can be rotated 90° to the left. The following steps rotate the 3-D Pie chart.

1

- Click the 3-D Rotation button (Chart Tools Layout tab | Background group) to display the Format Chart Area dialog box.

- Click the Increase X Rotation button in the Rotation area of the Format Chart Area dialog box until the X rotation is at 90° to rotate the chart (Figure 3–61).

Q&A

What happens as I click the Increase X Rotation button?

Excel rotates the chart 10° in a clockwise direction each time you click the Increase X Rotation button. The Y box in the Rotation area allows you to control the tilt, or elevation, of the chart. You can tilt the chart towards or away from your view in order to enhance the view of the chart.

Figure 3–61

2

- Click the Close button (Format Chart Area dialog box) to close the dialog box and display the rotated chart (Figure 3–62).

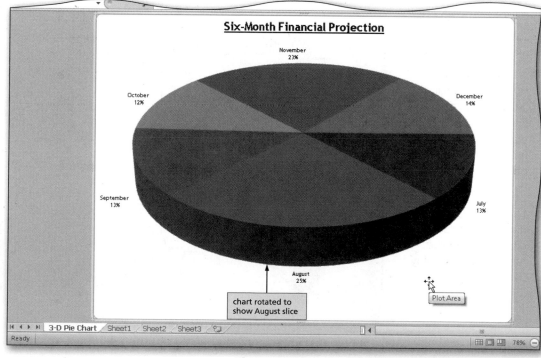

Figure 3–62

To Apply a 3-D Format to the Pie Chart

Excel allows you to apply dramatic 3-D visual effects to charts. The chart shown in Figure 3–62 could be enhanced with a bevel along the top edge. A bevel is a curve that is applied to soften the appearance of a straight edge. Excel also allows you to change the appearance of the material from which the surface of the chart appears to be constructed. The following steps apply a bevel to the chart and change the surface of the chart to a softer-looking material.

1

- Right-click the chart to display a shortcut menu and Mini toolbar (Figure 3–63).

Figure 3–63

2

- Click the Format Data Series command on the shortcut menu to display the Format Data Series dialog box and then click the 3-D Format category (Format Data Series dialog box) on the left side of the dialog box to display the 3-D Format panel.

- Click the Top button (Format Data Series dialog box) in the Bevel area to display the Bevel gallery (Figure 3–64).

Figure 3–64

3

- Click the Circle bevel button (column 1, row 1) in the Bevel gallery (Format Data Series dialog box) to add a bevel to the chart.

- Type 50 pt in the uppermost Width box in the Bevel area (Format Data Series dialog box) and then type 50 pt in the uppermost Height box in the Bevel area of the dialog box to increase the width and height of the bevel on the chart (Figure 3–65).

Figure 3–65

4

- Click the Material button in the Surface area (Format Data Series dialog box) to display the Material gallery (Figure 3–66).

Figure 3–66

- Click the Soft Edge button (column 2, row 2) in the Material gallery and then click the Close button (Format Data Series dialog box) to apply the desired material and close the Format Data Series dialog box (Figure 3–67).

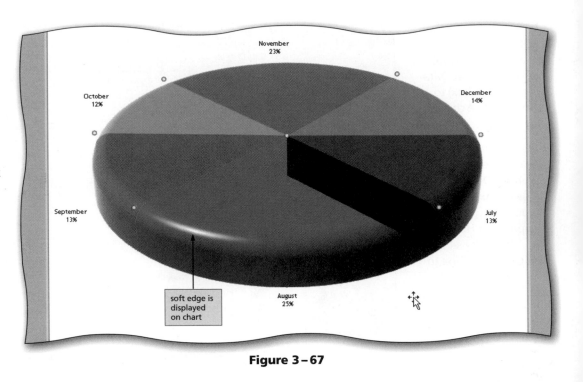

Figure 3–67

To Explode the 3-D Pie Chart and Change the Color of a Slice

The next step is to emphasize the slice representing August by offsetting, or exploding, it from the rest of the slices so that it stands out. The following steps explode the largest slice of the 3-D Pie chart and then change its color.

- Click the slice labeled August twice (do not double-click) to select only one slice of the 3-D Pie chart, the August slice in this case.

- Right-click the slice labeled August to display a shortcut menu and Mini toolbar (Figure 3–68).

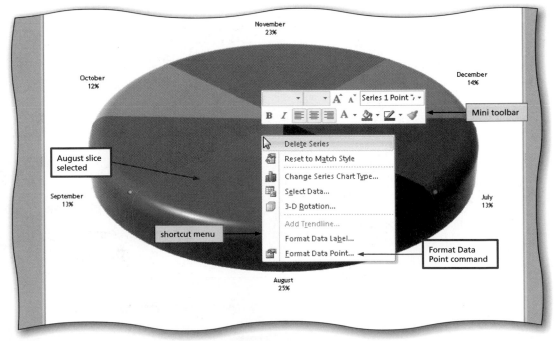

Figure 3–68

2

- Click Format Data Point on the shortcut menu to display the Format Data Point dialog box.

- Drag the Point Explosion slider (Format Data Point dialog box) to the right until the Point Explosion box reads 28% to set how far the slice in the 3-D Pie chart should be offset from the rest of the chart (Figure 3–69).

Q&A

Should I offset more slices?

You can offset as many slices as you want, but remember that the reason for offsetting a slice is to emphasize it. Offsetting multiple slices tends to reduce the impact on the reader and reduces the overall size of the Pie chart.

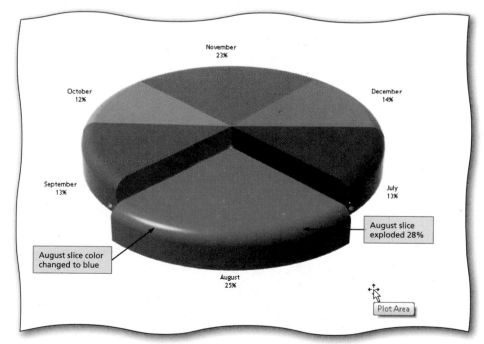

Figure 3–69

3

- Click the Fill category (Format Data Point dialog box) on the left side of the dialog box to display the Fill panel.

- Click Solid fill to display the Fill Color area and then click the Color button to display the Color gallery.

- Click the Blue color in the Standard Colors area of the color gallery and then click the Close button (Format Data Point dialog box) to change the color of the selected slice and close the dialog box (Figure 3–70).

Figure 3–70

Other Ways

1. Right-click slice, click Shape Fill Color button arrow on Mini toolbar, select color

To Change the Colors of the Remaining Slices

The colors of the remaining slices also can be changed to enhance the appeal of the chart. The following steps change the color of the remaining five chart slices.

1 Right-click the slice labeled July to select only the July slice, and display a shortcut menu and Mini toolbar.

2 Click the Shape Fill button arrow on the Mini toolbar to display the Color gallery.

3 Click the Yellow color in the Standard Colors area in the Color gallery to change the color of the slice.

4 Repeat Steps 1 through 3 for the remaining four slices. Assign the following colors in the Standard Colors area in the color gallery to each slice: September – Green; October – Dark Blue; November – Red; December – Purple.

5 Click anywhere outside the chart to deselect the December slice (Figure 3–71). The completed chart appears as shown in Figure 3–71.

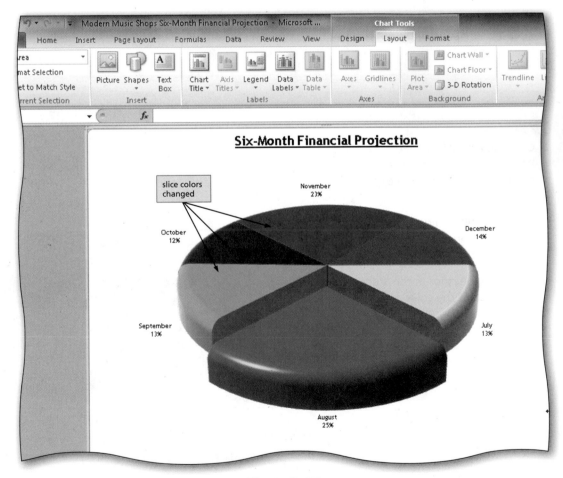

Figure 3–71

Renaming and Reordering the Sheets and Coloring their Tabs

The final step in creating the workbook is to reorder the sheets and modify the tabs at the bottom of the screen.

To Rename the Sheets and Color Their Tabs

The following steps rename the sheets and color the sheet tabs.

1 Change the sheet tab color of the 3-D Pie Chart sheet to Orange, Accent 6 (column 10, row 1).

2 Double-click the tab labeled Sheet1 at the bottom of the screen.

3 Type `Six-Month Financial Projection` as the new sheet name and then press the ENTER key.

4 Change the sheet tab color of the Six-Month Financial Projection sheet to Pink, Accent 1 (column 5, row 1) and then select cell D8 (Figure 3–72).

Figure 3–72

To Reorder the Sheet Tabs

Change the order sheets in a workbook so that they appear with the most important worksheets first. The following steps reorder the sheets so that the worksheet precedes the chart sheet in the workbook.

1

- Drag the Six-Month Financial Projection tab to the left in front of the 3-D Pie Chart tab to rearrange the sequence of the sheets (Figure 3–73).

		200,000.00	
3	Commission	5.75%	
4	Margin	57.50%	
5	Marketing	15.00%	
6	Research and Development	7.50%	
7	Sales Revenue for Bonus	3,500,000.00	
8	Support, General, and Administrative	18.75%	
9			

Modern Music Shops

Six-Month Financial Projection

		July	August	September	October
12	Six-Month Financial Projection tab moved to left of 3-D Pie Chart tab				
13	Revenue	$3,113,612.16	$7,962,235.53	$5,112,268.58	$2,924,62
14	Cost of Goods Sold	1,323,285.17	3,383,950.10	2,172,714.15	1,242,96
15	Gross Margin	$1,790,326.99	$4,578,285.43	$2,939,554.43	$1,681,661
16					
17	Expenses				
18	Bonus	$0.00	$200,000.00	$200,000.00	$0

Six-Month Financial Projection | 3-D Pie Chart | Sheet2 | Sheet3

Ready

Figure 3–73

Other Ways

1. To move sheet, right-click sheet tab, click Move or Copy on shortcut menu

To Check Spelling in Multiple Sheets

By default, the spell checker checks the spelling only in the selected sheets. It will check all the cells in the selected sheets, unless you select a range of two or more cells. Before checking the spelling, the following steps select both sheets in the workbook so that both worksheets in the workbook are checked for spelling errors.

1 With the Six-Month Financial Projection sheet active, press CTRL+HOME to select cell A1. Hold down the CTRL key and then click the 3-D Pie Chart tab to select multiple sheets.

2 Display the Review tab and then click the Spelling button (Review tab | Proofing group) to check spelling in the selected sheets.

3 Correct any errors and then click the OK button (Spelling dialog box or Microsoft Excel dialog box) when the spell check is complete.

4 Save the workbook.

BTW

Checking Spelling
Unless you first select a range of cells or an object before starting the spell checker, Excel checks the entire selected worksheet, including all cell values, cell comments, embedded charts, text boxes, buttons, and headers and footers.

To Preview and Print the Workbook

After checking the spelling, the next step is to preview and print the sheets. As with spelling, Excel previews and prints only the selected sheets. In addition, because the worksheet is too wide to print in portrait orientation, the orientation must be changed to landscape. The following steps adjust the orientation and scale, preview the workbook, and then print the workbook.

1 Ready the printer. If both sheets are not selected, hold down the CTRL key and then click the tab of the inactive sheet.

2 Click File on the Ribbon to open the Backstage view.

3 Click the Print tab in the Backstage view to display the Print gallery.

4 If necessary, click the Portrait Orientation button in the Settings area and then select Landscape Orientation to select the desired orientation.

5 If necessary, click the No Scaling button in the Settings area and then select 'Fit Sheet on One Page' to cause the workbook to print on one page.

6 If necessary, click the Printer Status button to display a list of available Printer options and then click the desired printer to change the currently selected printer.

7 Click the Print button in the Print gallery to print the worksheet in landscape orientation on the currently selected printer.

8 When the printer stops, retrieve the printed worksheet (Figure 3–74a and Figure 3–74b on the following page).

9 Right-click the Six-Month Financial Projection tab. Click Ungroup Sheets on the shortcut menu to deselect the 3-D Pie Chart tab.

10 Save the workbook.

Figure 3–74 (a) Worksheet

What-If Assumptions								
Bonus	200,000.00							
Commission	5.75%							
Margin	57.50%							
Marketing	15.00%							
Research and Development	7.50%							
Sales Revenue for Bonus	3,500,000.00							
Support, General, and Administrative	18.75%							

Modern Music Shops
Six-Month Financial Projection   12/23/2009

	July	August	September	October	November	December	Total	Chart
Revenue	$3,113,612.16	$7,962,235.53	$5,112,268.58	$2,924,627.87	$7,630,534.65	$3,424,270.23	$30,167,549.02	
Cost of Goods Sold	1,323,285.17	3,383,950.10	2,172,714.15	1,242,966.84	3,242,977.23	1,455,314.85	30,167,549.02	
Gross Margin	$1,790,326.99	$4,578,285.43	$2,939,554.43	$1,681,661.03	$4,387,557.42	$1,968,955.38	$30,167,549.02	
Expenses								
Bonus	0	200000	200000	0	200000	0	600000	
Commission	179,032.70	457,828.54	293,955.44	168,166.10	438,755.74	196,895.54	1,734,634.07	
Marketing	467,041.82	1,194,335.33	766,840.29	438,694.18	1,144,580.20	513,640.53	4,525,132.35	
Research and Development	233,520.91	597,167.66	383,420.14	219,347.09	572,290.10	256,820.27	2,262,566.18	
Support, General, and Administrative	583,802.28	1,492,919.16	958,550.36	548,367.73	1,430,725.25	642,050.67	5,656,415.44	
Total Expenses	$1,463,397.72	$3,942,250.70	$2,602,766.23	$1,374,575.10	$3,786,351.29	$1,609,407.01	$14,778,748.04	
Operating Income	$326,929.28	$636,034.73	$336,788.20	$307,085.93	$601,206.14	$359,548.37	$2,567,592.65	

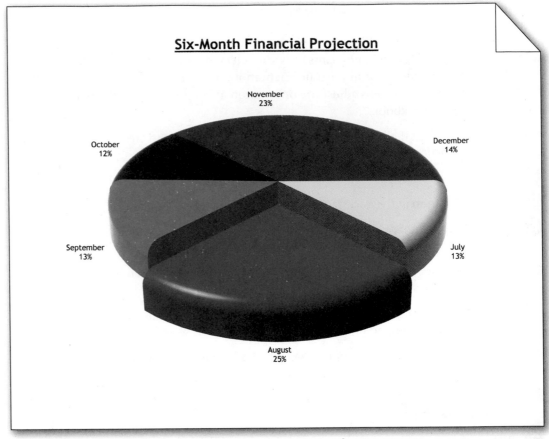

Figure 3–74 (b) 3-D Pie Chart

Changing the View of the Worksheet

With Excel, you easily can change the view of the worksheet. For example, you can magnify or shrink the worksheet on the screen. You also can view different parts of the worksheet through windowpanes.

To Shrink and Magnify the View of a Worksheet or Chart

You can magnify (zoom in) or shrink (zoom out) the appearance of a worksheet or chart by using the Zoom button (View tab | Zoom group). When you magnify a worksheet, Excel enlarges the view of the characters on the screen, but displays fewer columns and rows. Alternatively, when you shrink a worksheet, Excel is able to display more columns and rows. Magnifying or shrinking a worksheet affects only the view; it does not change the window size or printout of the worksheet or chart. The following steps shrink and magnify the view of the worksheet.

1

- If cell A1 is not active, press CTRL + HOME.

- Display the View tab and then click the Zoom button (View tab | Zoom group) to display a list of magnifications in the Zoom dialog box (Figure 3–75).

Figure 3–75

2

- Click 75% and then click the OK button (Zoom dialog box) to shrink the display of the worksheet (Figure 3–76).

Figure 3–76

3

- Click the Zoom In button on the status bar until the worksheet is displayed at 100% (Figure 3–77).

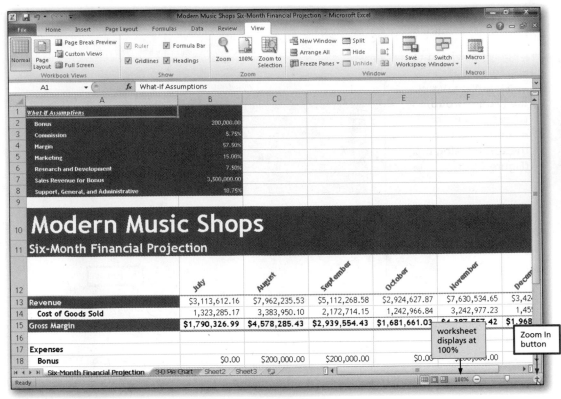

Figure 3–77

To Split a Window into Panes

When working with a large worksheet, you can split the window into two or four panes to view different parts of the worksheet at the same time. Splitting the Excel window into four panes at cell D13 allows you to view all four corners of the worksheet easily. The following steps split the Excel window into four panes.

1

- Select cell D13, the intersection of the four proposed panes, to select the cell at which to split the window.

- If necessary, display the View tab (Figure 3–78).

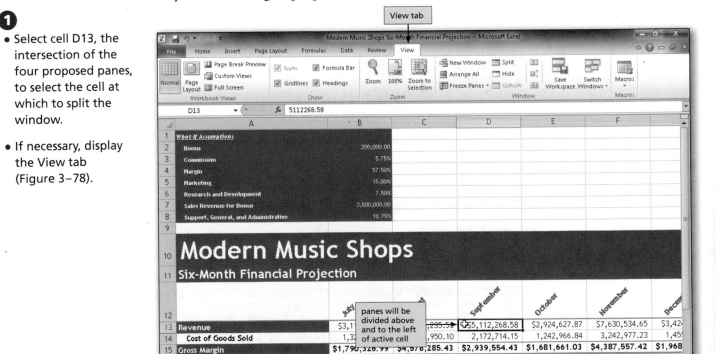

Figure 3–78

2

- Click the Split button (View tab | Window group) to divide the window into four panes.

- Use the scroll arrows to show the four corners of the worksheet at the same time (Figure 3–79).

Q&A

What is shown in the four panes?

The four panes in Figure 3–79 are used to show the following: (1) range A1:C12 in the upper-left pane; (2) range G1:I12 in the upper-right pane; (3) range A19:C24 in the lower-left pane; and (4) range G19:I24

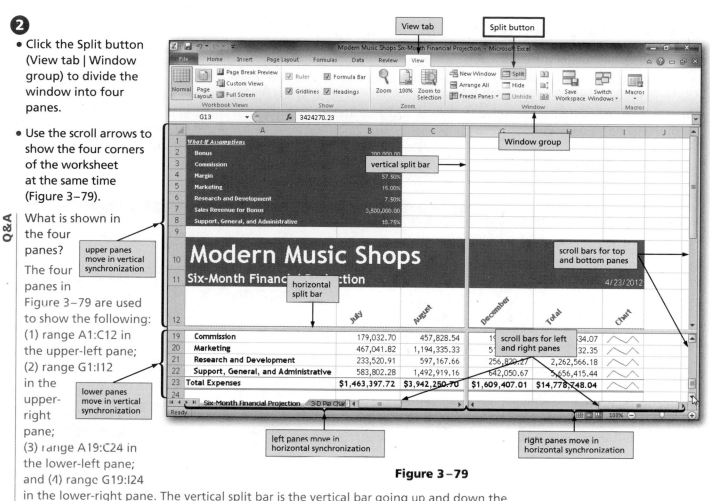

Figure 3–79

in the lower-right pane. The vertical split bar is the vertical bar going up and down the middle of the window. The horizontal split bar is the horizontal bar going across the middle of the window. If you use the scroll bars below the window and to the right of the window to scroll the window, you will see that the panes split by the horizontal split bar scroll together vertically. The panes split by the vertical split bar scroll together horizontally. To resize the panes, drag either split bar to the desired location in the window.

To Remove the Panes from the Window

1 Position the mouse pointer at the intersection of the horizontal and vertical split bars.

2 When the mouse pointer changes to a four-headed arrow, double-click to remove the four panes from the window.

Other Ways

1. Drag horizontal split box and vertical split box to desired locations

What-If Analysis

The automatic recalculation feature of Excel is a powerful tool that can be used to analyze worksheet data. Using Excel to scrutinize the impact of changing values in cells that are referenced by a formula in another cell is called what-if analysis or **sensitivity analysis**. When new data is entered, Excel not only recalculates all formulas in a worksheet but also redraws any associated charts.

In the workbook created in this chapter, many of the formulas are dependent on the assumptions in the range B2:B8. Thus, if you change any of the assumption values, Excel immediately recalculates all formulas. Excel redraws the 3-D Pie chart as well, because it is based on these numbers.

BTW

Zooming
You can use the Zoom in and Zoom out buttons on the status bar to zoom from 10% to 400% to reduce or enlarge the display of a worksheet.

To Analyze Data in a Worksheet by Changing Values

A what-if question for the worksheet in Chapter 3 might be *what* would happen to the six-month operating income in cell H25 *if* the Bonus, Commission, Support, General, and Administrative assumptions in the What-If Assumptions table were changed as follows: Bonus $200,000.00 to $150,000.00; Commission 5.75% to 4.00%; Support, General, and Administrative 18.75% to 15.75%? To answer a question like this, you need to change only the first, second, and seventh values in the What-If Assumptions table, as shown in the following steps. The steps also divide the window into two vertical panes. Excel instantaneously recalculates the formulas in the worksheet and redraws the 3-D Pie chart to answer the question.

1

- Press CTRL+HOME to select cell A1.

- Drag the vertical split box from the lower-right corner of the screen to the left so that the vertical split bar is positioned as shown in Figure 3–80 to split the screen vertically.

- Drag the horizontal split box from the upper-right corner of the screen down so that the horizontal split bar is positioned as shown in Figure 3–80 to split the screen horizontally.

- Use the scroll arrows in the lower-right pane to view the total operating income in column H in the lower-right pane.

Figure 3–80

- Enter `150000` in cell B2, `4%` in cell B3, and `15.75%` in cell B8 (Figure 3–80), which causes the six-month operating income in cell H25 to increase from $2,567,592.65 to $4,150,551.23.

To Goal Seek

If you know the result you want a formula to produce, you can use **goal seeking** to determine the value of a cell on which the formula depends. The following steps close and reopen the Modern Music Shops Six-Month Financial Projection workbook. They then use the Goal Seek command (Data tab | Data Tools group) to determine the Support, General, and Administrative percentage in cell B8 that will yield a six-month operating income of $3,000,000.00 in cell H25, rather than the original $2,567,592.65.

1

- Close the workbook without saving the changes and then reopen it.

- Drag the vertical split box from the lower-right corner of the screen to the left so that the vertical split bar is positioned as shown in Figure 3–81 to split the screen vertically.

- Drag the horizontal split box from the upper-right corner of the screen down so that the horizontal split bar is positioned as shown in Figure 3–81 to split the screen horizontally.

- Use the scroll arrows in the lower-right pane to view the total operating income in column H in the lower-right pane.

Figure 3–81

- Select cell H25, the cell that contains the six-month operating income.

- Display the Data tab and then click the What-If Analysis button (Data tab | Data Tools group) to display the What-If Analysis menu (Figure 3–81).

2

- Click Goal Seek to display the Goal Seek dialog box with the Set cell box set to the selected cell, H25 in this case.

- When Excel displays the Goal Seek dialog box, click the To value text box, type 3,000,000 and then click the 'By changing cell' box to select the 'By changing cell' box.

- Click cell B8 on the worksheet to assign the current cell, B8 in this case, to the 'By changing cell' box (Figure 3–82).

Figure 3–82

❸

- Click the OK button (Goal Seek dialog box) to goal seek for the sought-after value in the 'To value' box, $3,000,000.00 in cell H25 in this case (Figure 3–83).

Q&A

What happens when I click the OK button?

Excel immediately changes cell H25 from $2,567,592.65 to the desired value of $3,000,000.00. More importantly, Excel changes the Support, General, and Administrative assumption in cell B8 from 18.75% to 17.32% (Figure 3–83). Excel also displays the Goal Seek Status dialog box. If you click the OK button, Excel keeps the new values in the worksheet. If you click the Cancel button, Excel redisplays the original values.

Figure 3–83

❹

- Click the Cancel button in the Goal Seek Status dialog box to redisplay the original values in the worksheet.

BTW

Certification
The Microsoft Office Specialist (MOS) program provides an opportunity for you to obtain a valuable industry credential — proof that you have the Excel 2010 skills required by employers. For more information, visit the Excel 2010 Certification Web page (scsite.com/ex2010/cert).

Goal Seeking

Goal seeking assumes you can change the value of only one cell referenced directly or indirectly to reach a specific goal for a value in another cell. In this example, to change the six-month operating income in cell H25 to $3,000,000.00, the Support, General, and Administrative percentage in cell B8 must decrease by 1.43% from 18.75% to 17.32%.

You can see from this goal seeking example that the cell to change (cell B8) does not have to be referenced directly in the formula or function. For example, the six-month operating income in cell H25 is calculated by the function =SUM(B25:G25). Cell B8 is not referenced in this function. Instead, cell B8 is referenced in the formulas in rows 18 through 22, on which the monthly operating incomes in row 25 are based. Excel thus is capable of goal seeking on the six-month operating income by varying the value for the Support, General, and Administrative assumption.

To Quit Excel

With the workbook complete, the following steps quit Excel.

1 Click the Close button on the upper-right corner of the title bar.

2 If the Microsoft Excel dialog box is displayed, click the Don't Save button.

BTW

Quick Reference
For a table that lists how to complete the tasks covered in this book using the mouse, Ribbon, shortcut menu, and keyboard, see the Quick Reference Summary at the back of this book, or visit the Excel 2010 Quick Reference Web page (scsite.com/ex2010/qr).

Chapter Summary

In this chapter you learned how to work with large worksheets that extend beyond the window, how to use the fill handle to create a series, new formatting techniques, about the difference between absolute cell references and relative cell references, how to use the IF function, and how to rotate text in a cell, freeze titles, add Sparkline charts, change the magnification of the worksheet, show different parts of the worksheet at the same time through multiple panes, create a 3-D Pie chart, and improve the appearance of a 3-D Pie chart. This chapter also introduced you to using Excel to do what-if analysis by changing values in cells and goal seeking. The items listed below include all the new Excel skills you have learned in this chapter.

1. Rotate Text and Use the Fill Handle to Create a Series of Month Names (EX 145)
2. Increase Column Widths (EX 149)
3. Enter Row Titles (EX 150)
4. Copy a Range of Cells to a Nonadjacent Destination Area (EX 151)
5. Insert a Row (EX 154)
6. Enter Numbers with Format Symbols (EX 156)
7. Freeze Column and Row Titles (EX 157)
8. Enter and Format the System Date (EX 159)
9. Enter a Formula Containing Absolute Cell References (EX 162)
10. Enter an IF Function (EX 165)
11. Copy Formulas with Absolute Cell References Using the Fill Handle (EX 168)
12. Unfreeze the Worksheet Titles and Save the Workbook (EX 169)
13. Add a Sparkline Chart to the Worksheet (EX 170)
14. Format and Copy the Sparkline Chart (EX 171)
15. Assign Formats to Nonadjacent Ranges (EX 174)
16. Format the Worksheet Titles (EX 176)
17. Copy a Cell's Format Using the Format Painter Button (EX 178)
18. Draw a 3-D Pie Chart on a Separate Chart Sheet (EX 182)
19. Insert a Chart Title and Data Labels (EX 183)
20. Rotate the 3-D Pie Chart (EX 186)
21. Apply a 3-D Format to the Pie Chart (EX 188)
22. Explode the 3-D Pie Chart and Change the Color of a Slice (EX 190)
23. Reorder the Sheet Tabs (EX 194)
24. Check Spelling in Multiple Sheets (EX 194)
25. Shrink and Magnify the View of a Worksheet or Chart (EX 196)
26. Split a Window into Panes (EX 198)
27. Analyze Data in a Worksheet by Changing Values (EX 200)
28. Goal Seek (EX 200)

Learn It Online

Test your knowledge of chapter content and key terms.

Instructions: To complete the Learn It Online exercises, start your browser, click the Address bar, and then enter the Web address `scsite.com/ex2010/learn`. When the Excel 2010 Learn It Online page is displayed, click the link for the exercise you want to complete and then read the instructions.

Chapter Reinforcement TF, MC, and SA
A series of true/false, multiple choice, and short answer questions that test your knowledge of the chapter content.

Flash Cards
An interactive learning environment where you identify chapter key terms associated with displayed definitions.

Practice Test
A series of multiple choice questions that test your knowledge of chapter content and key terms.

Who Wants To Be a Computer Genius?
An interactive game that challenges your knowledge of chapter content in the style of a television quiz show.

Wheel of Terms
An interactive game that challenges your knowledge of chapter key terms in the style of the television show *Wheel of Fortune*.

Crossword Puzzle Challenge
A crossword puzzle that challenges your knowledge of key terms presented in the chapter.

Apply Your Knowledge

Reinforce the skills and apply the concepts you learned in this chapter.

Understanding Logical Tests and Absolute Cell Referencing

Instructions Part 1: Determine the truth value (true or false) of the following logical tests, given the following cell values: B4 = 30; W3 = 100; H5 = 32; L2 = 25; and M8 = 15. Enter true or false.

a. M8 > B4   Truth value: _____

b. W3 = L2   Truth value: _____

c. L2 + 15 * B4 / 10 <> W3   Truth value: _____

d. H5 − L2 < B4 / M8   Truth value: _____

e. (M8 + B4) * 2 <> W3 − (M8 / 3) * 2   Truth value: _____

f. M8 + 300 > B4 * H5 + 10   Truth value: _____

g. H5 * L2 >= 2 * (W3 + 25)   Truth value: _____

h. B4 = 10 * (M8 / 5)   Truth value: _____

Instructions Part 2: Write cell J49 as a relative reference, absolute reference, mixed reference with the column varying, and mixed reference with the row varying.

_____ _____ _____ _____

Instructions Part 3: Start Excel. Open the workbook Apply 3-1 Absolute Cell References. See the inside back cover of this book for instructions for downloading the Data Files for Students, or see your instructor for information on accessing the files required in this book. You will re-create the numerical grid pictured in Figure 3–84.

Perform the following tasks:

1. Enter a formula in cell C7 that multiplies the sum of cells C3 through C6 times cell C2. Write the formula so that when you copy it to cells D7 and E7, Excel adjusts all the cell references according to the destination cells. Verify your formula by checking it with the values found in cells C7, D7, and E7 in Figure 3–84.

2. Enter a formula in cell F3 that multiplies cell B3 times the sum of cells C3 through E3. Write the formula so that when you copy the formula to cells F4, F5, and F6, Excel adjusts all the cell references according to the destination cells. Verify your formula by checking it with the values found in cells F3, F4, F5, and F6 in Figure 3–84.

3. Enter a formula in cell C8 that multiplies the sum of cells C3 through C6 times cell C2. Write the formula so that when you copy the formula to cells D8 and E8, cell C2 remains absolute. Verify your formula by checking it with the values found in cells C8, D8, and E8 in Figure 3–84.

4. Enter a formula in cell G3 that multiplies the sum of cells C3, D3, and E3 times cell B3. Write the formula so that when you copy the formula to cells G4, G5, and G6, cell B3 remains absolute. Verify your formula by checking it with the values found in cells G3, G4, G5, and G6 in Figure 3–84.

5. Apply the worksheet name, Cell References, to the sheet tab and apply the Red, Accent 2 theme color to the sheet tab.

6. Change the document properties, as specified by your instructor. Change the worksheet header with your name, course number, and other information as specified by your instructor. Save the workbook using the file name, Apply 3-1 Absolute Cell References Complete, and submit the workbook as requested by your instructor.

Figure 3–84

Extend Your Knowledge

Extend the skills you learned in this chapter and experiment with new skills. You may need to use Help to complete the assignment.

Nested IF Functions and More About the Fill Handle

Instructions Part 1: Start Excel. You will use nested IF functions to determine values for sets of data.

1. Using the Insert Function dialog box, enter the following IF function in cell B1:

    IF(A1="TX", "Central", "Time Zone Error")

2. Select cell B1, select the text "Time Zone Error" in the Formula Bar, click the Logical button (Formulas tab | Function Library group), click IF, and enter the following IF function:

    IF(A1="OR", "Pacific", "Time Zone Error")

3. Select cell B1, select "Time Zone Error" in the Formula Bar, click Logical button (Formulas tab | Function Library group), click IF, and enter the following IF function:

    IF(A1="VA", "Eastern", "Time Zone Error")

4. Verify that the formula in cell B1 appears as follows:

    =IF(A1="TX","Central", IF(A1="OR","Pacific", IF(A1="VA","Eastern","Time Zone Error")))

5. Use the fill handle to copy the nested IF function down through cell B6. Enter the following data in the cells in the range A1:A6 and then write down the results that display in cells B1 through B6 for each set. Set 1: A1 = TX; A2 = NY; A3 = OR; A4 = MI; A5 = TX; A6 = VA. Set 2: A1= WI; A2 = OR; A3 = IL; A4 = VA; A5 = NJ; A6 = TX.

Set 1 Results: _____

Set 2 Results: _____

6. Save the workbook using the file name, Extend 3-1 Create Series Complete Part 1, and submit the workbook as specified by your instructor.

Instructions Part 2: Start Excel. Open the workbook Extend 3-1 Create Series. See the inside back cover of this book for instructions for downloading the Data Files for Students, or see your instructor for information on accessing the files required in this book.

Perform the following tasks:

1. Use the fill handle on one column at a time to propagate the twelve series through row 14, as shown in Figure 3–85. For example, in column A, select cell A2 and drag the fill handle down to cell A14. In column C, hold down the CTRL key to repeat Saturday through cell C14. In column D, select the range D2:D3 and drag the fill handle down to cell D14. Likewise, in columns G through L, select the two adjacent cells in rows 2 and 3 before dragging the fill handle down to the corresponding cell in row 14.

2. Select cell D19. While holding down the CTRL key, one at a time drag the fill handle three cells to the right, to the left, up, and down to generate four series of numbers beginning with zero and incremented by one.

3. Select cell H19. Point to the cell border so that the mouse pointer changes to a plus sign with four arrows. Drag the mouse pointer down to cell H21 to move the contents of cell H19 to cell H21.

4. Select cell H21. Point to the cell border so that the mouse pointer changes to a plus sign with four arrows. While holding down the CTRL key, drag the mouse pointer to cell K21 to copy the contents of cell H21 to cell K21.

Figure 3–85

5. Select cell K19. Drag the fill handle in to the center of cell K19 so that the cell is shaded and the cell contents are deleted.

6. Apply a worksheet name to the sheet tab and apply a color of your choice to the sheet tab.

7. Select cell range H2:I14, click the Pie button (Insert tab | Charts group) to display the Pie gallery, click Pie in 3-D chart in the Pie gallery, click the Move Chart button (Chart Tools Design tab | Location group), click the New sheet option button (Move Chart dialog box), and then click the OK button (Move Chart dialog box) to move the 3-D Pie chart to a new worksheet.

8. Click the Chart Title button (Chart Tools Layout tab | Labels group), click Above Chart in the Chart Title gallery, select the title, and change the chart title to "Yearly Breakdown".

9. Click the Data Labels button (Chart Tools Layout tab | Labels group), click Outside End in the Data Labels gallery to add data points to the chart.

10. Apply a chart sheet name to the sheet tab and apply a color of your choice to the tab.

11. Change the document properties, as specified by your instructor. Change the worksheet header with your name, course number, and other information as specified by your instructor. Save the workbook using the file name, Extend 3-1 Create Series Complete Part 2, and submit the workbook as specified by your instructor.

Make It Right

Analyze a workbook and correct all errors and/or improve the design.

Inserting Rows, Moving a Range, and Correcting Formulas in a Worksheet

Instructions: Start Excel. Open the workbook Make It Right 3-1 SpeedyOfficeSupply.com Annual Projected Net Income. See the inside back cover of this book for instructions for downloading the Data Files for Students, or see your instructor for information on accessing the files required for this book. Correct the following design and formula problems (Figure 3–86a) in the worksheet.

Figure 3–86 (a) Before

Assumptions

Shipping %	7.80%
Discount %	15.00%
Proc. Costs %	5.75%

SpeedyOfficeSupply.com Annual Projected Net Income

Contract	Sales	Shipping Costs	Discounts	Proc. Costs	Net Income
District Schools	$5,781,246.25	$450,937.21	$867,186.94	$332,421.66	$4,130,700.45
CMT Publishers	2,772,915.50	415,937.33	$159,442.64	$0.00	2,197,535.53
TVS Medical Offices	3,469,871.95	199,517.64	$0.00	$0.00	3,270,354.31
SuperRetail Outlets	2,348,638.75	-	$117,431.94	#VALUE!	#VALUE!
Total	$14,372,672.45	$1,066,392.17	$1,144,061.52	#VALUE!	#VALUE!

Figure 3–86 (b) After

SpeedyOfficeSupply.com Annual Projected Net Income

Contract	Sales	Shipping Costs	Discounts	Proc. Costs	Net Income
District Schools	$5,781,246.25	$450,937.21	$867,186.94	$332,421.66	$4,130,700.45
CMT Publishers	2,772,915.50	216,287.41	415,937.33	159,442.64	1,981,248.12
TVS Medical Offices	3,469,871.95	270,650.01	520,480.79	199,517.64	2,479,223.51
SuperRetail Outlets	2,348,638.75	183,193.82	117,431.94	135,046.73	1,912,966.26
Total	$14,372,672.45	$1,121,068.45	$1,921,036.99	$826,428.67	$10,504,138.34

Assumptions

Shipping %	7.80%
Discount %	15.00%
Proc. Costs %	5.75%

1. The Shipping Cost in cell C8 is computed using the formula =B2*B8 (Shipping % × Sales). Similar formulas are used in cells C9, C10, and C11. The formula in cell C8 was entered and copied to cells C9, C10, and C11. Although the result in cell C8 is correct, the results in cells C9, C10, and C11 are incorrect. Edit the formula in cell C8 by changing cell B2 to an absolute cell reference. Copy the corrected formula in cell C8 to cells C9, C10, and C11. After completing the copy, click the Auto Fill Options button arrow that is displayed below and to the right of cell C11 and choose Fill Without Formatting.

2. The Discount amounts in cells D8, D9, D10, and D11 are computed using the IF function. The Discount amount should equal the amount in cell B3*B8 (Discount % × Sales) if the corresponding Sales in column B is greater than or equal to $2,500,000. If the corresponding Sales in column B is less than $2,500,000, then the Discount amount is 5%*B8 (5% × Sales). The IF function in cell D8

was entered and copied to cells D9, D10, and D11. The current IF functions in cells D8, D9, D10, and D11 are incorrect. Edit and correct the IF function in cell D8. Copy the corrected formula in cell D8 to cells D9, D10, and D11. After completing the copy, click the Auto Fill Options button arrow that is displayed below and to the right of cell D11 and choose Fill Without Formatting.

3. The Processing Costs in cell E8 is computed using the formula =B4*B8 (Proc. Costs % × Sales). The formula in cell E8 was entered and copied to cells E9, E10, and E11. Although the result in cell E8 is correct, the results in cells E9, E10, and E11 are incorrect. Edit and correct the formula in cell E8 by changing cell B4 to an absolute cell reference. Copy the corrected formula in cell E8 to cells E9, E10, and E11. After completing the copy, click the Auto Fill Options button arrow that displays below and to the right of cell E11 and choose Fill Without Formatting. Ensure that the range B9:E11 is formatted with the Accounting Number format.

4. Change the design of the worksheet by moving the Assumptions table in the range A1:B4 to the range A14:B17, as shown in Figure 3–86b. To complete the move drag the Assumptions table to the range A14:B17. Use Figure 3–86b to verify that Excel automatically adjusted the cell references based on the move. Use the Undo button and Redo button on the Quick Access Toolbar to move the Assumptions table back and forth while the results of the formulas remain the same.

5. Apply a worksheet name to the sheet tab and apply the Orange, Accent 3 color to the sheet tab.

6. Change the document properties, as specified by your instructor. Change the worksheet header with your name, course number, and other information as specified by your instructor. Save the workbook using the file name, Make It Right 3-1 SpeedyOfficeSupply.com Annual Projected Net Income Complete, and submit the revised workbook as specified by your instructor.

In the Lab

Create a workbook using the guidelines, concepts, and skills presented in this chapter. Labs are listed in order of increasing difficulty.

Lab 1: Six-Year Financial Projection

Problem: Your supervisor in the Finance department at Med Supply Online Warehouse has asked you to create a worksheet that will project the annual gross margin, expenses, total expenses, operating income, income taxes, and net income for the next six years based on the assumptions in Table 3–9. The desired worksheet is shown in Figure 3–87 on the following page. In Part 1 you will create the worksheet. In Part 2 you will create a chart to present the data, shown in Figure 3–88 on page EX 213. In Part 3 you will use Goal Seek to analyze three different sales scenarios.

Table 3–9 Med Supply Online Warehouse Financial Projection Assumptions	
Units Sold in Prior Year	1,589,712
Unit Cost	$59.50
Annual Sales Growth	4.50%
Annual Price Decrease	3.80%
Margin	38.80%

Continued >

In the Lab *continued*

Figure 3–87

Instructions Part 1:

1. Start Excel. Apply the Civic theme to the worksheet by using the Themes button (Page Layout tab | Themes group). Bold the entire worksheet by selecting the entire worksheet and using the Bold button (Home tab | Font group).

2. Enter the worksheet title **Med Supply Online Warehouse** in cell A1 and the subtitle **Six-Year Financial Projection** in cell A2. Format the worksheet title in cell A1 to 36-point Copperplate Gothic Bold (or a similar font). Format the worksheet subtitle in cell A2 to 20-point Verdana (or a similar font). Enter the system date in cell G2 using the NOW function. Format the date to the 14-Mar-01 style.

3. Change the following column widths: A = 25.00 characters; B through H = 15.00 characters. Change the heights of rows 7, 15, 17, 19, and 22 to 18.00 points.

4. Enter the six column titles Year 1 through Year 6 in the range B3:G3 by entering Year 1 in cell B3 and then dragging cell B3's fill handle through the range C3:G3. Format cell B3 as follows: (a) increase the font size to 14; (b) center and italicize it; and (c) angle its contents clockwise. Use the Format Painter button (Home tab | Clipboard group) to copy the format assigned to cell B3 to the range C3:G3.

5. Enter the row titles in the range A4:A19. Change the font in cells A7, A15, A17, and A19 to 14-point Verdana (or a similar font). Add thick bottom borders to the ranges B3:G3 and B5:G5. Use the Increase Indent button (Home tab | Alignment group) to increase the indent of the row titles in cell A5, the range A8:A14, and cell A18.

6. Enter the table title **Assumptions** in cell A22. Enter the assumptions in Table 3–9 on page EX 209 in the range A23:B27. Use format symbols when entering the numbers. Change the font size of the table title in cell A22 to 14-point Verdana and underline it.

7. Select the range B4:G19 and then click the Format Cells: Number Dialog Box Launcher (Home tab | Number group) to display the Format Cells dialog box. Use the Number category (Format Cells dialog box) to assign the Comma style with no decimal places and negative numbers enclosed in parentheses to the range B4:G19.

8. Complete the following entries:

   a. Year 1 Sales (cell B4) = Units Sold in Prior Year * (Unit Cost / (1 – Margin)) or = B23*(B24/(1-B27))

   b. Year 2 Sales (cell C4) = Year 1 Sales * (1 + Annual Sales Growth) * (1 – Annual Price Decrease) or =B4*(1+$B$25)*(1-$B$26)

   c. Copy cell C4 to the range D4:G4.

   d. Year 1 Cost of Goods (cell B5) = Year 1 Sales * (1 – Margin) or =B4 * (1 - $B$27)

   e. Copy cell B5 to the range C5:G5.

   f. Gross Margin (cell B6) = Year 1 Sales - Year 1 Cost of Goods or =B4 – B5

   g. Copy cell B6 to the range C6:G6.

   h. Year 1 Advertising (cell B8) = 500 + 8% * Year 1 Sales or =500+8%*B4

   i. Copy cell B8 to the range C8:G8.

   j. Maintenance (row 9): Year 1 = 1,605,000; Year 2 = 4,378,000; Year 3 = 5,920,000; Year 4 = 5,050,000; Year 5 = 3,200,000; Year 6 = 4,250,000

   k. Year 1 Rent (cell B10) = 2,700,000

   l. Year 2 Rent (cell C10) = Year 1 Rent + (12% * Year 1 Rent) or =B10*(1+12%)

   m. Copy cell C10 to the range D10:G10.

   n. Year 1 Salaries (cell B11) = 17% * Year 1 Sales or =17%*B4

   o. Copy cell B11 to the range C11:G11.

   p. Year 1 Shipping (cell B12) = 3.9% * Year 1 Sales or =3.9%*B4

   q. Copy cell B12 to the range C12:G12.

   r. Year 1 Supplies (cell B13) = 1.3% * Year 1 Sales or =1.3%*B4

   s. Copy cell B13 to the range C13:G13.

   t. Year 1 Web Services (cell B14) = 250,000

   u. Year 2 Web Services (cell C14) = Year 1 Web Services + (15% * Year 1 Web Services) or =B14*(1+15%)

   v. Copy cell C14 to the range D14:G14.

   w. Year 1 Total Expenses (cell B15) = SUM(B8:B14)

   x. Copy cell B15 to the range C15:G15.

   y. Year 1 Operating Income (cell B17) = Year 1 Gross Margin - Year 1 Total Expenses or =B6-B15

   z. Copy cell B17 to the range C17:G17.

Continued >

In the Lab *continued*

    aa. Year 1 Income Taxes (cell B18): If Year 1 Operating Income is less than 0, then Year 1 Income Taxes equal 0; otherwise Year 1 Income Taxes equal 45% * Year 1 Operating Income or =IF(B17 < 0, 0, 45%*B17)

    bb. Copy cell B18 to the range C18:G18.

    cc. Year 1 Net Income (cell B19) = Year 1 Operating Income – Year 1 Income Taxes or = B17-B18

    dd. Copy cell B19 to the range C19:G19.

    ee. In cell H4, insert a Sparkline Column chart (Insert Tab | Sparklines group) for cell range B4:G4

    ff. Repeat step ee for the ranges H5:H6, H8:H15, and H17:H19

9. Change the background colors as shown in Figure 3–87. Use Teal, Accent 3, Lighter 40% for the background colors.

10. Zoom to: (a) 200%; (b) 75%; (c) 25%; and (d) 100%.

11. Change the document properties, as specified by your instructor. Change the worksheet header with your name, course number, and other information as specified by your instructor. Save the workbook using the file name, Lab 3-1 Med Supply Online Warehouse Six-Year Financial Projection.

12. Preview the worksheet. Use the Orientation button (Page Layout tab | Page Setup group) to fit the printout on one page in landscape orientation. Preview the formulas version (CTRL+`) of the worksheet in landscape orientation using the Fit to option. Press CTRL +` to instruct Excel to display the values version of the worksheet. Save the workbook again and close the workbook.

13. Submit the workbook as specified by your instructor.

Instructions Part 2:

1. Start Excel. Open the workbook Lab 3-1 Med Supply Online Warehouse Six-Year Financial Projection.

2. Use the nonadjacent ranges B3:G3 and B19:G19 to create a 3-D Cylinder chart. Draw the chart by clicking the Column button (Insert tab | Charts group). When the Column gallery is displayed, click the Clustered Cylinder chart type (column 1, row 3). When the chart is displayed, click the Move Chart button to move the chart to a new sheet.

3. Select the legend on the right side of the chart and delete it. Add the chart title by clicking the Chart Titles button (Chart Tools Layout tab | Labels group). Click Above Chart in the Chart Title gallery. Format the chart title as shown in Figure 3–88.

4. To change the color of the cylinders, click one of the cylinders and use the Shape Fill button (Chart Tools Format tab | Shape Styles group). To change the color of the wall, click the wall behind the cylinders and use the Shape Fill button to change the chart wall color. Use the same procedure to change the color of the base of the wall.

5. Rename the sheet tabs Six-Year Financial Projection and 3-D Cylinder Chart. Rearrange the sheets so that the worksheet is leftmost and color their tabs as shown in Figure 3–88.

6. Click the Six-Year Financial Projection tab to display the worksheet. Save the workbook using the same file name (Lab 3-1 Med Supply Online Warehouse Six -Year Financial Projection) as defined in Part 1. Submit the workbook as requested by your instructor.

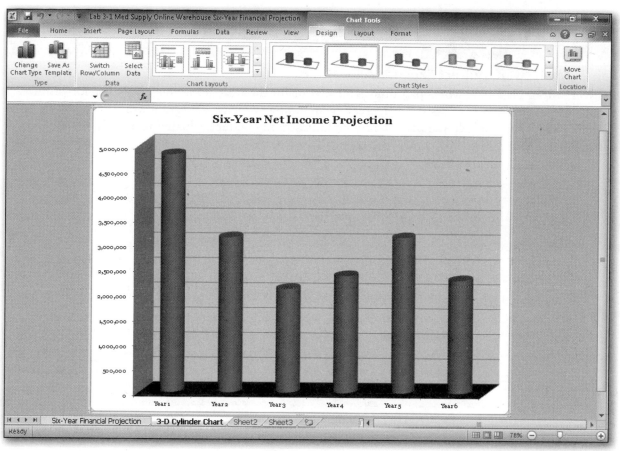

Figure 3–88

Instructions Part 3:

1. Start Excel. Open the workbook Lab 3-1 Med Supply Online Warehouse Six-Year Financial Projection. Do not save the workbook in this part of the In the Lab exercise. Divide the window into two panes by dragging the horizontal split box between rows 6 and 7. Use the scroll bars to show both the top and bottom of the worksheet. Using the numbers in columns 2 and 3 of Table 3–10, analyze the effect of changing the annual sales growth (cell B25) and annual price decrease (cell B26) on the net incomes in row 19. The resulting answers are in column 4 of Table 3–10. Submit the workbook or results of the what-if analysis for each case as requested by your instructor.

Table 3–10 Med Supply Online Warehouse Data to Analyze and Results			
Case	Annual Sales Growth	Annual Price Decrease	Year 6 Resulting Net Income in Cell G19
1	8.45%	5.75%	2,925,008
2	14.75%	23.00%	(2,353,532)
3	25.50%	2.65%	14,668,149

2. Close the workbook without saving it, and then reopen it. Use the What-If Analysis button (Data tab | Data Tools group) to goal seek. Determine a margin (cell B27) that would result in a Year 6 net income of $4,000,000 (cell G19). You should end up with a margin of 40.49% in cell B27. Submit the workbook with the new values or the results of the goal seek as requested by your instructor. Do not save the workbook with the latest changes.

In the Lab

Lab 2: Analysis of Indirect Expense Allocations

Problem: Your classmate works part time as an advisor for the ReachOut Neighbors not-for-profit group. She has asked you to assist her in creating an indirect expense allocation worksheet (Figure 3–89) that will help the not-for-profit administration better evaluate the branch offices described in Table 3–11.

ReachOut Neighbors

Analysis of Indirect Expenses   19-May-10

	Chicago Branch Office	Dallas Branch Office	Houston Branch Office	Jacksonville Branch Office	Los Angeles Branch Office	New York Branch Office	Reno Branch Office	Total
Total Donations	$735,356.00	$98,190.00	$178,435.00	$212,300.00	$175,350.00	$752,900.00	$1,845,230.00	$3,997,761.00
Distributed Goods and Services	529,750.00	60,891.00	135,589.00	150,895.00	96,050.00	589,590.00	1,629,350.00	$3,192,115.00
Direct Expenses	57,550.00	22,530.00	14,750.00	25,300.00	42,670.00	58,600.00	65,000.00	286,400.00
Indirect Expenses								
Administrative	$15,175.21	$2,026.30	$3,682.28	$4,381.14	$3,618.62	$15,537.26	$38,029.18	$82,500.00
Depreciation	15,930.38	296.52	7,759.63	8,479.07	976.38	6,449.23	8,838.29	49,230.00
Energy	10,355.93	1,382.80	2,512.88	2,989.80	2,469.43	10,603.00	25,986.16	56,300.00
Insurance	4,368.48	218.42	2,127.87	2,325.16	267.75	1,768.53	2,423.80	13,500.00
Maintenance	13,632.88	681.64	6,640.53	7,256.21	835.56	5,519.12	7,564.05	42,130.00
Marketing	12,554.04	1,676.31	3,046.25	3,624.40	2,993.59	12,853.55	31,501.87	68,250.00
Total Indirect Expenses	$72,016.92	$6,281.99	$25,269.45	$29,055.77	$11,161.32	$52,730.69	$114,393.85	$311,910.00
Net Income	$76,039.08	$7,987.01	$2,326.55	$7,049.23	$25,468.68	$51,979.31	$36,486.15	$202,336.00
Square Footage	15,500	775	7,550	8,250	950	6,275	8,600	47,900
Planned Indirect Expenses								
Administrative	82,500							
Depreciation	49,230							
Energy	56,300							
Insurance	13,500							
Maintenance	42,130							
Marketing	68,250							

Indirect Expenses Analysis / 3-D Column Chart / Sheet2 / Sheet3

Figure 3–89

Table 3–11 ReachOut Neighbor Worksheet Data							
	Chicago Branch Office	Dallas Branch Office	Houston Branch Office	Jacksonville Branch Office	Los Angeles Branch Office	New York Branch Office	Reno Branch Office
Total Donations	735356	98190	178435	212300	175350	752900	1845230
Distributed Goods and Services	529750	60891	135589	150895	96050	589590	1629350
Direct Expenses	57550	22530	14750	25300	42670	58600	65000
Square Footage	15500	775	7550	8250	950	6275	8600

Instructions Part 1: Do the following to create the worksheet shown in Figure 3–89.

1. Apply the Foundry theme to the worksheet. Bold the entire worksheet by selecting the entire worksheet and using the Bold (Home tab | Font group).

2. Change the following column widths: A = 30.00; B through I = 13.00; J = 20.00.

3. Enter the worksheet titles in cells A1 and A2 and the system date in cell I2. Format the date to the 14-Mar-01 style.

4. Enter the column titles, row titles, and the first three rows of numbers in Table 3–11 in rows 3 through 6. Add the column heading Total to cell I3. Center and italicize the column headings in the range B3:I3. Add a thick bottom border to the range B3:I3. Sum the individual rows 4, 5, and 6 in the range I4:I6.

5. Enter the Square Footage row as shown in Table 3–11 with the comma format symbol in row 16. Sum row 16 in cell I16. Use the Format Painter button (Home tab | Clipboard group) to format cell I16. Change the height of row 16 to 42.00. Vertically center the range A16:I16 through the use of the Format Cells dialog box.

6. Enter the remaining row titles in the range A7:A17 as shown in Figure 3–89. Increase the font size in cells A7, A14, and A15 to 14 point.

7. Copy the row titles in range A8:A13 to the range A18:A23. Enter the numbers shown in the range B18:B23 of Figure 3–89 with format symbols.

8. The planned indirect expenses in the range B18:B23 are to be prorated across the branch office as follows: Administrative (row 8), Energy (row 10), and Marketing (row 13) on the basis of Total Donations (row 4); Depreciation (row 9), Insurance (row 11), and Maintenance (row 12) on the basis of Square Footage (row 16). Use the following formulas to accomplish the prorating:

   a. Chicago Branch Office Administrative (cell B8) = Administrative Expenses * Chicago Branch Office Total Donations / ReachOut Neighbors Total Donations or =$B$18*B4/$I$4

   b. Chicago Branch Office Depreciation (cell B9) = Depreciation Expenses * Chicago Branch Office Square Footage / Total Square Footage or =$B$19*B16/$I$16

   c. Chicago Branch Office Energy (cell B10) = Energy Expenses * Chicago Branch Office Total Donations / ReachOut Neighbor Total Donations or =$B$20*B4/$I$4

   d. Chicago Branch Office Insurance (cell B11) = Insurance Expenses * Chicago Branch Office Square Footage / Total Square Footage or =$B$21*B16 /$I$16

   e. Chicago Branch Office Maintenance (cell B12) = Maintenance Expenses * Chicago Branch Office Square Footage / Total Square Footage or =$B$22*B16/$I$16

   f. Chicago Branch Office Marketing (cell B13) = Marketing Expenses * Chicago Branch Office Total Donations / ReachOut Neighbor Total Donations or =$B$23*B4/$I$4

   g. Chicago Branch Office Total Indirect Expenses (cell B14) = SUM(B8:B13)

   h. Chicago Branch Office Net Income (cell B15) = Total Donations - (Distributed Goods and Services + Direct Expenses + Total Indirect Expenses) or =B4-(B5+B6+B14)

   i. Copy the range B8:B15 to the range C8:H15.

   j. Sum the individual rows 8 through 15 in the range I8:I15.

9. Add a thick bottom border to the range B13:I13. Assign the Currency style with two decimal places and show negative numbers in parentheses to the following ranges: B4:I4; B8:I8; and B14:I15. Assign the Comma style with two decimal places and show negative numbers in parentheses to the following ranges: B5:I6 and B9:I13.

10. Change the font in cell A1 to 48-point Britannic Bold (or a similar font). Change the font in cell A2 to 22-point Britannic Bold (or a similar font). Change the font in cell A17 to 18-point italic Britannic Bold.

11. Use the background color Green, Accent 1, Lighter 40% and the font color Tan, Background 2, Darker 75% for cell A7 and the ranges A1:I2; A15:I15; and A17:B23 as shown in Figure 3–89.

12. Insert a Sparkline Win/Loss chart for the range B8:H8 in cell J8. Copy the cell J8 to the cell range J9:J13.

Continued >

In the Lab *continued*

13. Rename the Sheet1 sheet as Indirect Expenses Analysis and color its tab green.

14. Update the document properties with your name, course number, and name for the workbook. Change the worksheet header with your name, course number, and other information as specified by your instructor. Save the workbook using the file name, Lab 3-2 ReachOut Neighbor Analysis of Indirect Expenses.

15. Preview the worksheet. Use the Orientation button (Page Layout tab | Page Setup group) to fit the printout on one page in landscape orientation using the Fit to option. Preview the formulas version (CTRL+`) of the worksheet in landscape orientation using the Fit to option. Press CTRL+` to instruct Excel to display the values version of the worksheet. Save the workbook again and close the workbook.

16. Divide the window into four panes and show the four corners of the worksheet. Remove the four panes. Close the workbook but do not save the workbook.

Instructions Part 2: Start Excel. Open Lab 3-2 ReachOut Neighbor Analysis of Indirect Expenses. Draw a 3-D Column Chart (Figure 3–90) on a separate sheet that shows the contribution of each category of indirect expense to the total indirect expenses. That is, chart the nonadjacent ranges A8:A13 (category names) and I8:I13 (data series). Show labels that include value of the column. Do not show the legend. Format the 3-D Column Chart as shown in Figure 3–90. Rename the chart sheet 3-D Column Chart and color the sheet tab red. Move the chart tab to the right of the worksheet tab. Save the workbook using the file name, Lab 3-2 ReachOut Neighbor Analysis of Indirect Expenses. Submit the workbook as specified by your instructor.

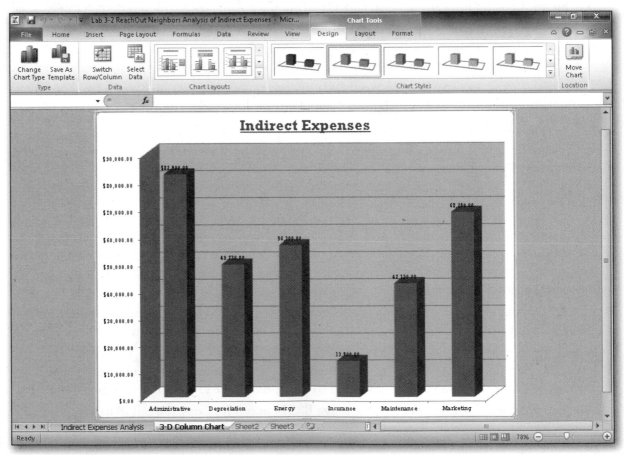

Figure 3–90

Instructions Part 3:   Start Excel. Open Lab 3-2 ReachOut Neighbor Analysis of Indirect Expenses.

1. Using the numbers in Table 3–12, analyze the effect of changing the planned indirect expenses in the range B18:B23 on the net incomes for each branch office. You should end with the following totals in cell I15: Case 1 = $5,846.00 and Case 2 = $124,346.00. Submit the workbook or results for each case as requested by your instructor.

2. Use the What-If Analysis button (Data tab | Data Tools group) to goal seek. Determine a planned indirect Marketing expense (cell B23) that would result in a total net income of $50,000 (cell I15). You should end up with a planned indirect Marketing expense of $225,586 in cell B23. Submit the workbook with the new values or the results of the goal seek as specified by your instructor.

Table 3–12 ReachOut Neighbor Indirect Expense Allocations What-If Data		
	Case 1	Case 2
Administrative	124000	66500
Depreciation	156575	75000
Energy	72525	56000
Insurance	46300	67000
Maintenance	75000	48000
Marketing	39000	82400

In the Lab

Lab 3: Modifying a Weekly Inventory Worksheet

Problem: As a summer intern at Dinah's Candle Depot, you have been asked to modify the weekly inventory report shown in Figure 3–91a on the following page. The workbook, Lab 3-3 Dinah's Weekly Inventory Report, is included with the Data Files for Students. See the inside back cover of this book for instructions for downloading the Data Files for Students, or see your instructor for information on accessing the files required for this book.

The major modifications to the payroll report to be made in this exercise include: (1) reformatting the worksheet; (2) adding computations of quantity to order based on reorder level and weeks to arrive; (3) adding calculations to suggest changes in ordering; (4) adding current and last month sales for inventory items; (5) adding and deleting inventory items; and (6) changing inventory item information. The final inventory report is shown in Figure 3–91b on the following page.

Continued >

In the Lab *continued*

Figure 3–91 (a) Before

Figure 3–91 (b) After

Instructions Part 1:

1. Start Excel. Open the workbook, Lab 3-3 Dinah's Weekly Inventory Report and then save the workbook using the file name Lab 3-3 Dinah's Weekly Inventory Report Complete.

2. Select the worksheet by clicking the Select All button. Click the Clear button (Home tab | Editing group) and then click Clear Formats on the Clear menu to clear the formatting. Bold the entire worksheet.

3. Delete rows 11 through 13 to remove the statistics below the Totals row. Change all the row heights back to the default height (12.75).

4. Insert four rows above row 1 by selecting rows 1 through 4, right-clicking the selection, and clicking Insert on the shortcut menu.

5. Change the row heights as follows: row 5 = 48.00; row 6 = 25.50; and 7 = 38.25. For the range B7:I7, change the format so that the text wraps. Center the range B7:I7.

6. Delete column B by right-clicking the column heading and clicking Delete on the shortcut menu.

7. Insert a new column between columns D and E. Change the column widths as follows: A = 25.00; E = 13.00; and F through I = 9.71. Enter the new column E title **Suggested Reorder** in cell E7.

8. Insert two new columns between columns F and G. Enter the new column G title **Last Month Sales** in cell G7. Enter the new column H title **Current Month Sales** in cell H7.

9. Enhance the worksheet title in cell A5 by using a 36-point purple Cooper Black (or a similar font) font style as shown in Figure 3–91b.

10. Assign the NOW function to cell B6 and format it to the 3/14/2001 style.

11. Delete item Car Air Freshener (row 13). Change Mini Jar Candle's (row 12) cases on hand to 6. Change Large Candle's (row 8) items per case to 8 and cost per case to $131.00. Change Incense Stick's (row 10) sale price per item to $2.00 and Incense Holder's (row 9) sale price per item to $4.75.

12. Freeze column A and rows 1 through 7 by selecting cell B8, clicking the Freeze Panes button (View tab | Window group), and then clicking Freeze Panes on the Freeze Panes gallery.

13. In columns G and H, enter the current month and last month sales values listed in Table 3–13.

14. Insert three new rows immediately above the Totals row. Add the new items data as listed in Table 3–14.

Table 3–13 Dinah's Candle Depot Monthly Sales Values

Inventory Item	Last Month Sales	Current Month Sales
Large Candle	851.6	1703.2
Incense Holder	37.5	56.25
Incense Stick	90	100
Candle Topper	390	260
Mini Jar Candle	1208	1208

Table 3–14 Dinah's Candle Depot New Items

Inventory Item	Cases On Hand	Items Per Case	Reorder Level	Order Time (Weeks)	Last Month Sales	Current Month Sales	Cost Per Case	Sale Price Per Item
Votive Candle	3	18	4	1	300	450	20	1.5
Taper Candle	2	16	3	2	350	612.5	35	3.5
Candle Warmer	2	5	1	3	638	797.5	100	15.95

15. Center the range B8:F15. Use the Currency category in the Format Cells dialog box to assign a Comma style (no dollar signs) with two decimal places and negative numbers within parentheses to the range G8:K16. Draw a thick bottom border in the ranges A7:K7 and A15:K15.

16. As shown in Figure 3–91b, enter and format the Increase Reorder Amt (2), the Decrease Reorder Amt (1), and the Sales Threshold % (25%) information in the range A1:B3. Use format symbols where applicable.

Continued >

In the Lab continued

17. Remove any Totals in the range B16:F16. Update and add totals as necessary so that totals appear in the range G16:K16.

18. In cell E8, enter an IF function that applies the following logic and then copy it to the range E9:E15. If (Current Month Sales – Last Month Sales) / Current Month Sales >= Sales Threshold %, then Reorder Level + Increase Reorder Amt, otherwise Reorder Level – Decrease Reorder Amt or =IF((H8-G8)/H8 >= $B$3, D8+$B$1,D8-$B$2).

19. In cell L8, insert a Sparkline Line chart for range G8:H8. Copy cell L8 to the range L9:L16.

20. Unfreeze the worksheet by clicking the Freeze Panes button (View tab | Window group), and then clicking Unfreeze Panes on the Freeze Panes gallery.

21. Preview the worksheet. Use the Orientation button (Page Layout tab | Page Setup group) to fit the printout on one page in landscape orientation.

22. Change the document properties, as specified by your instructor. Change the worksheet header, adding your name, course number, and other information as specified by your instructor. Save the workbook.

23. Use the Zoom button (View tab | Zoom group) to change the view of the worksheet. One by one, select all the percents on the Zoom dialog box. When you are done, return the worksheet to 100% magnification.

24. Preview the formulas version (CTRL+`) in landscape orientation. Close the worksheet without saving the latest changes.

25. Submit the workbook as specified by your instructor.

Instructions Part 2: Start Excel. Open Lab 3-3 Dinah's Weekly Inventory Report Complete. Do not save the workbook in this part. Using the numbers in Table 3–15, analyze the effect of changing the Sales Threshold in cell B3. The first case should result in a Suggested Reorder in cell E15 of 0. The second case should result in a Suggested Reorder in cell E15 of 3. Close the workbook without saving changes. Submit the results of the what-if analysis as specified by your instructor.

Table 3–15 The Dinah's Candle Depot's Sales Threshold Cases	
Case	Sales Threshold
1	30%
2	15%

Instructions Part 3: Submit results for this part as requested by your instructor.

1. Start Excel. Open Lab 3-3 Dinah's Weekly Inventory Report Complete. Select cell E8. Write down the formula that Excel displays in the formula bar. Select the range D8:D15. Point to the border surrounding the range and drag the selection to the range E17:E24. Click cell E8, and write down the formula that Excel displays in the formula bar below the one you wrote down earlier. Compare the two formulas. What can you conclude about how Excel responds when you move cells involved in a formula? Click the Undo button on the Quick Access Toolbar.

2. Right-click the range D8:D15 and then click Delete on the shortcut menu. When Excel displays the Delete dialog box, click Shift cells left and then click the OK button. What does Excel display in cell D8? Click cell D8 and then point to the Trace Error button that is displayed to the left of the cell. Write down the ScreenTip that is displayed. Click the Undo button on the Quick Access Toolbar.

3. Right-click the range D8:D15 and then click Insert on the shortcut menu. When Excel displays the Insert dialog box, click 'Shift cells right' and then click the OK button. What does Excel display in the formula bar when you click cell F8? What can you conclude about how Excel responds when you insert cells next to cells involved in a formula? Close the workbook without saving the changes.

Cases and Places

Apply your creative thinking and problem solving skills to design and implement a solution.

1: Bachelor Degree Expense and Resource Projection

Academic

Attending college with limited resources can be a trying experience. One way to alleviate some of the financial stress is to plan ahead. Develop a worksheet following the general layout in Table 3–16 that shows the projected expenses and resources for four years of college. Use the formulas listed in Table 3–17 and the concepts and techniques presented in this chapter to create the worksheet.

Table 3–16 Bachelor Degree Expense and Resource Projection

Expenses	Freshman	Sophomore	Junior	Senior	Total
Room & Board	$12,550.00	Formula A ———————————→			—
Tuition & Books	16,450.00	Formula A ———————————→			—
Clothes	785.00	Formula A ———————————→			—
Entertainment	1,520.00	Formula A ———————————→			—
Miscellaneous	936.00	Formula A ———————————→			—
Total Expenses	—	—	—	—	—

Resources	Freshman	Sophomore	Junior	Senior	Total
Savings	Formula B ———————————→				
Parents	Formula B ———————————→				—
Job	Formula B ———————————→				—
Loans	Formula B ———————————→				—
Scholarships	Formula B ———————————→				—
Total Resources	—	—	—	—	—

Assumptions	
Savings	10.00%
Parents	12.00%
Job	11.00%
Loans	35.00%
Scholarships	32.00%
Annual Rate Increase	8.25%

Table 3–17 Bachelor Degree Expense and Resource Projection Formulas

Formula A = Prior Year's Expense * (1 + Annual Rate Increase)
Formula B = Total Expenses for Year * Corresponding Assumption

After creating the worksheet: (a) perform what-if analysis by changing the percents of the resource assumptions; (b) perform a what-if analysis to determine the effect on the resources by increasing the Annual Rate Increase to 9.95% (answer = $149,520.41); and (c) with the original assumptions, goal seek to determine what the Annual Rate Increase would be for the total expenses to be $175,000 (answer = 20.77%). Submit the workbook and results of the what-if analysis as specified by your instructor.

Continued >

Cases and Places *continued*

2: Fuel Cost Analysis

Personal

You are thinking about buying a new vehicle, and you want to make sure that you get the most fuel savings you can find. You know that there are hybrid vehicles available and so you decide to research them as well as gas-only cars. Your friends also are interested in the results. Together, you decide to research the fuel costs associated with various types of vehicles. Research the gas mileage for six vehicles: three should run only on gas, and the others should be hybrid vehicles, combining gas and battery power. After you find the gas mileage for each vehicle, you will use formulas to calculate the fuel cost for 1 month, 1 year, and three years. Assume that in a typical month, you will drive 400 miles and that the average price of gas is $2.69 per gallon. Develop a worksheet following the general layout in Table 3–18 that shows the fuel cost analysis. Use the formulas listed in Table 3–19 and the concepts and techniques presented in this chapter to create the worksheet. Add a 3-D line chart showing the cost comparisons as an embedded chart.

Table 3–18 Fuel Cost Analysis				
Vehicle	**Miles Per Gallon**	**1 Month**	**1 Year**	**3 Year**
Ford Expedition	17	Formula A	Formula B	Formula C
Dodge RAM 1500	20	---	---	---
Honda Civic	31	---	---	---
Chevy Silverado Hybrid	21	---	---	---
Ford Fusion Hybrid	41	---	---	---
Honda Civic Hybrid	45	---	---	---
Assumptions				
Distance per Month	400			
Price of Gas	$2.69			

Table 3–19 Fuel Cost Analysis Formulas
Formula A = (Distance per Month / Miles per Gallon)*Price of Gas
Formula B = ((Distance per Month / Miles per Gallon)*Price of Gas)*12
Formula C = ((Distance Per Month / Miles per Gallon)*Price of Gas)*36

3: Quarterly Income Projections

Professional

Notable Web Site Design is one of the largest Web site design and Web site hosting companies in the Midwest. The company generates revenue from Web site design and selling Web site hosting space on their Web servers. A fixed percentage of the total net revenue is spent on administrative, equipment, marketing, payroll, and production expenses. A bonus is expensed if the total net revenue for the quarter exceeds $14,000,000. The company's projected receipts and expenditures for the next four quarters are shown in Table 3–20.

With this data, you have been asked to prepare a worksheet similar to Figure 3–87 on page EX 210 for the next management team meeting. The worksheet should show total net revenues, total expenditures, and operating income for each quarterly period. Include a 3-D Pie chart on a separate sheet that shows the quarterly income contributions to the annual operating income. Use the concepts and techniques presented in this chapter to create and format the worksheet and chart.

During the meeting, one manager lobbied to reduce marketing expenditures by 1.25% and payroll costs by 2.75%. Perform a what-if analysis reflecting the proposed changes in expenditures. The changes should result in an operating income of $22,425,581 for the year. Using the original assumptions shown in Table 3–20, another manager asked to what extent marketing would have to be reduced to generate an annual operating income of $21,000,000. Marketing would to be reduced from 13.50% by 1.92% to 11.58%.

Submit the workbook and results of the what-if analysis as specified by your instructor.

Table 3–20 Notable Website Design Operating Income Projection by Quarter				
Revenues	**Quarter 1**	**Quarter 2**	**Quarter 3**	**Quarter 4**
Site Design	12,247,999	15,234,813	16,567,102	10,619,201
Web Hosting	1,678,153	5,901,988	4,718,231	1,569,378
Expenditures				
Administrative	10.50%			
Bonus	250,000.00			
Equipment	17.75%			
Marketing	13.50%			
Payroll	22.50%			
Production	6.30%			
Revenue for Bonus	14,000,000.00			

NOTES

NOTES

NOTES

NOTES

Appendix A

Project Planning Guidelines

Using Project Planning Guidelines

The process of communicating specific information to others is a learned, rational skill. Computers and software, especially Microsoft Office 2010, can help you develop ideas and present detailed information to a particular audience.

Using Microsoft Office 2010, you can create projects such as Word documents, PowerPoint presentations, Excel spreadsheets, and Access databases. Productivity software such as Microsoft Office 2010 minimizes much of the laborious work of drafting and revising projects. Some communicators handwrite ideas in notebooks, others compose directly on the computer, and others have developed unique strategies that work for their own particular thinking and writing styles.

No matter what method you use to plan a project, follow specific guidelines to arrive at a final product that presents information correctly and effectively (Figure A–1). Use some aspects of these guidelines every time you undertake a project, and others as needed in specific instances. For example, in determining content for a project, you may decide that a chart communicates trends more effectively than a paragraph of text. If so, you would create this graphical element and insert it in an Excel spreadsheet, a Word document, or a PowerPoint slide.

Determine the Project's Purpose

Begin by clearly defining why you are undertaking this assignment. For example, you may want to track monetary donations collected for your club's fund-raising drive. Alternatively, you may be urging students to vote for a particular candidate in the next election. Once you clearly understand the purpose of your task, begin to draft ideas of how best to communicate this information.

Analyze Your Audience

Learn about the people who will read, analyze, or view your work. Where are they employed? What are their educational backgrounds? What are their expectations? What questions do they have?

PROJECT PLANNING GUIDELINES

1. DETERMINE THE PROJECT'S PURPOSE
Why are you undertaking the project?

2. ANALYZE YOUR AUDIENCE
Who are the people who will use your work?

3. GATHER POSSIBLE CONTENT
What information exists, and in what forms?

4. DETERMINE WHAT CONTENT TO PRESENT TO YOUR AUDIENCE
What information will best communicate the project's purpose to your audience?

Figure A–1

Design experts suggest drawing a mental picture of these people or finding photos of people who fit this profile so that you can develop a project with the audience in mind.

By knowing your audience members, you can tailor a project to meet their interests and needs. You will not present them with information they already possess, and you will not omit the information they need to know.

Example: Your assignment is to raise the profile of your college's nursing program in the community. How much do they know about your college and the nursing curriculum? What are the admission requirements? How many of the applicants admitted complete the program? What percent pass the state board exams?

Gather Possible Content

Rarely are you in a position to develop all the material for a project. Typically, you would begin by gathering existing information that may reside in spreadsheets or databases. Web sites, pamphlets, magazine and newspaper articles, and books could provide insights of how others have approached your topic. Personal interviews often provide perspectives not available by any other means. Consider video and audio clips as potential sources for material that might complement or support the factual data you uncover.

Determine What Content to Present to Your Audience

Experienced designers recommend writing three or four major ideas you want an audience member to remember after reading or viewing your project. It also is helpful to envision your project's endpoint, the key fact you wish to emphasize. All project elements should lead to this ending point.

As you make content decisions, you also need to think about other factors. Presentation of the project content is an important consideration. For example, will your brochure be printed on thick, colored paper or posted on the Web? Will your PowerPoint presentation be viewed in a classroom with excellent lighting and a bright projector, or will it be viewed on a notebook computer monitor? Determine relevant time factors, such as the length of time to develop the project, how long readers will spend reviewing your project, or the amount of time allocated for your speaking engagement. Your project will need to accommodate all of these constraints.

Decide whether a graph, photo, or artistic element can express or emphasize a particular concept. The right hemisphere of the brain processes images by attaching an emotion to them, so audience members are more apt to recall these graphics long term rather than just reading text.

As you select content, be mindful of the order in which you plan to present information. Readers and audience members generally remember the first and last pieces of information they see and hear, so you should place the most important information at the top or bottom of the page.

Summary

When creating a project, it is beneficial to follow some basic guidelines from the outset. By taking some time at the beginning of the process to determine the project's purpose, analyze the audience, gather possible content, and determine what content to present to the audience, you can produce a project that is informative, relevant, and effective.

Appendix B

Publishing Office 2010 Web Pages Online

With Office 2010 programs, you use the Save As command in the Backstage view to save a Web page to a Web site, network location, or FTP site. **File Transfer Protocol (FTP)** is an Internet standard that allows computers to exchange files with other computers on the Internet.

You should contact your network system administrator or technical support staff at your Internet access provider to determine if their Web server supports Web folders, FTP, or both, and to obtain necessary permissions to access the Web server.

Using an Office Program to Publish Office 2010 Web Pages

When publishing online, someone first must assign the necessary permissions for you to publish the Web page. If you are granted access to publish online, you must obtain the Web address of the Web server, a user name, and possibly a password that allows you to connect to the Web server. The steps in this appendix assume that you have access to an online location to which you can publish a Web page.

To Connect to an Online Location

To publish a Web page online, you first must connect to the online location. To connect to an online location using Windows 7, you would perform the following steps.

1. Click the Start button on the Windows 7 taskbar to display the Start menu.
2. Click Computer in the right pane of the Start menu to open the Computer window.
3. Click the 'Map network drive' button on the toolbar to display the Map Network Drive dialog box. (If the 'Map network drive' button is not visible on the toolbar, click the 'Display additional commands' button on the toolbar and then click 'Map network drive' in the list to display the Map Network Drive dialog box.)
4. Click the 'Connect to a Web site that you can use to store your documents and pictures' link (Map Network Drive dialog box) to start the Add Network Location wizard.
5. Click the Next button (Add Network Location dialog box).
6. Click 'Choose a custom network location' and then click the Next button.
7. Type the Internet or network address specified by your network or system administrator in the text box and then click the Next button.
8. Click 'Log on anonymously' to deselect the check box, type your user name in the User name text box, and then click the Next button.
9. If necessary, enter the name you want to assign to this online location and then click the Next button.
10. Click to deselect the Open this network location when I click Finish check box, and then click the Finish button.

11. Click the Cancel button to close the Map Network Drive dialog box.

12. Close the Computer window.

To Save a Web Page to an Online Location

The online location now can be accessed easily from Windows programs, including Microsoft Office programs. After creating a Microsoft Office file you wish to save as a Web page, you must save the file to the online location to which you connected in the previous steps. To save a Microsoft Word document as a Web page, for example, and publish it to the online location, you would perform the following steps.

1. Click File on the Ribbon to display the Backstage view and then click Save As in the Backstage view to display the Save As dialog box.

2. Type the Web page file name in the File name text box (Save As dialog box). Do not press the ENTER key because you do not want to close the dialog box at this time.

3. Click the 'Save as type' box arrow and then click Web Page to select the Web Page format.

4. If necessary, scroll to display the name of the online location in the navigation pane.

5. Double-click the online location name in the navigation pane to select that location as the new save location and display its contents in the right pane.

6. If a dialog box appears prompting you for a user name and password, type the user name and password in the respective text boxes and then click the Log On button.

7. Click the Save button (Save As dialog box).

The Web page now has been published online. To view the Web page using a Web browser, contact your network or system administrator for the Web address you should use to connect to the Web page.

Appendix C

Saving to the Web Using Windows Live SkyDrive

Introduction

Windows Live SkyDrive, also referred to as **SkyDrive**, is a free service that allows users to save files to the Web, such as documents, spreadsheets, databases, presentations, videos, and photos. Using SkyDrive, you also can save files in folders, providing for greater organization. You then can retrieve those files from any computer connected to the Internet. Some Office 2010 programs including Word, PowerPoint, and Excel can save files directly to an Internet location such as SkyDrive. SkyDrive also facilitates collaboration by allowing users to share files with other SkyDrive users (Figure C–1).

Windows
Live SkyDrive

Figure C–1

Note: An Internet connection is required to perform the steps in this Appendix.

To Save a File to Windows Live SkyDrive

You can save files directly to SkyDrive from within Word, PowerPoint, and Excel using the Backstage view. The following steps save an open Excel spreadsheet (Brain Busters, in this case) to SkyDrive. These steps require you to have a Windows Live account. Contact your instructor if you do not have a Windows Live account.

1

- Start Excel and the open a workbook you want to save to the Web (in this case, the Brain Busters workbook).
- Click File on the Ribbon to display the Backstage view (Figure C–2).

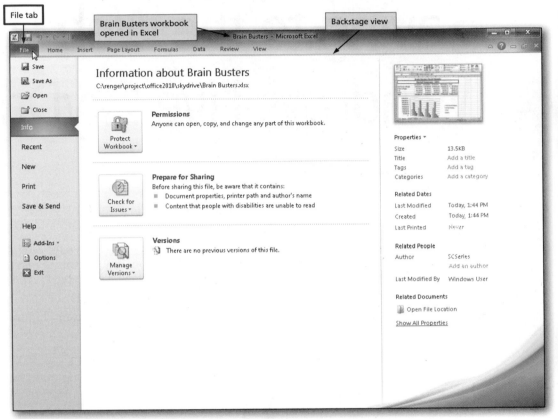

Figure C–2

2

- Click the Save & Send tab to display the Save & Send gallery (Figure C–3).

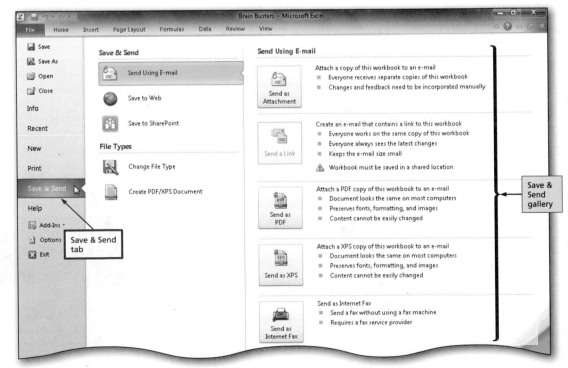

Figure C–3

3

- Click Save to Web in the Save & Send gallery to display information about saving a file to the Web (Figure C–4).

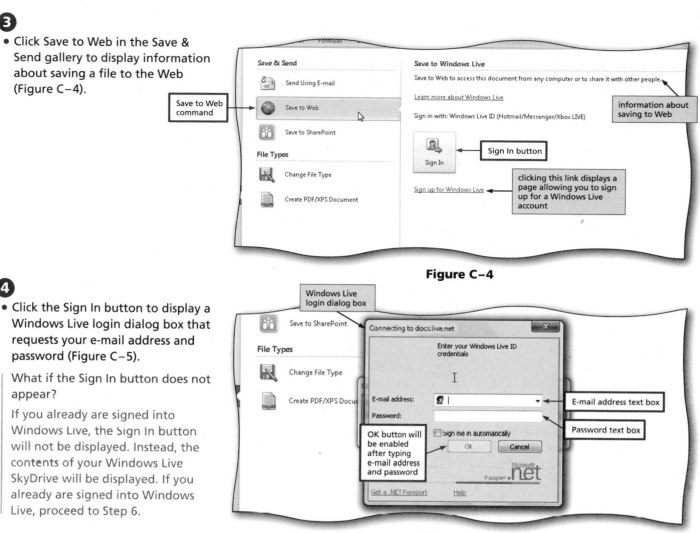

Figure C–4

4

- Click the Sign In button to display a Windows Live login dialog box that requests your e-mail address and password (Figure C–5).

Q&A What if the Sign In button does not appear?

If you already are signed into Windows Live, the Sign In button will not be displayed. Instead, the contents of your Windows Live SkyDrive will be displayed. If you already are signed into Windows Live, proceed to Step 6.

Figure C–5

5

- Enter your Windows Live e-mail address in the E-mail address text box (Windows Live login dialog box).

- Enter your Windows Live password in the Password text box.

- Click the OK button to sign into Windows Live and display the contents of your Windows Live SkyDrive in right pane of the Save & Send gallery.

- If necessary, click the My Documents folder to set the save location for the document (Figure C–6).

Q&A What if the My Documents folder does not exist?

Click another folder to select it as the save location. Record the name of this folder so that you can locate and retrieve the file later in this appendix.

Q&A What is the difference between the personal folders and the shared folders?

Personal folders are private and are not shared with anyone. Shared folders can be viewed by SkyDrive users to whom you have assigned the necessary permissions.

Figure C–6

6

- Click the Save As button in the right pane of the Save & Send gallery to contact the SkyDrive server (which may take some time, depending on the speed of your Internet connection) and then display the Save As dialog box (Figure C–7).

Figure C–7

7

- Type **Brain Busters Web** in the File name text box to enter the file name and then click the Save button (Save As dialog box) to save the file to Windows Live SkyDrive (Figure C–8).

Q&A

Is it necessary to rename the file?

It is good practice to rename the file. If you download the file from SkyDrive to your computer, having a different file name will preserve the original file.

Figure C–8

8

- If you have one Excel spreadsheet open, click the Close button on the right side of the title bar to close the spreadsheet and quit Excel; or if you have multiple Excel spreadsheets open, click File on the Ribbon to open the Backstage view and then click Exit in the Backstage view to close all open spreadsheets and quit Excel.

Web Apps

Microsoft has created a scaled-down, Web-based version of its Microsoft Office suite, called **Microsoft Office Web Apps,** or **Web Apps**. Web Apps contains Web-based versions of Word, PowerPoint, Excel, and OneNote that can be used to view and edit files that are saved to SkyDrive. Web Apps allows users to continue working with their files even while they are not using a computer with Microsoft Office installed. In addition to working with files located on SkyDrive, Web Apps also enables users to create new Word documents, PowerPoint presentations, Excel spreadsheets, and OneNote notebooks. After returning to a computer with the Microsoft Office suite, some users choose to download files from SkyDrive and edit them using the associated Microsoft Office program.

To Open a File from Windows Live SkyDrive

Files saved to SkyDrive can be opened from a Web browser using any computer with an Internet connection. The following steps open the Brain Busters Web file using a Web browser.

①

- Click the Internet Explorer program button pinned on the Windows 7 taskbar to start Internet Explorer.

- Type **skydrive.live.com** in the Address bar and then press the ENTER key to display a SkyDrive Web page requesting you sign in to your Windows Live account (Figure C–9).

Q&A
Why does the Web address change after I enter it in the Address bar?

The Web address changes because you are being redirected to sign into Windows Live before you can access SkyDrive.

Q&A
Can I open the file from Microsoft Excel instead of using the Web browser?

If you are opening the file on the same computer from which you saved it to the SkyDrive, click File on the Ribbon to open the Backstage view. Click the Recent tab and then click the desired file name (Brain Busters Web, in this case) in the Recent Workbooks list, or click Open and then navigate to the location of the saved file (for a detailed example of this procedure, refer to the Office 2010 and Windows 7 chapter at the beginning of this book).

Figure C–9

②

- Click the Sign in link to display the Windows Live ID and Password text boxes (Figure C–10).

Q&A
Why can I not locate the Sign in link?

If your computer remembers your Windows Live sign in credentials from a previous session, your e-mail address already may be displayed on the SkyDrive Web page. In this case, point to your e-mail address to display the Sign in button, click the Sign in button, and then proceed to Step 3. If you cannot locate your e-mail address or Sign in link, click the Sign in with a different Windows Live ID link and then proceed to Step 3.

Figure C–10

3

• If necessary, enter your Windows Live ID and password in the appropriate text boxes and then click the Sign in button to sign into Windows Live and display the contents of your SkyDrive (Figure C–11).

Q&A

What do the icons beside the folders mean?

The lock icon indicates that the folder is private and is accessible only to you. The people icon signifies a folder that can be shared with SkyDrive users to whom you have assigned the necessary permissions. The globe icon denotes a folder accessible to anyone on the Internet.

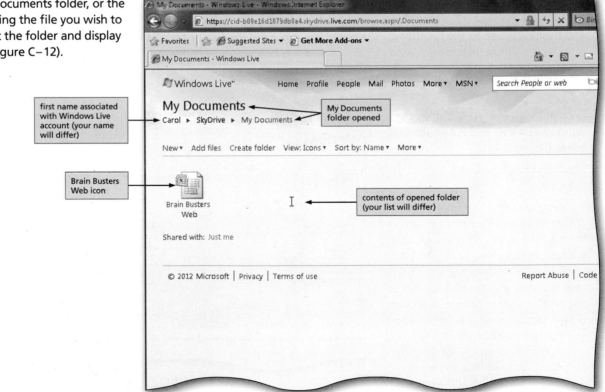

Figure C–11

4

• Click the My Documents folder, or the folder containing the file you wish to open, to select the folder and display its contents (Figure C–12).

Figure C–12

5

- Click the Brain Busters Web file to select the file and display information about it (Figure C–13).

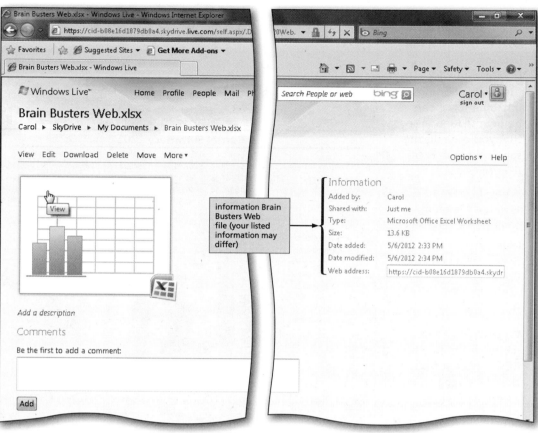

Figure C–13

6

- Click the Download link to display the File Download dialog box (Figure C–14).

Figure C–14

7

- Click the Open button (File Download dialog box) to open the file in Microsoft Excel. If necessary, click the Enable Editing button if it appears below the Ribbon so that you can edit the spreadsheet in Excel (Figure C–15).

Q&A What if I want to save the file on my computer's hard disk?

Refer to the Office 2010 and Windows 7 chapter at the beginning of this book.

Q&A Why does the file name on the title bar look different from the file name I typed when saving the document?

Because you are opening the file directly from SkyDrive without first saving it to your computer, the file name may differ slightly. For example, spaces may be replaced with "%20" and a number in parentheses at the end of the file name may indicate you are opening a copy of the original file that is stored online.

Figure C–15

Collaboration

In today's workplace, it is common to work with others on projects. Collaborating with the members of your team often requires sharing files. It also can involve multiple people editing and working with a certain set of files simultaneously. Placing files on SkyDrive in a public or shared folder enables others to view or modify the files. The members of the team then can view and edit the files simultaneously using Web Apps, enabling the team to work from one set of files. Collaboration using Web Apps not only enables multiple people to work together, it also can reduce the amount of time required to complete a project.

Index

Quick Reference Summary

Microsoft Excel 2010 Quick Reference Summary

Task	Page Number	Mouse	Ribbon	Shortcut Menu	Keyboard Shortcut
Accounting Number Format, Apply	100		Accounting Number Format button (Home tab | Number group)		
All data in a cell, Select	51	Double-click if there are no spaces in data			
Auto Fill	18	Drag fill handle	Auto Fill Options button (Home tab | Editing group)		
AutoCalculate	48	Select range | right-click AutoCalculate area | click calculation			
Average Function	84	Insert Function box in formula bar | AVERAGE in Select a function list | OK | range | OK	Sum button arrow (Home tab | Editing group) or Sum button arrow (Formulas tab | Function Library)		Type =av | press DOWN ARROW | ENTER
Background Color, Change	96		Format Cells Dialog Box Launcher (Home tab | Font group) | Fill tab | click color | click OK	Format Cells on shortcut menu	CTRL+1
Best Fit	107	Select columns | point to boundary until arrow is split double arrow | double-click			
Bold	25	Bold button on Mini toolbar	Bold button (Home tab | Font group)	Format Cells on shortcut menu | Font tab | Bold	CTRL+B
Cell Entries, Clear Selected	52	Drag fill handle from empty cell through cells with entries	Clear button (Home tab | Editing group) | Clear Contents	Clear Contents on shortcut menu	DELETE
Cell Reference, Add	78	Click cell			
Cell Style, Change	52		Cell Styles button (Home tab | Styles group)		
Cell, Highlight	19	Drag mouse pointer			
Cell, Select	34	Click cell or click Name box, type cell reference, press ENTER			Use arrow keys
Cells, Merge and Center	28	Merge & Center button on Mini toolbar	Merge & Center button (Home tab | Alignment group)	Format Cells on shortcut menu | Alignment tab	

Microsoft Excel 2010 Quick Reference Summary *(continued)*

Task	Page Number	Mouse	Ribbon	Shortcut Menu	Keyboard Shortcut
Characters to left of insertion point, Delete	50				BACKSPACE
Characters to right of insertion point, Delete	50				DELETE
Characters, Highlight	51	Drag through adjacent characters			SHIFT+RIGHT ARROW or SHIFT+LEFT ARROW
Chart, Add	38		Charts group | Insert tab		
Color Text	27	Font Color button on Mini toolbar	Font Color button arrow (Home tab | Font group)		
Column Width	33	Drag column heading boundary		Column Width on shortcut menu	
Comma Style Format, Apply	100		Comma Style button (Home tab | Number group)		
Complete an Entry	8	Click Enter box			Press ENTER
Conditional Formatting	104		Conditional Formatting button (Home tab | Styles group)		
Copy Range of Cells	80	Select range | drag fill handle |	Copy button (Home tab | Clipboard group) |	Copy on shortcut menu	CTRL+C
Currency Style Format, Apply	100		Format Cells: Number Dialog Box Launcher (Home tab | Number group)		CTRL+1 OR CTRL+SHIFT+ DOLLAR SIGN ($)
Date, Format	98		Format Cells: Number Dialog Box Launcher on Home tab	Format Cells on shortcut menu | Number tab (Format Cells dialog box)	
Document Properties, Change	43		Properties button (File tab | Info tab)		
Document Properties, Print	45		File tab | Print tab, first box arrow (Settings area)		
Document Properties, Set or View	43		File | Info tab		
Entry, Complete	8	Click Enter box			Press ENTER
Font Color	27	Font Color box arrow on Mini toolbar	Font Color button arrow (Home tab | Font group)	Format Cells on shortcut menu | Font tab	
Font Size, Decrease	26	Font Size box arrow on Mini toolbar	Decrease Font Size button (Home tab | Font group)	Format Cells on shortcut menu | Font tab	
Font Size, Increase	26	Font Size box arrow on Mini toolbar	Increase Font Size button (Home tab | Font group)	Format Cells | Font Tab	
Font Type	24	Font box arrow on Mini toolbar	Font box (Home tab | Font group)	Format Cells | Font tab	
Font, Change	24	Font Size box arrow on Mini toolbar	Font box arrow (Home tab | Font group)	Format Cells | Font tab	
Formulas Version	119				CTRL+ACCENT MARK (`)
Highlight Cells	18	Drag mouse pointer			SHIFT+ARROW KEY
In-Cell Editing	50	Double-click cell			F2

Microsoft Excel 2010 Quick Reference Summary (continued)

Task	Page Number	Mouse	Ribbon	Shortcut Menu	Keyboard Shortcut
Insert and Overtype modes, Toggle between	50				INSERT
Insertion point, Move	8	Click			Use arrow keys
Insertion point, move to beginning of data in cell	51	Point to left of first character and click			HOME
Insertion point, move to ending of data in cell	51	Point to right of last character and click			END
Margins, Change	114	Page Layout button on status bar | Page Layout tab | Margins button	Page Setup Dialog Box Launcher | Margins tab (Page Layout tab | Page Setup group)		
Max Function	86	Insert Function box in formula bar | MAX in Select a function list | OK | range | OK	Sum button arrow (Home tab | Editing group) or Sum button arrow (Formulas tab | Sum group)		
Min Function	87	Insert Function box in the formula bar | MIN in Select a function list | OK | range | OK	Sum button arrow (Home tab | Editing group) or Sum button arrow (Formulas tab | Sum group)		
New Line in Cell, Start	71				ALT+ENTER
Numbers, Format	31	Accounting Number Format, Percent Style, or Comma Style button on Mini toolbar	Cell Styles button (Home tab | Styles group) or Accounting Number Format, Percent Style, or Comma Style button (Home tab | Number group), or Format Cells: Number dialog box launcher | Accounting, or Percentage or Number Format list arrow | Accounting or Percentage		
Open a Workbook	48		Open or Recent (File tab)		CTRL+O
Percent style format	103		Percent Style button (Home tab | Number group)	Format Cells on shortcut menu | Number tab | Percentage (Format Cells dialog box)	CTRL+SHIFT+ percent sign (%)
Print Scaling Option	120		Page Setup Dialog Box Launcher (Page Layout tab | Page Setup group)		
Print Section of Worksheet	118		File | Print tab | Print Active Sheets or Print Area button (Page Layout tab | Page Setup group)		
Print Worksheet	46		File tab | Print tab		CTRL+P
Quit Excel	47	Close button on right side of title bar	Exit (File tab)		
Range Finder	91	Double-click cell			
Range, Deselect	18	Click outside range			
Range, Select	28	Drag fill handle through range			

Microsoft Excel 2010 Quick Reference Summary *(continued)*

Task	Page Number	Mouse	Ribbon	Shortcut Menu	Keyboard Shortcut
Redo	51	Redo button on Quick Access Toolbar			CTRL+Y
Row Height	110	Drag row heading boundary		Row Height on shortcut menu	
Save Workbook	20	Save button on Quick Access Toolbar	Save (File tab | Save button)		CTRL+S
Save Workbook, New Name	20	Save button on Quick Access Toolbar			
Save Workbook, Same Name	20	Save button on Quick Access Toolbar	Save (File tab | Save button)		CTRL+S
Select Cell	7	Click cell or click Name box, type cell reference, press ENTER			Use arrow keys
Select Entire Worksheet	52	Click Select All button			CTRL+A
Select Nonadjacent Cells	100	Select first cell, hold down CTRL key while selecting second cell			
Selected characters, Delete	50		Cut button (Home tab | Clipboard group)		DELETE
Selected Chart, Delete	53				DELETE
Sheet Name, Change	42	Double-click type name		Rename on shortcut menu	
Spelling	112		Spelling button (Review tab | Proofing group)		F7
Sum	15	Click Insert Function button in formula bar | SUM in Select a function list | OK | range | OK	Sum button (Home tab | Editing group)		ALT+EQUAL SIGN (=) twice
Text, Delete after typing but before pressing the ENTER key	8	Click Cancel box in formula bar			Press ESC
Text, Delete while typing	8				Press BACKSPACE
Undo	51	Undo button on Quick Access Toolbar			CTRL+Z
Workbook Theme, Change	94		Themes button (Page Layout tab | Themes group)		
Worksheet Name, Change	42	Double-click sheet tab, type name		Rename on shortcut menu	
Worksheet, Clear	52		Select All button | Clear button (Home tab | Editing group)		CTRL A, press DELETE
Worksheet, Preview	46		File tab | Print tab		CTRL+P